I, SHITHEAD

I, SHITHEAD

a life in punk

JOEY KEITHLEY

ARSENAL
PULP PRESS
Vancouver

Third printing: 2010

ARSENAL PULP PRESS
#102-211 East Georgia St.
Vancouver, BC Canada V6A 1Z6

arsenalpulp.com

The publisher gratefully acknowledges the support of the Canada Council for the
Arts and the British Columbia Arts Council for its publishing program, and
the Government of Canada through the Book Publishing Industry
Development Program for its publishing activities.

Design by Solo
Cover photography by Sylvie E. Thorne
Editing by Barbara Pulling

Printed and bound in Canada

National Library of Canada
Cataloguing in Publication Data

Keithley, Joe, 1956–
I, Shithead : a life in punk / Joe Keithley.
Includes index.
ISBN 978-1-55152-148-0

1. Keithley, Joe, 1956– 2. D.O.A. (Musical group) 3. Punk rock
musicians – Canada – Biography. I. Title.
ML420.k28a3 2003   782.42166'092   c2003-911198-9

CONTENTS

Hey folks, it is a given in almost every rock band that there is some form of substance abuse. D.O.A. was no exception to this. At times, it was rampant with members of the band as well as people working with the band. At times, substance abuse led to people being forced out of playing and working with D.O.A. I've lost too many friends to put up with that shit.

But out of respect for people's privacy, and because stories about people being drunk and stoned are a waste of time, I'm not going into detail about it in this book.

D.O.A. touring Hardcore 81. *photo: Bev Davies*

WE'RE ALL D.O.A.!

Jack Rabid

Joey Shithead is a Canadian institution. He's the man who put the Canadian underground rock/punk scene on the map. He's also damn interesting and hilariously funny. His perseverance in the face of constant chaos and adversity has been crucial to the survival and ultimate triumph of his band D.O.A. (Well, *that* plus more than his share of Molsons, Mooseheads, Labatts, the occasional American swill, and lots of stronger brew overseas.) Were it not for Joe, most of us in the East Coast wouldn't even know the geography of Western Canada, let alone the musical riches of the city of Vancouver.

Joey Shithead? That's Joey Keithley to you! Whereas I still get to call him the old name – my rights are grandfathered, kind of like the old hockey players who played without helmets after the rule change. Then again, the one time my wife and I visited him in Vancouver, it seemed as if he knew every passerby in town, as one and all alike called out from across the street, "Hey, Shithead!" Some things you can't outlive.

Anyway, I first met the Mr Shithead in question over two decades ago (May 8, 1981) when the original lineup of D.O.A. made its third foray to New York. (And what a rewarding acquaintance that has been since, both personally and musically!) I introduced myself to him in-between their two long, hardworking, awe-inspiring sets that night at the Peppermint Lounge, a historic old joint off Times Square on 45th Street (of Joey Dee & the Starlighters 1961 #1 hit "Peppermint Twist" fame). Nowadays, amazingly enough, D.O.A. sells a DVD called *Greatest Shits* with vivid footage from that night, showing them playing a typically hellacious version of "Get Out of My Life." I just about fell down laughing when I watched this recently, and saw the back of my 19-year-old head and torso as it pogoed senselessly in my customary place, at the front of the six-foot stage! But, given the blistering assault captured so well in that footage, who could have done anything else?

I'd seen this incredible band before, though I was still stuck in high

school in the suburbs. I still thought of touring musicians as grand exalted wizards sequestered in magical, hidden, sidestage drawing rooms full of free alcohol and girls, and had no access. But by 1981 I was in college and in a local punk band myself. I was also putting out my own fanzine. So by 1981, I thought it nothing to just saunter right into the sanctum, where they were indeed consuming copious amounts of their beer allowance along with their old West Coast friend Jello Biafra – in town for his own smokin' Dead Kennedys shows. While giving Joe issue five of *Big Takeover*, I told him that the copy of the brand new D.O.A. second LP *Hardcore 81* he'd thrown off the stage into the crowd had been wrestled out of my hand by some jerk twice my size. (The cover got all twisted and bent, served the jerk right.) So Joe promptly just handed me another one. Hey, thanks Joe! I think that copy is worth a few hundred bucks now. What a pal!

I wish there was some way to convey how truly stunning a D.O.A. show was back then. There was only one other band in the world who could touch them, and that was the (early) Bad Brains, who thankfully shared New York stages with D.O.A. twice. The effect of the original lineup of Joe on guitar and lead vocals, Dave Gregg on second guitar, Randy Rampage on bass, and Chuck Biscuits on drums was like being thrown off a bridge and living to tell about it. They were an absolute whirlwind of lightning guitars, gut-smacking bass lines, and the hottest drumming I've ever seen in twenty-five years of live concerts. (I never saw The Who's Keith Moon, but from movies like *The Kids Are Alright*, I swear the young Biscuits gave the young Moon a run for his money.) No one could forget the band's raw abandon on stage: I think Rampage leaped so high so many times he nearly hit the balcony overhang to his right. And clad in his usual Airborne T-shirt, Joe was putting his considerable chest into his vocals, as Gregg was bent over (he appeared to be giving birth) from playing so hard.

And D.O.A. weren't just hitting you over the head for fun. It's also impossible to forget the band's utter conviction. Whether playing politically aware anthems such as "New Age" or "The Enemy" in the best Clash and Stiff Little Fingers tradition, or belting out their equally charged hardcore thrash-rockers such as "Slumlord" ("It's all laid out like a prison plot/Each little peasant with their plot/Slumlord your title fits your deed!"), or showing off their *bonhomie* with their clownish-yet-high-octane cover of Led Zeppelin's "Whole Lotta Love" and wry party tunes such as "Middle Class Television Family Daughter" – D.O.A. were always the most formidable thing I've witnessed on a stage.

They made you proud to say you were a punk rocker while all your clueless classmates were still thinking that the Doobie Brothers and Kansas and Foghat and Foreigner were, like, rock 'n' roll, man. D.O.A. were straight up moonshine whiskey in a Bartles and James' world. And the most amazing thing is that pretty much every lineup of D.O.A. that has succeeded that seminal first one has also been fucking great live, right up to the distant present. Thus, for a quarter century, they've had a massive effect on the worldwide audiences they've roasted.

It is impossible to underestimate the band's impact on the underground rock community. Firstly because they've played in more countries than there are pages to fill on a dozen passports, inspiring thousands of bands to form and take a stand for what they believe in – a far more important concept in the less apolitical and apathetic parts of the world that ours. But the group has had an equally trailblazing impact here, because D.O.A. toured the U.S. and Canada more than anyone in punk back when that just *wasn't* done!

I could count on two hands the number of West Coast punk bands that came to New York to play back before 1980 (among them X, Zeroes, Screamers, Dils, original lineup Dead Kennedys, and Plugz). Most of these groups either flew straight here or played only a handful of gigs on their way and back. It's not that they were lazy, it's just there were so few established gigs to be had, since there was so little precedent for punk outside the half-dozen cities with actual thriving punk scenes – Austin, Toronto, Cleveland, New York, Boston, L.A., and San Francisco. Whereas, as you'll read in these pages, D.O.A. were constantly going where no other independent-label-affiliated, politically oriented punk-rock group had gone before. With a band this great, with a message this strong, they were bound to plant some pretty big seeds. They showed by brute example what could be done if you didn't mind a starvation diet, uncertain transport, accommodations that might be called "Triple z" (as opposed to AAA), and gigs whose actual existence could never be assured, booked as they were through shady and often criminal promoters whose payouts often failed to match their contractual promises.

Indeed, it's a shame how few were driven to test those inhospitable waters. Someday someone will write a book about the wonderful Vancouver scene of 1978–1981 of which D.O.A. were the biggest stars, and which remains the best kept secret in North American underground music history. This is probably because only the two best bands of that scene, D.O.A. and the Subhumans, ever made it east of the Mississippi to play (and the Subhumans only did it once)! How I wish we *could* have seen all the other Vancouver bands these two spawned, like Young Canadians, Pointed Sticks, Modernettes, Wasted Lives, Dishrags, Active Dog, Uj3rk5, I Braineater, Dave Gregg's old band Private School, and their funny sidebands like Sgt. Nick Penis Band and Rude Norton. But this point just underscores how lucky we were that D.O.A. put up with all the crap, to use Joey's favorite word, out of a pure unadulterated desire to spread the punk rock ethic, and have done it so long. (When I was DJing at their big Rock Hotel shows, I would make a point of playing all these too-obscure Vancouver bands songs before D.O.A. went on, to help psyche them up for the show. And people would keep coming up to the booth, saying excitedly, "Who is this?!")

Frankly, if anything is clear in this book, it's that nothing, repeat, nothing, stopped (stops) D.O.A. (Not even the worst sad calamities, like fire and death.) Even breaking up after eleven years failed to slay them – they came back shortly thereafter with a vengeance, and are plotting yet another huge tour and another album as I write this. Which can only mean a second book's worth of incredible stories of having to change on the fly (another hockey term), of improvising when everything goes wrong, and most of all, of living up to their most sacred creed, "Talk minus action equals zero." Few have talked more – that's for sure! – and few have acted more, either, and not just when it was convenient or safe to do it. I've often thought it was a good thing that through the years nearly every member of D.O.A. has been so physically imposing. They've sure had their share of dealing with drunks, skunks, skinheads, pinheads, creeps, sheep, cops, border guards, promoters, and even firemen who've wanted to start something with them, and often did.

How different all this is to today! Here we are in a time when punk rock is just another peer-approved lifestyle or ho hum musical choice, for an-easily bored MTV generation who has little idea how substantive, radical, and small the movement once was. Now indie rock in general is a safe and predictable pursuit. Hundreds of punk and indie bands have strong, efficient, and even deep-pocketed record labels that put them on the road playing clubs that book this sort of thing all the time, with good vans, clean hotel rooms, CDs in the store, and support from local radio and Internet-fed fanbases. Whereas none of that was out there when D.O.A. bravely hit the road. They traveled with little more than their unshakeable belief in their music and the punk rock scene. Not only did they make friends with everyone everywhere they went, D.O.A. exchanged ideas and music and furthered the whole "alternative" (in the real sense of the word) culture. In their songs, stances, and benefit concerts, their world was very unlike the one I was used to as a kid in the suburbs. It was and is one where we actually confront our problems societally, culturally, politically, and globally, instead of just getting stoned and buying what the ads tell us to. It was both the absolute spirit of those amazing punk rock times, when so much of the point of the new movement was to meet and congregate with the few others around who knew about and loved this phenomenal (but "uncommercial!" ha!) music, as well as a measure of the man.

Joe is, after all, gregarious, a great ambassador/commentator for the music and the causes he supports. He's a big, warm-hearted, funny bear of a man who plays and sings on stage with amazing intensity and tells tall tales off it. Joe has more ribald remembrances of crazy stunts, wild behavior, bizarre depravations, hangover cruelties, and comical-in-retrospect tour nightmares than anyone I've even met. And Joe has no intention of giving you a dry history of his band or his life, though he peppers his commentary with the relevant facts, dates, names, places, and events required to give you the total picture. What he's clearly more interested in is relating the total experience . . . of all the amazing places his belief in punk, rock 'n' roll in general, and social justice has taken him, all the great shows and great people he's met and played with, and, most of all, all the nutty things that have happened to him and his bandmates. Pure entertainment, at that.

Some I can vouch for myself. I was there when the fire department tried to shut down the World show with the Dead Kennedys, and the wee morning jam with Steve Jones of the Sex Pistols at A7, and the huge Staten Island Paramount concert, and the Ritz Rock Hotel shows where they blew everyone away. Heck, my friend Sumishta Brahm and I almost got D.O.A. killed in L.A. the night of a 1982 Whiskey-a-Go-Go show, driving them around the steep Hollywood Hills in a tiny car they barely fit in (big lugs), a car which had brakes that were nearly failing from the strain. (Now that was a white-knuckle ride!) So lest you disbelieve what you read herein, guess again! If anything, Joe's *left out* some of the craziness for space, rather than embellishing anything. You know what's really amazing? It's that Joe is still alive, after all the rigors, beer, and travel, the proud papa of three sharp and aware children, and here to tell his tale.

Enjoy this book, it really is a surefire pleasure. And if you want to get another laugh, ask Joe about the first time his eldest son Jake came home from school saying the kids down there claimed his dad used to have a different last name.

I, Shithead, indeed. We are all shitheads, all proud members of the extended, worldwide Shithead family. And as their *Hardcore 81* classic exclaims, "We're all D.O.A.!"

Jack Rabid has been the editor and publisher of The Big Takeover *since 1980.*

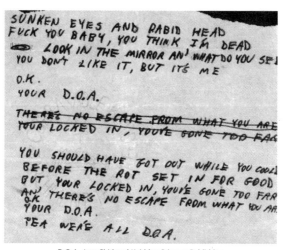

D.O.A. *Joey Shithead Keithley, Prisoner Publishing*

To Laura, Jake, Georgia, and Clayton
All my love

D.O.A.

IF YOU
FIGHT FOR
A LITTLE
YOU DON'T
GET A LOT.

It was January 1978. My first punk band, the Skulls, had broken up, and I'd just moved back to Vancouver from Toronto. I was glad to be home. The winter and the attitude had really sucked out there. Yeah, I was back home, but I was completely broke with few prospects. It was obvious I was never going to fit into the regular world. I had dropped out of university two years earlier, and I would never be the civil rights lawyer I had dreamed of being. None of that stuff was going to work for me. I just didn't fit in.

But the short-lived career of the Skulls had been fucking great. I knew that. It was great because punk was great. The mainstream music scene was full of pretenders – bands like Styx and Journey and my own personal least-favourite, Prism – that were enough to make you gag. To top it off, disco was at its peak. It should have been mandatory to make free barf bags available on every corner.

Punk was different. It was anti-establishment, it made fun of everything, and it was powerful, loud, and obnoxious, the way rock was meant to be. Punk was political, too. But what the fuck was I going to do? It took me less than a week to figure it out: I needed to start a new band. The only things I had going for me were my trusty old Gibson SG guitar and my intuition. But punks were rebellious and believed we could change the world. I set out to prove that theory right. I didn't know I was in for twenty-five years of trouble-making.

CHAPTER ONE
G R O W I N G   U P

Like Bob Marley said, "In this bright future, you can't forget your past," and I have not. I grew up in Burnaby, British Columbia. At the time it was known as Canada's biggest suburb. What a fucking claim to fame! We lived on Burnaby Mountain. It was a rural outpost then, complete with small farms, swamps, bears, and cougars, even though it was only ten miles from downtown Vancouver.

I was an average kid, with an older brother, Jef, and an older sister, Karen. My parents were worn out from raising kids by then, I think, so they didn't pay much attention to me. My early years were directionless, you might say, but by the time I was eight, some influential things had started to happen. We were seeing the Vietnam war on TV every night. Sucked into the brainwashing, I would get out my toy machine gun and crouch and shoot those Viet Cong.

When I was ten we got a colour TV, and things suddenly became a lot more graphic. Right in our front room, in full living colour, were images of soldiers holding their guts in with dinner plates and monks setting themselves on fire. We saw neighbourhoods burning during the race riots in Watts and Detroit, and hundreds of thousands of people protesting the war in Washington. It all made a deep impression on me.

The other event that had a profound effect was my sister Karen's wedding in 1965, when I was nine. That was the night I fell in love with music. As the wedding guests danced and partied, I sat with my eyes glued to the drummer, banging along on the chair beside me to keep time.

Warmonger

I was 8 years old
I watched a black & white TV
I had a toy machine gun
And I aimed it at the screen
I shot at Viet Cong
While the general's medal gleamed
They stood there like heroes
While the napalm dropped like rain

chorus:
Warmonger – don't make us count the dead
Warmonger – waste your own life instead
I hope you get, get what you deserve
Warmonger – will you help us to bury the dead

When I turned 10 years old
We got a colour TV
And it showed how a tin plate
Could hold a soldier's guts inside

And it showed monks burning
And villages ripped apart
And it showed me hatred
Every nite at 6 o'clock

chorus

Joey Shithead Keithley, Prisoner Publishing

From then on, I wanted a drum kit. My brother agreed to let me work part of his paper route to get the dough. I did the steepest third of his route for ten percent of his pay. (Jef has since gone on to be a great union organizer and negotiator.) Finally I had saved up $125, half of what I needed. I asked my parents for the rest.

My dad yelled and screamed. "You want to become a drummer? Goddammit! You'll end up being a hophead like Gene Kruppa." Not knowing what a hophead was, I wasn't deterred one bit. A couple of days later, when my father was at work, my dear old mom took me down to the music shop. She made up the cash shortfall, and I had my first drum kit. The drum lessons started, and then the practicing, which, over the next few years, would just about drive my parents nuts.

Shortly after I got to high school, some friends and I started our first band. Scott Flear and Ken McLeod were the only two guys I knew who had guitars and amps. We called ourselves Lead Balloon; that was definitely the way we were going to go over, because we sucked so much. We chickened out of our first and only gig.

By the time I was sixteen, though, a core part of the future punk rock scene in Vancouver had started jamming together. Brian Goble, Gerry Hannah, and I had all been friends since grade two, and Ken had moved into the area when I was eleven. Brian and I played a lot of hockey. I was a rough and tumble defenseman; penalties seemed to be my specialty. Brian was a good digger on the forward line, but he wasn't loud or brash. I also spent every summer playing lacrosse. Gerry was the hip outcast among us. He had long hair and sideburns and occassionally got kicked out of school. He was also the only one of our pals who managed to get a girlfriend. Ken was the unhip outcast. He had long hair and fucked-up clothes and his family were really different: they were the only Americans in our neighbourhood.

At fifteen, Ken ran away to Alberta with his pal Dave Noga for six months. They lied about their age and got jobs working in an asylum. When he came back, he had changed. He called Brian and me "rubbernecks," a term for kids who were really regular, with short hair; I was the only guy in school with a crew cut. He had turned onto mind-altering substances. But he also discovered something else that was mind-blowing. He had a copy of the epic album *Paranoid* by Black Sabbath. We had never heard anything like it.

Soon we were jamming every chance we could get. Our instrumentation was bizarre; the only part that made sense was the drumming. Ken and I both had drum kits. Brian played a chord organ. (If you've never heard one, let's just say it is one of the worst-sounding pieces of shit going.) Brian also had an acoustic six-string guitar until the top half of the neck broke off. We just strummed the three remaining strings. If we were over at Gerry's house, Gerry would play the organ that his ultra-religious mother practiced on for church. Nobody had an amp, so the drums drowned everything else out. We had no vehicle either, so we constantly carried our drum sets up and down the mountain.

Our practices drove my father so insane that he rigged up a separate power switch for my room. Whenever he had had enough, he would hit the switch and cut our power, then yell at the top of his lungs, "Goddammit, Joe! I can't hear myself think!" That was always our cue to move on.

Sometimes we practiced at Brian's place on the back porch. I remember us doing a tortured version of "Sweet Leaf" by Black Sabbath there. But sooner or later Brian's father would come running out and implore us to quit because the noise stopped the chickens from laying eggs. Chickens, for christ's sake, when we were trying to make rock 'n' roll history. Next we would try Ken's garage, but his dad would scream, "Kenny, what is this awful fuckin' noise? Why don't you get a real trade? You won't get anywhere with this music bullshit!" So that would leave Gerry's place, and we could only go there when his mom was at church or working at the hospital. As soon as we got the green light, Gerry would bust out with the massive water pipe and the wild jam would start.

After a while, we managed to borrow an Ace Tone amp and an electric guitar. We would plug the organ, guitar, and vocals into this poor defenseless amp, then max the distortion. Gerry, who had developed into our singer, lived on the main road to Simon Fraser University, built on top of Burnaby Mountain in 1965. On a hot summer day, with the SFU students walking up and down the hill, the real fun would begin. The students always looked perplexed as our wildly distorted jam blared out the open windows. Inside, Gerry would be writhing around on the floor, screaming, "Burn in hell! Burn in hell!"

Around this time, in 1971, the U.S. government announced that they were planning to test a series of nuclear devices on Amchitka Island, part of the Aleutian Islands chain off the tip of Alaska. Members of Greenpeace, which had been founded in Vancouver a few years earlier, started passing out pamphlets, urging people to come to the American consulate in Vancouver and demonstrate against the nuclear testing. They also approached local high schools with the idea that kids from each area would march down to the consulate on a rotating basis. Every day that week, high-school students from all over Greater Vancouver marched and chanted at the consulate. It was an all-out barrage. When our day came, about 300 students from Burnaby North and Kensington high schools walked out of their classes and headed downtown. Our route led us past some other Burnaby and East Vancouver schools, and we shouted up to the kids in their classes to join us. By the time we arrived at the U.S. consulate, we were 1,500 strong. What made it even more special for us was that Ken Montgomery had strapped on his bass drum and was leading the demonstration.

The next day, actor John Wayne, "the Duke," happened to be in town, on his way to a fishing trip somewhere in B.C. He stopped in at a local radio station to talk to right-wing smear-tactic host Pat Burns. Burns asked Wayne what he thought about all these Vancouver kids voicing their opinions, to which the Duke replied, "I think these goddamn Canadians should mind their own goddamn business!" That was infuriating and funny, but the topper for me was when I got home from school that afternoon and I checked the *Vancouver Sun* for coverage of the demonstration. My father read the paper fanatically; he was the type of guy who would berate the paperboy if our paper was so much as five minutes late. That day I beat my father home, though, and you can imagine my panic when I discovered a picture of Ken and me on the front page, leading the fucking march! I hadn't told my parents I'd skipped school to go, and at that moment I thought I was a dead fifteen-year-old. So I grabbed the paper and hid it in my closet. You should have heard my old man ranting and raving that night about his missing newspaper. Little did he know!

That demonstration really politicized me. Like John Sinclair said, "You got to decide if you're part of the problem or part of the solution." Another thing that changed my perspective on the world was my trip to Jamaica. My brother Jef had gone to a little town there to teach building construction to high school students, and in the summer of '73 my parents and I flew down to visit him. What a culture shock. Jamaica is a great country, but what really got me was the music. I had never listened to reggae or even heard of Rasta culture. My brother loaded me up with a bunch of a records like the soundtrack to *The Harder They Come*, and I was hooked. Little did I realize that a whole amalgamation of reggae and punk rock lay just a couple of years down the road.

High school eventually came to an end. I had a good idea of what I wanted to do: go to Simon Fraser University to become a lawyer. Not a slimy corporate hack who twisted and deflated the truth for his own ill-gotten gains, but rather a man with principles, a civil rights lawyer like William Kunstler, famous for defending the Chicago Seven. SFU appealed to me not only because I knew every inch of Burnaby Mountain, but because radical students had occupied the campus there in the early seventies. I wanted to be one of them.

In the summer of 1974, I worked on the green chain in a sawmill, pulling 2x4s and 2x6s off the conveyor belt. I quit when my dad, a machinist, got me a job working with him at Osborne Propellers. I love my father, but working with him was tough sledding. He had this unending temper which he inherited from his own father, an English salesman and miner who had been the black sheep of his family back in Yorkshire. I was lucky there was a balance, though; I got my compassionate side from my mother and her family of Finnish immigrants, who had been involved in the radical Fisherman's Union.

The day after I enrolled at SFU, I bought my first guitar from San Francisco Pawnbrokers on Hastings Street. During the fall, I worked a lot harder at learning to play it than I did at my courses. I spent too much time at the school pub and the university radio station, and it seemed as if the radical element that had drawn me there had either left or gone silent. I dropped out after four months – so much for being a lawyer.

I idled away the first few months of 1975 at my parents' house. Then Gerry Hannah started talking about moving out of the city to the country. Brian, Ken, and I were stunned.

"How the fuck are we going to be a rock band out in the country?" we demanded.

Gerry had an answer for that. "We'll all play acoustic instruments, and that way we won't be supporting the evil BC Hydro power corporation and their ability to flood valleys at the drop of a kilowatt. Back to the land, man!"

Gerry started to peruse the *Georgia Straight*, Vancouver's local alternative weekly, for places in the country. Before long, we got word from some commune (this was way before punk rock, remember!) that a forty-acre farm near Lumby, in British Columbia's interior, was going to be open for squatting.

Me and Fast Eddie, another colourful character from north Burnaby, were the vanguard. So we hitchhiked up there. Now, if you've never been to a small, forestry-based town in British Columbia, you haven't missed much. Lumby is one of those towns. The first thing you see when you drive into it are thousands and thousands of dead trees, and everybody in the whole fucking place is proud of it.

The farm was four miles out of town, on Cooper Mountain, and it had two cabins, no running water, and no electricity. Eddie and I squatted it, and shortly after, we were joined by Brian, Ken, Gerry, and Bruce Coleman, another neighbourhood friend. They had all quit high school just short of graduation for this idyllic paradise. (Really bloody smart.) The best thing on the farm was the outhouse; you could leave the door open as you did your business and enjoy a panoramic view of surrounding mountains. Sometimes when I would be taking a crap, Gerry would nudge the outhouse with his truck while honking the horn.

We were like junior hippies, and as we got to know the townsfolk, we found ourselves growing more unpopular by the day. The town had two cops; the head of the constabulary had apparently been demoted because of a despicable incident that involved kicking a sixty-year-old First Nations man to death in the mud. The other cop we nicknamed Carl the Cow, since he bore an uncanny resemblance to a cow we had run into. I looked up "redneck town" in the dictionary, and there was a picture of Lumby.

To make things worse, there was a brewery strike that summer. Hardly a drop of beer to be got in the entire province. Everybody was desperate. There were huge lineups at the liquor store whenever word got out that a rare shipment of suds was coming in from Alberta. People even lined up for American beer. Like I said, they were desperate.

After the strike had been going for a while, somebody stole the only beer truck to reach our area in over a month. A day or two later, a cop car roared up Cooper Mountain. Carl the Cow jumped out with a bovine look of satisfaction on his face. He started shouting at us. "All right! Come clean with me! Where's that beer truck?"

We could only look bewildered and collectively scratch our heads, which further infuriated him. Right around the time the beer truck was stolen, somebody had seen Gerry's truck in town, Carl explained accusingly. We told him to check the local garage, where Gerry's truck had been in pieces for the last week. Now he was really pissed. He jumped back in his cruiser and raced off. Great bit of police work. (Carl was an inspiration when I wrote the D.O.A. song "Royal Police.")

After three months of ongoing tension with the locals, including threats that they were going to beat the crap out of us and rip off all our musical gear – by this point, we had told Gerry to screw the accoustic thing and rented some electric amps – we got evicted. We were turfed because some real hippie had rented the farm legally. Shit! Imagine that!

We decided to move further into the Monashee Mountains, to a tiny burg called Cherryville. The only things there were a general store, a community hall, and a bridge. But the place we rented five miles up the road was huge; it had power and water, and we could make as much noise as we wanted with our obnoxious rock band. Nobody had a job, but Gerry and I were collecting unemployment enjoyment. We had lots of time to practice.

We landed our first gig at a wake at the Cherryville Hall. The name of our band at that point was The Resurrection; maybe that's why they hired us. The wake was for a logger who had been crushed by a tree in the bush, and it was attended by everybody in the vicinity: aunts, uncles, grandmothers, you name it. There were maybe a hundred people all told.

The first musicians on stage were the Foise Family Band. The band featured the entire fucking Foise family, right down to grandpa on the fiddle and the little kid on the drums. Then it was our turn to play. We played one Beatles song, one Black Sabbath song, and a couple of others. After each song, the crowd stood and stared in disbelief. One guy clapped, but it was our friend Derek, the guitar repairman, and eventually he stopped, too. After the fourth song, we were asked to stop playing altogether. To add to the embarrassment, the next band, the Cherryvillains, went over like gangbusters. Shit! What a first gig.

As the months went by, we landed a few more shows, and got into plenty of hassles with the cops and the locals, who just didn't get us. One night our house was attacked by a bunch of drunk rednecks. We started up the chainsaw to chase them away, and you could almost hear them shitting their pants as they took off.

Fall turned to winter, and it got very, very cold. First we ran out of money, then firewood. One night we were drinking and smoking at the Lumby Hotel, and when we got kicked out I was way too loaded for the twenty-mile car ride back to Cherryville. I slept in the doorway of the hotel that night. About five in the morning I woke up feeling like a Popsicle. I had on an old ratty coat, and there was about a foot of snow on the ground. I had eleven cents in my pocket. That was it – I couldn't take that clean country living any more. So I decided to hitchhike back to Vancouver.

It was 250 miles to get home. It usually took three to four hitched rides to make it back, maybe ten hours. On this frozen January day, it took me a day and a half and eleven stinkin' rides, the same number of pennies I had in my pocket. One well-groomed young couple kicked me out in the middle of nowhere after I told them I was an atheist. I got off one good line when they insisted on calling me a Satanist: "I'd rather be a king in hell, than a stooge in heaven!"

Soon thereafter, the rest of the gang moved back to North Burnaby as well. Brian, Ken, Gerry, and I rented a big house and kept practicing. We played a few high schools as Stone Crazy. When we

Stone Crazy (l-r Brad Kent, Brian Goble, Joe Keithley, Ken Montgomery), 1976.

were forced to move by our slumlords, we found a new house farther out in the suburbs, in a town called Coquitlam.

To keep ourselves going, the four of us got hired on at Royal City Foods, a food processing company. They would hire anybody. Brad Kent, a rock 'n' roller from South Burnaby who we had met in Cherryville and who would become our lead guitar player, also worked at Royal City. Brad would chuck his cigarette butts into the blueberry hopper for fun. Ken worked in the room where they made creamed corn. It was a mundane job; at more or less the appropriate time, he was supposed to dump certain ingredients into the vat: a hundred-pound sack of cornstarch, a fifty-pound sack of sugar, and so on. One night, he came home from the late shift and said, "Hey, you guys. Guess what? I pissed into the vat of creamed corn!" Like I said, they hired anybody. To this day I have never eaten another can of the stuff.

Finally, Stone Crazy got its first paying gig, four nights at the Grasslands Motor Inn in Merritt, B.C., for the royal sum of $125 a night. By this point, we had changed the line-up. There was Ken, Brian, Gerry, and I as usual, as well as a new guitar player, Simon Werner. Originally a Brit, Simon had been in Canada for a while, but he never lost that dry, English wit. We drove to Merritt on my twenty-first birthday, June 3, 1977. It's another one of those towns where the first thing you see is piles of dead trees. The Grasslands' manager, Big Joe, demanded that we play a Steve Miller song during the sound check, so we launched into a shakey rendition of "Rock 'N Me" ("Keep on-a rockin' me, baby"). He was suitably unimpressed.

Nighttime drew in swiftly, and we headed on stage for the first of four sets. I can't remember exactly when the booing and the catcalling started. Let me think . . . was it after our first song, or our second? What a way to start! Big Joe, the nauseating prick boss, came backstage and threatened us if we didn't get better. But our second set proved to be even worse. Snuck into the set, along with the predictable rock standards of the day, was our cover of "Beat on the Brat" by the Ramones, and the first song I ever wrote: "Disco Sucks." These gems went over like Scud missiles. Then we launched into "Paranoid." As we got to the lead section, a solo by me, I reached over to my Marshall amp and cranked everything up to ten. When the song was over, two huge lumberjacks jumped up on the stage, yelling, "Turn it down or we'll tear it down!" Not impressed, I told them to fuck off. One of the lumberjacks, now frothing at the mouth, shouted back, "Turn it down or we'll cut you down like a Douglas Fir!" Despite this, we managed to get to the end of our set, exiting to a chorus of boos.

Unfortunately, all the excitement caused me to take temporary leave of my senses. I walked back on stage and grabbed the mike. "The problem with you people is, you don't have the balls to accept this kind of music!" I yelled. As I walked off, one of the lumberjacks in the audience yelled: "I'll have your balls for bookends, buddy!" Backstage, the rest of the band admonished me. "Joe, are you fucking crazy? You're going to get us killed!"

That night, Big Joe fired us. When I protested that we had a contract for four nights, he laughed in my face and threw thirty bucks at me. Shit! That wouldn't cover the gas, let alone the van rental. The next day, as we were being thrown out of the hotel, Joe came around one last time. "I'm gonna be a nice guy," he said. "You only have to pay half on your meal last night." Goddamn it! Fuck Big Joe and fuck Merritt. On our way back to Vancouver, we stopped at a high mountain pass and talked about the whole experience. "This rock 'n' roll trip ain't all it's cracked up to be," somebody said. The rest of us seconded that. Then Simon said, "Maybe we should become a punk rock band."

Simon was right. That would be cool.

Stone Crazy (l-r Joe Keithley, Brian Goble, Ken Montgomery, Brad Kent), 1976.

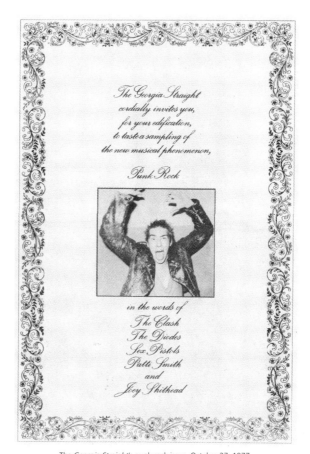

The Georgia Straight
cordially invites you,
for your edification,
to taste a sampling of
the new musical phenomenon,

Punk Rock

in the words of
The Clash
The Diodes
Sex Pistols
Patti Smith
and
Joey Shithead

The *Georgia Straight*'s punk rock issue, October 27, 1977.

CHAPTER TWO
THE SKULLS

It was a raunchy scene around our joint on North Road in Coquitlam in 1977. The neighbourhood had a bus loop, a mall, five fast-food joints, and a bar, the Caribou Hotel, where we hung out nightly. Various lowlifes were always coming by our place, trying to sell us hot goods or to rip us off when the house was empty. We practiced a lot, blasting day and night, and anybody who was walking by or had heard about the band house would feel free to pop in the door with a case of beer and start partying. We would pay Ken's fourteen-year-old brother Chuck and fifteen-year-old Bill Chobatar to guard the place while we were at work. They would skip school and jam all day long or just plain slack.

At that point, there was no punk scene in Vancouver, as far as we knew. We'd been listening to the Ramones' first album and to a bunch of stuff by Iggy Pop, the greatest stage guy/wildman I have ever seen. We had also seen short news clips of the Damned, the Clash, and the Sex Pistols. We figured that punk rock was the snarling, confrontational, kick-in-the-teeth rebellion that rock 'n' roll was always meant to be. Punk was the antithesis of the rock business that included performers so despicable they made us feel embarassed to be a member of the human race. Gerry wasn't too heavy into punk, though, so we needed a new singer. We put an ad in the *Georgia Straight*, and we ended up with Lee Kendall, a lunatic Australian. What other kind are there?

Now we had a line-up. We called ourselves the Skulls. It was mean! What we needed next were punk rock nicknames; our given names would never do. Ken suggested the name "Joey Shithead and the Marching Morons" for the band, and I gratefully adopted Shithead for myself. Simon figured that Brian looked like the famous chess master La Bourdonnais. It was a poor punk name, but you have to start somewhere. Ken thought up his own moniker: Dimwit. He and I tried to give Simon the name Ring Wormer, but Simon wouldn't go for it. He was a little touchy, as well as a bit of a Bible thumper. Lee was just plain Lee. Brad Kent became Brad Kunt.

As summer rolled along, I heard something that would change my life forever. A local radio station announced that the Ramones were going to play Vancouver's Commodore Ballroom, Canada's best live venue. The great thing was that the tickets were free. They had only sold about 100 tickets for a venue that holds 1,200 people, so it was time to paper the place. Fuckin-A! Bubba! The Ramones for free!

We got down there at eight PM, along with about 400 other would-be punks and thrillseekers. The Ramones came on stage an hour later, and they blew the doors off that fuckin' joint. I had never seen anything so alive in all my life. They played for thirty-five minutes, and then it was over. Everybody was drenched with sweat and bruised from all the fun on the dance floor. For me, that was it. I knew I was on the right path.

The Skulls' first gig as a punk band was a free show on the beach at White Rock, twenty miles south of Vancouver. When we arrived in mid-afternoon, Art Bergmann (the K-Tels, the Young Canadians, Los PopulBros) was already on stage with his band, the Smorgs. The audience was a mix of people to be sure, but the most prominent type was what I would call the greaseball hippie: you know, guys with long greasy hair and beards and Jack Daniel's T-shirts who like to sit on the beach and smoke and drink away as many brain cells as possible.

Our set consisted of a few early originals that all of us had written together. They had a heavy punk sound. We also played some Iggy and some Ramones covers. Those greaseball hippies sure weren't ready for it. After a couple of songs, they started hucking their garbage at us. Soon the bandshell was littered. Lee, our Australian lead singer, started throwing the garbage right back at the crowd and telling them to fuck off. At one point, Buck Cherry (AKA John Armstrong of the Modernettes) jumped up on stage and tried to sing along on Brad Kunt's mike. A pushing and shoving match ensued, and Buck was ejected from the stage. More garbage was thrown, there was more pushing and shoving, and general ill will set in.

The Skulls (l-r Dimwit, Shithead, Wimpy), 1977.   The Skulls (l-r Wimpy, Dimwit, Simon, Shithead), 1977.

After the show, we figured we needed some publicity, so the next day I phoned Tom Harrison, a Vancouver rock critic who wrote for the *Georgia Straight* at the time. "Tom," I said, "I want to tell you about a big riot that happened at the open air show in White Rock on Sunday with my band, the Skulls."

Tom said, "Who is this?"

I gulped, never having said my new stage name aloud. I finally stammered, "This is Joey Sh- Sh- Sh- Shithead."

"Well, Mr Shithead," Tom said, "can you tell me what happened?"

The following Thursday we raced out to grab the new issue of the *Straight*. There it was, in black and white, an article on the Skulls. "The Skulls, undoubtedly Vancouver's most hated rock band, started a riot in White Rock last Sunday," Tom had written. The article went on to say that Brad Kunt had shoved local musician Buck Cherry off the stage and told him he'd have it out with him anywhere anytime anyplace. As I read Tom's article aloud, everybody screamed and guffawed. Then we all looked at each other. Wow! Vancouver's most hated band! We're on our way, motherfuckers!

Shortly after this, both Lee and Brad left the band. Lee did the usual wandering Australian thing and Brad just didn't fit in. He was never really a punk. The Skulls became streamlined: Simon on guitar, Brian on bass, Dimwit on drums, and me on vocals.

Vancouver had its first local punk rock show on July 30, 1977 at the Japanese Hall. It featured the Furies, the city's first punk rock band, and Dee Dee and the Dishrags, the first punk band from Victoria, just across the water. I missed that show, but soon we heard about another one, scheduled for September 2 at the Japanese Hall. The posters were already up, but I phoned and got us on the bill. The Lewd were the headliners, and the Furies had the middle spot. Dee and the Dishrags were supposed to open, but we, the last-minute addition, opened for them. None of the bands had really developed a following, but lots of curious music fans came to the show. The Skulls started the show. We played fourteen songs, seven covers, a mix of Sex Pistols and Iggy songs, and seven original songs. I had played maybe ten shows in my lifetime, always as the rhythm guitar player. This was the first time I had been the front man, the lead singer, the shit disturber. I can't remember much about the show, except that I was screaming a lot. I do remember feeling fucking exhilarated. But we were starting to get some cohesion as a band. Simon was good on guitar, and Brian's bass playing was really coming along. Dimwit was well on his way to becoming one of the top five drummers Canada has ever produced.

The Dishrags came on second, and were incredibly rough and amazing

at the same time. These three fifteen-year-old Victoria girls ripped it up. The Furies were on third, with Chris Arnett on guitar, Malcolm Hasman (later Simon Werner's older brother Jonathan) on bass, and Jim Walker (PiL) on drums. They seemed a little out of sync to me. The show was headlined by the obviously more experienced band, the Lewd, from Seattle, who played a slicker set than the rest of us.

The most memorable part of the night for me occurred after the show. The Labour Day weekend was coming up, and the Satan's Angels (who later became the Vancouver chapter of the Hell's Angels) had hired the Furies, the Lewd, and the Skulls to play at a giant gathering they were holding on a farm in Matsqui, forty miles east of Vancouver. The bikers had heard about the burgeoning punk scene, but they were under the major misconception that the Furies were actually called the Fuhrers, as in Adolf. As for the other two bands, I think they just liked our names.

After the show at the Japanese Hall, one of the head Angels showed up backstage. He had liked the show, and he wanted to confirm that we would all be at the bikers' event. "Fuck, yeah!" I said. It sounded great to me – $200 a day and all the beer we could drink; three days of straight nonstop party. When the Angel turned to the Furies' Chris Arnett, however, Chris looked kind of pale. He mumbled something, then said, "I have to fly to South America tomorrow," one of the lamest excuses I have ever heard. The biker called Chris on his bullshit and started to chase him around the room. He caught Chris and smacked him a couple of times. Finally Chris managed to wriggle out of the room and escape a royal boot fucking. I just looked at the Angel and said, "See you tomorrow."

My only previous dealings with a bike gang had been as a gas jerk a few years earlier. One quiet summer's day, forty bikes and a parts truck pulled into the full-serve station where I worked. That was a lot of filling to do. Bike tanks are small, and the design painted on the tank is really fucking important; it's where the owner shows off the bike's soul, so to speak. While filling the first guy's tank, I accidentally spilled gas on his tank. He swore at me and gave me a look that said, "I am going to cut your balls off and shove them down your throat as soon as I am finished cleaning this up!" He grabbed the nozzle from me, and at that moment we became a self-serve station.

But I digress. I got a ride out to the Labour Day bike run with my friend Brett in his Mustang. As soon as we pulled off the highway, we were met by two RCMP officers who were noting everybody coming and going. Further up the road, we ran into a biker lying down on the seat of his bike. He was like the palace guard. Once we identified ourselves, he let us pass without incident. We didn't get another 100 metres, though, before we were assailed by a gang of bikers. I got out of the car, and a guy starts yelling, "Hey, it's Shithead and the Skulls." Then they all yelled, "Hey, Shithead!" and stuff like "Are you going to take a shit on stage?" (I gave that a try later in the weekend, but I was not able to duplicate the feat of the mighty Frank Zappa.)

Now we had to wait for the rest of the band. So far there was only Dimwit, Bill Chobatar, my girlfriend Cheryl Thompson (whom I had met a couple of months earlier at the Coquitlam jam house), myself, and the gear. Brett headed back to Vancouver to pick up Simon and Brian, but we learned later he was scared shitless of the bikers and refused to come back; Simon and Brian had to bum a ride with someone else. The only other entertainer there at the time was Dave Freeburn, a solo piano act. Dave started the show off with some raunchy blues, but when he was done, the Lewd still hadn't showed up. The bikers were restless and demanded music, so Dimwit, Chobatar (who was just along for the ride), and I got up and did a makeshift set.

Eventually Simon and Brian arrived. Now the crowd – 600 to 700 bikers and various hangers-on – wanted to hear the Skulls. No problem, we said, but first we needed the libations we had been promised. I walked down to the farm utility building that housed the bar, the prize Harley that somebody was going to win that weekend, and round-the-clock blue movies. The guy behind the bar was about 6'5" and must have weighed about 300 pounds. I went up to him and said, "Hey, I'm in the Skulls, and we need some beer." He looked at me with violent disgust. "It's two bucks a beer, puke!" I knew I had to stick to my guns or get run out of the joint. So I shot back, "Hey, I'm in the band, man, and we're supposed to get free beer."

He was having none of it. "Two bucks a beer, puke!"

"No, no, no. It's all the beer we can drink."

"It's two bucks, kid."

A small crowd had started to gather, and I figured I was in for a right pounding. Finally, the bartender smiled, then handed me a case of beer. "Have a good time, kid!" he said with a laugh.

I got back to the stage and we launched into our set. It got a mixed reaction, but the event was young, and we were still warming up. The stage was a flatbed trailer up on a hill looking north across the Fraser River. They had a huge sound system that was cranked. It must have been torture on the other side of the river in those God-fearing little farmhouses. It was as if satanic beasts were roaring out a call for all pagans to come and join in the ritual.

The Lewd were scheduled to go on after us, but there was a bit of a hold up. It seems that their manager, Robert the Weasel, was busy trying to renegotiate the deal the band had made with the bikers. Instead of $200, they wanted $300, so the Weasel had suggested that the Skulls' fee be cut back to $100 to make up the difference. The negotiations were being conducted in a helicopter, since a helicopter jockey was giving the bikers rides for twenty dollars a pop, and the Weasel was lucky he didn't get a Bre-X kind of ride down. When the copter landed, a few bikers told me about the Weasel's sliminess.

The Lewd got up and played their set. It was cool, but I'm not sure the crowd liked it much. Part of the problem was that the Lewd only *had* one set, and they were scheduled to play all night. The other part was that they dressed a little on the New Wave side. Some of the crowd was cat-calling the band and calling them fags.

I'm not certain if the Lewd got paid, but I do know one thing. They played one set that night and then made an unceremonious exit. After their last song, they threw their gear into their van as fast as they could and then jumped in after it. As their van pulled away, some of the bikers started to chase it, hurling beer bottles and swearing at them. The van bumped wildly across the field with about twenty guys in pursuit. I don't think I ever saw the Lewd back in Canada again.

So the Skulls and Dave Freeburn were left to entertain the troops. We only had one set of tunes, but all we had to do was change the order we played them. We played set after set till about four in the morning. My girlfriend Cheryl and I wanted to crash out, but it was tough to sleep on the stage, with the gas-powered generator roaring beside us, not to mention the general mayhem still going on. It looked like a fine night for sleeping under the stars, so we grabbed our sleeping bags and headed out across the field. It was very peaceful till about five in the morning, when a rainstorm passed over us and we got fucking soaked. We headed back to the stage where the rest of the band was passed out, and used Dimwit's dirty drum carpet (that doubled as a spittoon) as a blanket. Lovely.

We enjoyed a restful hour, till six AM, when about a dozen bikers came up and started banging their beer bottles on the stage, yelling, "Wake up music! Wake up music!" Finally Dave Freeburn got up and played "Saran Wrap" by the Fugs on his electric piano. That got the day started.

We met a friend of Freeburn's that weekend who became a lifelong friend of mine and Dimwit's. He was Al Steadman, but we quickly gave him the nickname, Al Dopeman. Al would play a key role in some early D.O.A. trips.

We alternated with Freeburn, basically playing the same set all day long. The only sustenance around was an endless supply of pills and beer. Brian got so wasted that he would pass out between sets on the side of the stage. He didn't bother taking his bass off, but just lay there there comatose with the bass across his gut.

One benefit of playing the same songs over and over again was that the crowd got to know them and began yelling for their favourites. We finished our final set at around four-thirty in the morning on Sunday, with a half dozen bikers up on stage, singing along and beating on the mikestands with spare drumsticks. They were really getting the hang of it by the end. I have never done anything like that since. That was one of the wildest gangs I've ever encountered. What an extraordinary weekend!

Like any young new band, the Skulls needed more shows, but we had no manager, no booking agent, not even a scummy, run-down, roach-infested club to play in. It was a desert out there. So I decided to take matters into my own hands. These days, people always ask me, "What did punk rock accomplish?" Let me tell you, punk went a long ways towards reinventing and reinforcing the DIY ethic: DO IT YOURSELF. We realized we could achieve many things by running our own lives and rejecting the modern western version of the "slave" mentality.

In September 1977, I went out and rented a hall, the Port Moody Legion Hall, to be exact. I told the old guy who ran it that we were putting on a young

Disco Sucks

I was walkin', walkin' around
walkin' round, round downtown
saw some people stompin' around,
sayin' disco sucks,like shit
lots of plastic people
building a plastic steeple
disco sucks, disco sucks, disco sucks, like shit

Joey Shithead Keithley, Prisoner Publishing

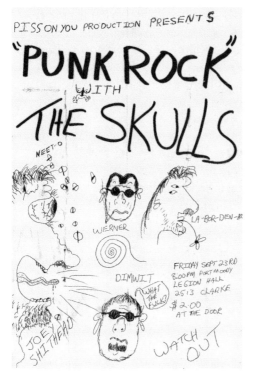

people's concert. Next I got Bob Montgomery – Dimwit and Chuck's middle brother and a fine fellow in his own right – to design a poster. "Piss on You Productions presents the Skulls," it read. It featured caricatures of each of us, and there were flies buzzing around the Shithead likeness.

My old man had always drilled a work ethic into me, so I was a real go-getter. I knew things had to get done, so I put in the time and the elbow-grease that was required. I phoned the local papers, then began postering the city. I would jam my backpack full of posters, squeezing in a bag of flour and a staple gun, and take along my trusty bucket. Then I would hop on a bus and go to it. When there was nowhere to use the staple gun, I would stop at a gas station for some water and mix up a thick, gooey mixture of flour and water. I'd spread the goo on metal light standards with my hands, and stick up the poster. *Voilà!* (Some of those posters stayed up for years, which is saying something when you think of the long periods of rain we endure on the West Coast.) After a short while my jeans and leather jacket were so covered with the shit I looked like a drywaller. On the return trip, I always got my own seat on the bus, no problem.

Finally the day of the gig arrived. We drove out to the hall and started setting up our gear. We hadn't been there long when two guys in ill-fitting suits came in. "Who's in charge of this shindig?" one of them asked. After a pregnant pause, I turned around and said, "I guess I am." The two turned out to be plainsclothes policemen. The first one continued, "We've been seeing your posters everywhere, and you know what?"

"What?"

"They're obscene."

I played dumb. "What do you mean?"

"You know what I mean," the cop snarled. "This is sick stuff, really sick stuff!"

The hall was silent as we glared at each other.

"You better run a tight ship tonight. We'll be keeping a close eye on the hall!" With that, the cops left in a huff. That was the last we saw of them.

Before we knew it, it was time to open the doors. We got about forty people: twenty punks and twenty bikers, who sat on opposite sides of the hall. Cheryl, ever the loudmouth, almost got me killed by taking the largest biker's chair and telling him to get another one. He said, "That's my fucking chair!"

"There's another bloody chair right there!" Cheryl yelled back. I took her by the hand and we got out of there.

But then the same biker came backstage and saw that Dimwit had a fake hypodermic needle pinned to his shirt. The hulking mass of a man irately ripped the hypo off Dimwit's shirt and grabbed him by the throat. "I ought to shove this down your throat!" he barked, but nothing came of it.

Somehow, the show went off okay, and I put on a few more hall shows that fall. At one of them, a bunch of the bikers showed up and offered to run the door for me. That was a tough offer to refuse. It worked okay until the bikers started charging kids to get in the door, and then charging them on the way out as well.

Meanwhile, I had to make some decisions. I wasn't making a dime off the music, so I needed another job. One day Al Dopeman suggested I go along with him and become a taxi driver. The company he worked for said they would hire me, but not until I got a cab licence. Al said that was no problem, though, since he and Dave Freeburn, who also drove cabs for the company, didn't have licences either. The company never bothered to check. All you had to do was go to the motor vehicle office and tell them you'd lost your driver's licence. When you got the temporary one, you could put a little sticker over the part of the licence that specified what class it was, then write in the one you wanted to have. Instant licence! Instant job!

I started with the night shift. Every night the same thing: drunken loogans who could barely remember where they lived and had often drunk away the money to pay the fare. At least I got beer as a tip almost every night. My caper finally ended when a Port Moody cop pulled me over for an illegal turn and suspected that my licence was phony. He gave me three hours to come back with a proper one. But I never did. For the next month, the Port Moody cops pulled over every single Coquitlam cab looking for me. I wasn't in any of them.

The Skulls had written a bunch of original songs by this point, and we decided to make a demo. We went to Psi-cord Studios, an 8-track outfit in Vancouver. I had a hand in writing or had written the three songs we recorded: "No Escape," "Waiting for You," and "Fucked Up Baby." We sent the tape to Bomb Records in Toronto, but nothing ever came of it.

Near the end of October 1977, the *Georgia Straight* invited us to play at their tenth anniversary bash, to be held at the Commodore Ballroom. There were a few other bands there too, the standard boring rock shit of the day. The Skulls were out to cause trouble that night, but we didn't have to try very hard. When we hit the stage, the collective jaw of the audience immediately dropped. The joint was full of Vancouver's old hippie establishment. These people had never heard of punk rock, and it was obvious they were not going to like it anytime soon.

During our fourth song, the club turned the power off. By then, about a third of the audience had already left the venue. Dimwit kept drumming. I ran over and got into a screaming match with the stage manager. He and I ended up in a tug of war with our power supply box. Then it turned into a pushing and shoving match. That was it. We told the organizers to fuck off and left.

At this point we decided we were not going to get anywhere by hanging out in Vancouver. So we made a plan. We would all keep working at Royal City Foods and save up some dough. Then we'd move to Toronto for a while and then on to London, the punk rock capital of the world, to make our big break. Cheryl and I decided we would stay together and she would come along. This was not greeted by a chorus of cheers by the rest of the band.

By the time we were ready to hit the road for Toronto, Gerry Hannah had fuck all to do in Vancouver, so he came along for the ride. Gerry, Dimwit, Brian, and I were still the "gang of four."

We decided to put on one last show in Vancouver, and it turned out to be a seminal one for Vancouver punk rock. It was a punk show and we were the only punk band in town, so everyone connected to the scene showed up. Since the Furies' last line-up (with Jim Walker on drums) had broken up, there were no other bands to play with. So we just traded instruments and started another band. This gave birth to what Vancouver calls a "fuck band": a band dedicated to pure fun. We became Victorian Pork, with Dimwit on bass, Brad Kunt on guitar, Dave Noga on vocals, and me on drums as "Flab Jiggle." (Victorian Pork still play to this day, albeit with a completely different line-up.)

We lined up a "drive-through" motorhome to take us and our gear to Toronto. (It used to be easy to get these; you'd drive a rental vehicle back to its point of origin, having to pay only for the gas.) It was November 1977, and it was the first time any of us had traversed our home and native land. We soon found out what a big-ass country Canada is. The ground in Saskatchewan was covered with snow, and it was so fucking flat that you could see a grain elevator miles away. It looked like the earth had been run over by a giant bulldozer! Let's just say the beauty of the heartland is an acquired taste. The road was like a skating rink through eastern Manitoba. I drove through a flotilla of cop cars and tow trucks, my knuckles white from grippin' the wheel.

Finally, we arrived in Toronto. Hogtown. The Big Smoke, as First Nations people used to call it back when it was still Fort Toronto. We had no place to stay, no gigs, and no jobs. As *Road Warrior*'s Lord Humungous, the ruler of the wasteland, would say, "What a puny plan." We ended up in what was then the most beat-up area of the city, Lawrence Avenue, and got six beds at the Lawrence Hotel. Boy, it was cheap – $2.33 per person per night. A real luxury joint. The only drawback was that you had to step over the puddles of blood in the doorway of the common bathroom and the guys passed out in the hall. As it turned out, Toronto was entering the coldest winter it had had for thirty years, and in the room Cheryl and I had, there were two small holes in the window. (I don't know if they were from bullets or not.) When I complained, the hotel gave us a blanket that was half my height. Just ducky.

On our second night in town, we decided to cruise Yonge Street, the main drag, hoping like hell our guitars and amps would not get ripped off from the hotel in our absence. Yonge Street, the longest and most famous street in the country, is completely overrated by Torontonians. We walked by Maple Leaf Gardens, just off the strip, and past the Eaton's Centre shopping mall before coming to a hoary old rock club called the Gasworks. On stage was a famous Canadian band called GODDO, fronted by a bass player named Greg Godovitz. Their music was the typical rock of the day.

Then the band stopped, and Greg announced that they were going to do their "punk" set. We sure as hell paid attention. But the music sounded just like their other stuff, only sped up a bit. When they had done a couple of songs, I ran up to the stage and said to Greg, "Hey! Why don't you let a real punk band get up there and play?" To my surprise, he said sure.

We hopped up on stage and ripped into a mini-set using GODDO's gear. The audience – well, talk about a bunch of slack-jawed gawkers. Those rock fans were shocked. After about five songs, somebody from the management came up and screamed for us to stop. Apparently, all alcohol sales had ground to a standstill. We gave up, thanked the band for letting us play, and left. I've got to say that was ultra-cool of them; for all they knew, we might have pulled a "Who" on their gear.

After about a week in Toronto, we found a house to rent on the west side. It was an Italian neighbourhood with lots of churches. Cheryl and I had the upper floor, the rest of the band moved into the basement, and smack dab in the middle was Ed, our drunken fifty-five-year-old landlord. At first Ed was cool; he would come downstairs and dance around with a beer in one hand and a smoke in the other while we were practicing. But before long he started calling the cops on us whenever we practiced or had parties. Sometimes he would knock on our door and ask to use the bathroom, saying, "I think I just shit my pants." He must have thought we were going to kill him, because he would push his mattress and chair up against his door when he went to bed.

The Skulls finally got on a bill. We opened for the Viletones and the Ugly at Club David's, a gay club that showcased punk a couple of nights a week. Right in the centre of the club was a reproduction of Michelangelo's *David* pissing into a fountain. It was a good bill. The Ugly and the Viletones both had a lot of energy on stage. We played well, but we got the cold shoulder from the Toronto punks. We came across like a bunch of lumberjacks, I guess, and most of the people in the scene liked to act as if they were from

New York. But we had our way of making a mark. One night at David's I dragged Nazi Dog (Steven Leckie) of the Viletones through a pool of urine I had deposited on the dance floor.

I became quite fond of spraypainting in Toronto, and I always had my handy-dandy can at the ready. It was the one thing I could do to drum up some publicity for the band. The power of intelligent grafitti cannot be underestimated. I'm not sure mine fell into that category, but graffiti is the voice of the people nonetheless. I would spraypaint the band's name and various slogans outside clubs, on churches, on walls, anywhere I could. It was fun to be provocative and destructive at the same time. A rumour started around town that the cops were looking for the Skulls, but I guess they never bothered to look at the street posters. We were not too bloody hard to find.

In one sense Toronto was like Vancouver: there were very few places to play. We had heard about the Crash 'n' Burn, a place the Diodes had helped make famous, but it was closed by the time we arrived. We did go to a couple of parties the Diodes threw, but they came across as art school posers to me.

We continued to play at David's once in a while, and also at another establishment called the Shock Theatre. Our first show there, we opened for what must have been the original line-up of the Misfits. I hadn't heard of them, but I knew they had driven up from New York City. About forty people showed up for the show. While on stage in between songs I found the Misfits set list that they had left during soundcheck. I thought it was an old set list from some previous gig and I started reading out and ridiculing the song titles, then I ripped them up. When we were finished, some big guy from the Misfits gave me a hard time about it. It turns out the set list was theirs and he was downright pissed, you might say, in the American sense of the word.

I don't know what it was about our gang, but we seemed to rub people the wrong way. A lot of Toronto punks hated us, although we got along with most of the bands. We really liked the Ugly, and played three or four shows with them.

THE **SHOCK THEATRE**
565 college st
SKULLS
SAT.
JAN. 7
$ 2.99
9:00 P.M.
WITH
SPECIAL
GUESTS
WIMPY
AND THE
BLOATED
COWS
FROM LONDON, EN

Most of the band later relocated to Vancouver. Mike Nightmare, their singer, came up with one of the great rock 'n' roll quotes of all time on his thirtieth birthday when he told me, "Fuck, Joey! I'm thirty years old, and what have I got? A beat-up car and a bunch of scratched Iggy Pop records!" That should be in the *Official Rock 'n' Roll Book of Quotes*. They should put his quote right next to mine.

We hunted around Toronto for a record deal but never got a bite. Gerry Hannah was working on some cool songs there, though, and he penned two classics while playing bass in our basement: "Slave to My Dick" and "Fuck You." Gerry had no band of his own, so we formed Wimpy and the Bloated Cows: Gerry on bass, Simon on guitar, and me, Flab Jiggle, on drums. Brian was the vocalist, becoming Wimpy, his first punk nickname at last. (Brian's middle name is Roy, so later he took to calling himself Wimpy Roy, sometimes Sunny Boy Roy.) Hannah also got his punk name at this time, becoming Gerry Useless.

Now we had two punk bands and a fanzine I had put together called *Drones*. We only ever put out one issue; it had photos and stories about the local punk scene from the Skulls' warped point of view. We needed a show of our own, though, so we got Billy from the Shock Theatre to book us. We started postering like mad; on the poster, we announced that the opening act was Wimpy and the Bloated Cows "from London." We figured if anybody called us on the "London" thing, we would say we meant London, Ontario. But the day of our show, Billy phoned up and said he was cancelling the gig. He claimed that people were mad about the "London" bullshit. Piss on them. And on Billy!

Somewhere along the way, we learned that there was another band called the Skulls, from Los Angeles. "Shit!" we said collectively. "They're from L.A., they'll get a bunch of free publicity, and we'll be fucked." So we toyed with the idea of changing our name. We came up with the Numbskulls, then the Red Skulls. In the end it didn't matter; the end was near. (Strangely enough,

D.O.A. played a show at the Tiki Bar in Costa Mesa, California, in November 2002 with a reformed version of L.A.'s Skulls. They were good.)

We had been in Toronto for five months, and our time there was coming swiftly to an end. Simon and Wimpy caught a flight to the U.K., as originally planned, and Dimwit and I were supposed to join them soon after. But Dimwit and I changed our minds. Cheryl and I caught a flight back to Vancouver. Dimwit hung out in Toronto for a bit. I think his last act was to host a bowling tournament at our house on Edwin Avenue. He and our friend Kier took all the ketchup bottles we had been saving – there were lots, because we lived on potatoes and ketchup – and smashed them together to get back at our landlord Ed.

Wimpy and Simon stayed for a while in a squat in Brixton. Wimpy finally got tired of freezing and starving and waiting for Dimwit and me, so he caught the plane back home. Simon was so broke that he took Wimpy's bass to a pawn shop.

And that was it. The Skulls were kaputsville, finito, done like dinner. It was a funny thing. Even though Dimwit and I were the fuckheads who broke up the Skulls, somehow I got all the blame. Well, Jesus H. Christ. I didn't worry about it too much. It just set the table for the feast of fury to come.

D.O.A. (l-r Randy Rampage, Joey Shithead, Chuck Biscuits, Dave Gregg)
at the Greyhound Club in London (U.K.), 1981. *photo: Bev Davies*

CHAPTER THREE

D . O . A . :   T H E   B E G I N N I N G S

While we had been living in Toronto, the Vancouver punk scene had grown by leaps and bounds. It was now 1978; there were new bands, more people at shows, and even a fanzine called *Snot Rag*. So now that I was back in Vancouver, I started working on forming a new band. I've never been the type to sit on my fuckin' ass for too long.

First things first. I needed a drummer, the bedrock of any band. I had heard about a guy named Randy Archibald, who was drumming for a band called Looney Tunes. I arranged to meet him. He was seventeen years old, a greasy-looking rock 'n' roll type from North Vancouver. We started jamming, and it didn't take me long to realize that Randy was no Bill Ward.

But then somebody told me that Chuck, Dimwit's little brother, was interested in my band. It took me a while to get my head around the idea. The last time I'd seen Chuck play drums he was about eleven, sitting in his family's old garage, hitting the bongos while Brian, Gerry, Ken, and I made some horrible concoction of sound. Chuck would be playing along while Dimwit and Chuck's old man pounded on the garage door, yelling at us to stop. But when Chuck and I jammed this time around, I was amazed. He was only fifteen, but he had a lot of chops; he had really developed as a drummer. Chuck had been playing with the revamped line-up of Victorian Pork. He took punk influences like the Clash and the Sex Pistols and mixed those in with Keith Moon wild-man rolls. That was great, 'cause to me Keith Moon was the King.

Once Chuck was in, we needed a bass player. So I thought, why not teach Randy? If you're a drummer you've got timing, which is the first order of business. I didn't know if he was musical, but how tough could it be? It's only eighth notes, only about four or five positions on the neck of a guitar. It turned out that Randy learned pretty quick. So the three of us got together and started practicing.

One night Chuck, Randy, and I were jamming at 343 Railway, the infamous hangout/gig joint on Vancouver's grubby waterfront. It was home to a jam space, a studio, an artists' hangout, and a boozecan. (In those days, all of us who were looking for a scene had this weird punk-rock radar. Like a heat-seeking missile, we always hit our target – wherever there were punks or people who thought they were punks in town, we would find them.) In the middle of rehearsing, we stopped to grab a beer, and in came a slick guy maybe twenty years old, with a girl on each arm. He hung around as we started playing again. After a couple of songs, he said, "Hey, you guys are good. My name's Harry Homo. You be the band, I'll be the singer, we'll make a million dollars, and we'll call it D.O.A."

The three of us stepped out into the hallway to have a private pow-wow. Randy, a happy-go-lucky type, was easy about the proposal. Chuck was thoughtful: "Well, why don't we try it and see if it works?" For a fifteen-year-old he was really on top of it. So we came back and said to Harry, "Hey, what the fuck. It sounds good to us."

Before you could say Iggy Pop, the four of us were practicing almost every night. We would play for hours and then run down to the liquor store to grab more beer before it closed. Just for something to do, we would dance around on the crosswalk, blocking traffic and waving our empties at annoyed motorists. Sometimes drivers would yell or threaten us. One guy wanted to have it out with us freaks. It was a dumb move on his part – we bombarded his shitbox Toyota with our empties.

Things were going good, and we decided that everybody in the band needed a punk rock name. I already had mine, Joey Shithead. Harry called himself Harry Homo. We figured Chuck's name was like "upchuck," like you were going to puke, hence, Chuck Biscuits. Randy was the wild man of the group, a really hard partier, so he became Randy Rampage.

We'd only learned a couple of songs when we heard about a gig that was happening at the Japanese Hall on Alexander Street. Old Japantown had been a prosperous place until the Second World War, when the government interned all the Japanese, confiscated their property, and sent them to camps in the interior of British Columbia. (It took fifty years before they were even apologized to.) The Japanese Hall was one of those places that was cheap to rent because it was near the waterfront, with no tourists around. Bands had just started renting it out.

On the night of the gig, February 20, the four of us headed down to the hall. We didn't have any gear, but we talked one of the bands, the Generators, into lending us their amps and drums. We hit the stage with an electronic belch of noise that made the hundred or so punks and assorted scenemakers scratch their heads. Rampage, Biscuits, Harry, and I didn't look like everyone else, who were mostly copies of the punk scenes in New York, L.A., or London. We wore ripped-up pants and jean vests and had spiky hair. Randy wore a dog collar around his throat. And we were full of piss and vinegar. We lurched into "Fucked Up Baby":

> Yeah, you're fucked up, baby
> Your eyes are like glass
> Your mind's like a beer bottle filled with butts
> You're fucked up, baby.

Next we hit them with another Skulls tune called "No Escape." As we finished, we were greeted by sneers and guffaws. Undeterred, we moved right into Harry's classic song "Sick Baby." Harry belted out the vocals while drinking a 40-ouncer of Canadian rye. He would turn his mouth to the mike to sing but keep the bottle tilted and let the rye slop over his shoulder as he delivered his lines. It was either a great stage ploy or a pathetic waste of rye.

As the crowd drunkenly leered and jeered, I yelled to the others, "Cool! Let's play those songs again!" What the hell, it was all we knew. So away we went. When the Generators realized we were playing the same shit over again, however, all hell broke loose. They grabbed as many of their friends as they could and bum-rushed us off the stage. I jumped before I got pushed, with my trusty Gibson SG still strapped on. "Hey, that's cool," I was thinking to myself. "We really caused some trouble. We're D.O.A.!"

We realized after that first show that Harry Homo was a great guy and a good frontman, but he lacked something essential to all music: timing. So it was not going to work out with him. I became the singer/guitarist, and Chuck and I started working seriously on writing songs.

Our second gig, in March 1978, was also at the Japanese Hall. On the bill with us were the Chumps and Victorian Pork. Victorian Pork had a totally different line-up now, except for Brad Kunt on guitar. Tony Bardach played bass (Tony, later part of Pointed Sticks, still plays in the current version of the Pork; his daughter Alex is the vocalist/guitarist. Talk about generations of punk!), Ian Tiles was on vocals, and Dimwit was on drums. Tim Ray and AV, with Bill Napier-Hemy (Pointed Sticks) on guitar, were headlining the show; they were new wave and they were good. (In those

D.O.A. (l-r Shithead, Biscuits, Rampage), 1979. *photo: Bev Davies*

days, new wave and punk bands always played together because the scene had not yet split; later on, as bands got more serious, the divisions began.) As soon as the three of us launched into our first song, some fuckin' geek started winging eggs at me. It was quite dark in the hall, but after a few of these portable omelettes, I had a fairly good idea who was doing the chuckin'. Without warning, I dropped my guitar, jumped off the stage, and throttled the guy. When I threw him to the ground, he just lay there and clucked. In the end, D.O.A. played eight or nine songs, and the cool thing was that they were all originals.

We did a number of shows that month at halls in Vancouver and Burnaby – one with Victorian Pork, one with the Stiffs (Sid Sick on vocals, Gerry Useless on bass, Mike Normal on guitar, and Zippy Pinhead on drums), and one with a new band, the Subhumans. For their first show, the Subhumans were Dimwit, Wimpy, and Brad Kunt. Shortly after that, they kicked Brad out and Wimpy moved over to vocals. Once they got Gerry Useless and Mike Normal (AKA Mike Graham), both from the Stiffs, on bass and guitar, the Subhumans were solidified. This was the normal state of affairs. Bands would flip-flop their lineups until they got the right mix.

On March 31, we played the South Concourse Lounge at my old alma mater, Simon Fraser University. The show was presented by the university radio station and Phil "God Save the Queen" Smith (later with Corsage). We had our first manager by then, George Young. George was a doorknob. He suggested we should try to sound more like Boston, the big rock band of the time ("More Than a Feeling")! He hired three toughs to be our security, and when it was time to go on stage, these toughs formed a wedge and pushed their way through the crowd with us right behind them. Just in case we were attacked by those skinny punks, I suppose. Anyway, it turned out

The Smiling Buddha Cabaret. *photo: Bev Davies*

to be a great show, with people pulling out the ceiling tiles as we played.

Another key thing happened around this time: we discovered the Smilin' Buddha. For any punk scene to grow, there had to be a regular place to play. New York had CBGBS, a grubby club in the Lower East Side that gave bands like the Ramones, Television, and Blondie their start; London had the 100 Club, a really plain-looking former jazz club that became home to bands like the Sex Pistols and the Damned, and later, the Roxy; San Francisco had the Mabuhay Gardens, which started as a Filipino nightclub. Those were the legendary punk clubs of the early days. And now Vancouver had the Smilin' Buddha, smack downtown at 109 East Hastings, a less-than-savory neighbourhood. Over a year earlier, I'd been driving around town with a buddy and complaining that there was nowhere for our band Stone Crazy to play. Just as I finished my lament, we happened to pass by the Buddha.

"Why don't you get a gig in there?" my buddy asked.

"Are you fucking crazy?" I burst back. "People get stabbed there every night!" Now, less than fourteen months later, it became our regular hang-out.

I think I went to what was only the second-ever night of punk rock at the Buddha. Victorian Pork had booked themselves in there for a week, and during one set Ian Tiles started ridiculing the tiny railing that circled the stage. He reached down and ripped off a piece, then several of us in the audience ran up to help him finish the job. The Buddha's owners, Nancy and Lachman Jir, didn't seem to mind; they had fifty punks there drinking beer at two dollars a pop. This was fucking heaven to them, since their usual crowd was four drunks, three hookers, one drug dealer, and two undercover cops.

We sure raised a lot of shit at the Buddha over the years. As the club's popularity grew, I talked Lachman into renting a sound system on a full-time basis. Now we could play anytime we wanted, and play we did. We were usually there on Thursdays, Fridays, and Saturdays, with extra early shows sometimes thrown in because there was now a regular crowd. The Vancouver scene had started to grow, and while before there were only four bands, now there were ten. It never cost more than $2.50 to get in. Because the club was only a block from Vancouver's main police station, the Buddha was careful not to exceed their legal capacity of 115 people. Inevitably too many people would show up, but Rampage and I had it scoped. He would gather up a bunch of people waiting to get in and escort them around to the back alley. I was the inside guy; I'd wait until Lachman and his staff were looking the other way, then I would pop open the back door. As I did this, Rampage would be collecting two bucks from everybody who wanted to enter.

The cast of characters at the Buddha was like something out of a 1940s dime-store detective novel. Lachman was a sixty-year-old South Asian whose only two occupations seemed to be playing chess with the locals at the end of the bar and periodically shouting, "Joey! Joey! You have too many people in here!" He would occasionally yell at his long-suffering wife Nancy to grab more beer for the punks. Nancy, also from India, was a terrific person, and she seemed to do all the work that kept the bar going. Then there was Igor, the huge Yugoslavian doorman. He was perfect for the job, so big that he took up the whole door with his body. Steve, the clean-up guy, seemed to live in the cellar of the club. He had a bum leg, a hunched back, and an unfortunate lisp, and that was enough to get a lot of stories about him started. I know a few punks who snuck into Steve's lair to see if there were any bodies down there. Poor old Steve. To top it all off, the Smilin' Buddha was right in the heart of Vancouver's Downtown Eastside, Canada's poorest neighbourhood. The area wasn't quite as rough then as it is now, but you still had to watch your step.

After a short period of unabashed, unfiltered punk rock mayhem, the police began to take exception to what was happening under their noses. They started harassing the Buddha's owners and its patrons more and more. But sometimes the numbers were too much for them. D.O.A. was onstage one night when the joint was crammed tighter than a Tokyo subway during rush hour. We had just finished a song when the back door flew open. In walked these four cops, all wearing moustaches and hideous smirks. There was a strange silence as the audience realized this might be the end of a fuckin' great time. A couple of people in the audience started chanting, "Fuck off! Fuck off!" and soon everybody joined in. Rampage and I had been busy stuffing the joint that night, so there were some 250 punks raising their voices (only more than double the legal capacity). The cops looked nervously at each other and then left without saying a word.

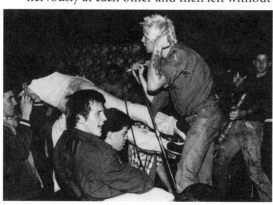

Rampage rocks the Buddha. *photo: Bev Davies*

D.O.A. was starting to make some headway. People were coming to see our shows and we were developing an actual fan base. Our first out-of-town gig, on a bill with Tim Ray and AV, and Dee Dee and the Dishrags, was in Esquimalt, a suburb of Victoria, B.C. right next to a Canadian

Forces naval base. Only sixty people showed, but the best part of the trip was when we invaded a high school. The three girls in the Dishrags were only fifteen, so we thought we should get some of their classmates out to the show. We met the band members out front and then went inside, where we all started running through the classrooms throwing flyers around. Teachers were yelling and the principal was chasing us. It was complete chaos, but good promotion!

Another way of getting gigs in those days was to play the Gong Shows that various bars hosted. The TV show of the same name, hosted by Chuck Barris, was a big hit at the time, and the idea was that you would get up, perform your talent in front of the audience and the judges, and try to avoid getting gonged off the

D.O.A. at a Gong Show, 1978. *photo: Bev Davies*

stage. There was also a chance to win some dough. One or all of the judges would inevitably hate us, but we'd keep playing while some disco queen or fisherman wildly banged the gong. Needless to say, we never won the cash prize.

Nobody had any gear in those days, so we had to rent from a music shop called Long & McQuade. Say what you will about L&M, a lot of bands would never have gotten anywhere without them. Nobody else trusted us with their stuff. To be honest, I don't know why they didn't pull the plug on D.O.A. after a while; everything we returned was fucked up in some way or other. I was always twisting the mike stands into various contortions, strongman style. Our favourite trick was to take the cymbals, which Chuck always beat the shit out of and broke, and try to slip them under some other cymbals available for rent. The staff eventually got wise to this, though.

We did a big show at the Japanese Hall with the Avengers, a great punk band from San Francisco led by Penelope Houston. The day after the second show, we had a party with the Avengers and a whole pile of hangers-on in the basement at the punk rock house on Randolf Street in Burnaby. D.O.A.'s gear was set up, so we jammed for a bit. Then things got looser, with me playing drums and Jimmy from the Avengers playing bass. All the lightbulbs in the basement had been smashed out earlier, so we lit candles for light. As we were jamming, the candle on top of the bass cabinet tipped over and the top speaker in the cabinet caught fire. I was still drumming furiously when I saw the flames and it dawned on me that we might burn the house down. Jimmy, smiling away, kept playing. I kept the bass drum going while dousing the fire with my beer. The bass sound got more and more distorted the wetter the speaker got. When we brought the bass cabinet back to Long & McQuade, half of it destroyed, all the staff did was stare at me in silence. I told them we had had a real smokin' jam. They were speechless and I quickly hustled out of there.

The credit manager at Long & McQuade was a slimy creature known as Kenny Mack. Whenever we went to the shop we would duck behind the amps, because Mack had a two-way mirror in his office that looked out over the main floor. We used to see a lot of grafitti around town that read, "Kenny Mack, lick my crack." (Gee, I wonder if it was musicians wielding those spray cans.) Sometimes Mack would sneak up on me and say, "You know, Joe, you're going to have to pay for that gear you destroyed. You know Neil Young still owes us

$2,000. Eventually we'll make him pay and you'll pay too." We never did.

By now, later in 1978, Vancouver was starting to get a pretty cool punk scene happening. There were plenty of bands starting up, and *Snot Rag*, the zine run by Don Betts, Steve Taylor, Wilberta Taylor (married to Steve), and brother-and-sister Grant and Lynn McDonagh, legitimized the scene and, like other zines across North America, helped everybody keep tabs on what was going on locally. Quintessence Records, which later became Zulu Records, was the shop to read zines from other cities, and the information we gleaned was what allowed us to organize our tours later on.

During a D.O.A. show at the Indian Centre, a First Nations cultural centre, my old Gibson sg got ripped off. Now you must understand, this was no ordinary guitar. I've owned about twenty guitars in my lifetime, but the sound and feel of that one was special. I bought it used in 1974 and knew right then it was the guitar for me. That night at the Indian Centre, I was outside having a beer when Biscuits came up and says, "I got some bad news!"

"What's that?" I said.

"Somebody stole your guitar!"

"Why the fuck didn't you stop him?"

Biscuits didn't really have an answer. I then ran back inside and around the hall raising hell, threatening to beat the shit out of anybody who knew anything about the rip-off. I kicked doors and slammed things around. Finally this guy came up and said, "Hey, I think I know where your guitar is." It was stashed outside, in a bush beside the hall. He also pointed out the drunk geek who had grabbed it. He got seriously thumped by Cheryl and some of her girlfriends; they kicked and punched the geek for a block down the street, until we could all hear him begging for mercy. The same guitar was later ripped off in Portland, Oregon, but Zippy Pinhead caught the thief red-handed in an elevator. The last time it was stolen was after a show in the Basque country of northern Spain; it was gone for about six months before I got a letter from the contrite robber. It cost me $400 to fly the guitar back on Iberia, Spain's national airline, which just happened to be how much I had paid for it in the first place.

In June of 1978, the *Georgia Straight* selected D.O.A. to appear in a Battle of the Bands. The event was to be held at Vancouver's most notorious meat market, a nightclub called the Body Shop. That was where semi-well-heeled, cocaine-toting, monkey-suit-wearing slimeballs would go to pick up big-haired disco queens. The night we played we shared the bill with No Fun, who are still putting on creative shows around Vancouver, and Doug and the Slugs, who went on to a fair bit of success in Canada themselves. The bill was rounded out by a nauseating bunch of rock 'n' roll pretenders called Sapphire.

The joint that night was packed with posers, pukes, disco-ites, stockbrokers, *bon vivants*, and the entire Vancouver punk scene – all one hundred of us. The scene was set. Doug and the Slugs were up first, followed by No Fun. Both bands got fairly decent reactions. Then it was our turn. Rampage, Biscuits, and I hit the stage hard, and the punks went berserk. They were spitting and tossing beer everywhere, and every so often somebody would jump up on stage and sing along. The four big guys doing security were completely bewildered. We finished up our usual twelve-song, twenty-five-minute set to punks chanting, "D.O.A.! D.O.A.! D.O.A.!"

Sapphire closed the evening with some hackneyed disco/rock tunes. Once they were done, it remained only for the judges to pick the winner. The dreaded chore of making the announcement fell to Tom Harrison, who was the emcee. He started out cautiously, telling the crowd that Biscuits had won a new snare drum as the best drummer in the battle. Then he announced the grand winner. It was Sapphire.

Well, hell! Tom should have stopped by Niagara Falls on the way and picked up some rain gear. As soon as those words came out of that honourable man's mouth, he was showered in beer and spit. D.O.A. fans and friends had been whipped into a frenzy, and they were pissed!

We didn't realize it at the time, but something definitive had just happened. The Battle of the Bands made the cultural clash between the Vancouver punks and everybody else official. After that, there was no going back. One cool thing that came out of the whole fiasco was that Tom Harrison ended up with a two-track recording of our set.

July 1, 1978 was the date of the first Vancouver outdoor anarcho/punk event. D.O.A., the Subhumans, and Private School were to play in Vancouver's Stanley Park. The organizers of the anti-Canada Day event were Ken Lester, later to become D.O.A.'s manager, David Spaner, later to become manager of the Subhumans, Brent Taylor, Bob Sardi, and others involved with the anarchist publications *B.C. Blackout* and *Open Road*.

The rally/show was supposed to start at noon at Prospect Point inside the park, but the cops stopped that from happening since there was no permit, so the organizers moved the flatbed truck and the sound system down the road to a big field. A church group had a permit to use the field until six PM, and we talked them into lending us their permit once their function was finished. Right Christian of them, I would say. The cops were not crazy about this, and they spent the afternoon haranguing the four hundred people that showed up.

When the show finally got underway, D.O.A. played first; our set lasted about forty-five minutes. During it, Dave Spaner got up on stage and burned a copy of the Canadian constitution. Then Ken Lester came on and started burning money (we tried to grab it from him, being so broke). We had a gnarly set, highlighted by "Disco Sucks." Another highlight was "Trident," written by Brad Kunt, whom we had just selected to become our guitar player. I was back to just singing again. The crowd yelled and cheered at us and jeered at the cops who were watching.

Private School were up next. Their set wasn't quite punk, but what the hell; they were more on the art school side of things. By the time the Subhumans came on, it was dark. There were no stage lights, so you could barely see them, but their set was strong and the crowd ate it up. Politics and music moved closer together that day, contradicting the media stereotype that punk rock was only a nihilistic pursuit. That event showed that punk rock had guts, purpose, and direction.

During this period, we all had time on our hands because we were all on welfare, except for Rampage, who worked at his old man's import-export company. My usual schedule was to wake up late, have Kraft Dinner or potatoes for lunch, then write songs and play guitar. Dinner was usually the same as lunch, although sometimes we'd throw in a hunk of bologna to spruce it up.

In the evenings, I would meet up with the guys and practice for a couple of hours, or go out postering, then we would try to see a band or go to a party at one of the punk houses. Eventually the whole gang would head over to the house on Randolf or over to the shack that Cheryl and I rented around the corner. On our two-channel television, we would watch shows like *Emergency* or *McMillan and Wife* – the only shows that were on – until four in the morning. The next day, the whole process would start all over again.

All of the bands got their posters from Dave Gregg, who worked at a construction company as the printer. He had the keys to the printing shop, and used to sneak in at three AM to print posters, zines, comics, and other stuff. He called his sideline Rebel Crime Press.

But it was time to get a record out. Since the existing record labels were run by a bunch of dicks, we decided to produce it ourselves. More of the DIY ethic. I booked nine hours at the old Ocean Sound Studios in North Vancouver, a cinderblock building that looked like a bunker. We arrived with our guitars and Chuck's rented drum kit. The studio had told us on the phone that they had amps we could use, but they neglected to say that they were so fucking old they almost predated electricity; they were Ampegs from the fifties. I plugged my guitar into one and it just farted.

But we were able to get our basic sound up in about half an hour. None of us had ever been in a studio before, and we weren't quite sure what we were doing. The engineer, Dave Thomas (not the scTV guy), was very low-key; he kept saying, "Sounds good, keep going." Once we had all the bed tracks done, it was time for the vocals. But then I remembered I only had about half of the lyrics written. Fuck! So I grabbed a pen and paper and finished all four songs in about fifteen minutes. Then I hollered at Dave, "Okay, let's do it!" Dave took about an hour to mix it all after that, then we were through.

The next day I got the tape in my hot little hands and raced down to Imperial Records to order 500 7-inch pieces of vinyl. I designed the cover myself; we had our photographer friend Lori Holland take a picture of Cheryl lying under a sheet on a rented stretcher outside a graveyard. I censored us and put an X through the word "Shithead" on the back cover, because I thought it might stop the records from getting into some stores. We bagged them so soon after the covers got off the press that you could see our fingerprints on the white portions of the cover.

So there we had it: the *Disco Sucks* 7-inch EP, featuring "Disco Sucks," "Nazi Training Camp," "Royal Police," and "Woke up Screaming." That little record kicked open the door for D.O.A. and became our passport to travel the world. The title song caught a trend at the right time, being released during the disco backlash. A lot of people felt that disco did suck.

It was also the beginning of Sudden Death Records, which was ours alone. We did all the local distribution by car and bus, and I mailed out promotional copies to fanzines and college radio stations across Canada and the U.S. We were in good shape. All we needed now was a road trip.

CHAPTER FOUR

THE EARLY DAYS

Soon after the release of *Disco Sucks* in the summer of 1978, I got a letter from KUSF, one of the college radio stations in San Francisco, informing me that it was #1 on their chart. I immediately called down to the Mabuhay Gardens, San Francisco's punk rock mecca, to book some shows. I had never planned a road trip before (other than the one-off forays to Toronto and the B.C. interior), so I learned how to do it on the fly. When I got Dirk Dirksen, the Mabuhay's head cheese, on the phone, I told him about *Disco Sucks'* airplay on KUSF. He was a hard ass about it at first – "Who the fuck are you?" – but to my amazement, he booked us in for a weekend in August.

So our first tour was on, small as it was. We were really excited. San Francisco had a big punk scene. Ken Lester had been to the big Sex Pistols show when the Avengers opened for them and returned raving about the city. Our modes of transport were varied, to say the least: Brad hitchhiked to San Francisco with his guitar, Rampage and Biscuits took a Greyhound, and I took a train – such luxury. My trip was uneventful until we crossed the mighty Columbia River. At that point, two young women who were hanging out in the bar car pulled out a joint and started smoking it. I couldn't believe it, but they said not to worry, smoking pot was only a misdemeanor in the state of Oregon. Wow! How times have changed in the U.S. of A.

I arrived in SF on Friday morning, August 11. It was cold and foggy. I had never been there before and I didn't know a soul, so I wandered around all day, waiting for my bandmates to arrive. I had twenty dollars and fifty *Disco Sucks* EPs. The Mabuhay Gardens was in the sleazy North Beach district, right near all the strip clubs. During the day, the Mabuhay was a Filipino/Polynesian restaurant owned by Nes Aquino; at night, they would move the tables out and the punk rock would start. I introduced myself to Nes, who gave me a bowl of something unidentifiable to eat. Lucky for me, I was starving. When I got hold of Dirk Dirksen, I told him that we needed amps and drums for our shows. Dirksen, a showbiz veteran who had produced television shows, couldn't believe that these rubes from Canada had showed up with almost no gear. "You have no gear?" he sputtered. "Are you guys fucking stupid or what?" I thought he was going to have a heart attack.

Once he had recovered, Dirksen phoned up Will Shatter from Negative Trend, a great early San Francisco band, to see about us borrowing their gear. They were cool. Will came down to the club, we hailed a cab and grabbed the gear from Negative Trend's practice space, and made it back to the club in time for the show.

That night D.O.A. played with Novak, who I don't remember a goddamn thing about, and Roxz, an all-girl hard rock band. They were a Runaways clone from San Francisco. Very so-so. About 150 people showed up; there were fashion punks, and tourists, and a bit of an s&m scene thrown in. Our set got off to a good start, but Brad Kunt broke a string on the second song. I hadn't brought a guitar, and Brad Kunt had no spare. Shit! I was sure our momentum was going to be lost. So much for mowing over the crowd with a

Shithead gaffs his head at the Mabuhay Gardens, 1978.

blitzkrieg-type approach. However, I thought of a way to save the moment while Brad Kunt took some time to change his string. I grabbed a roll of gaffer tape and proceeded to wrap my head and body, mummy fashion, with the sticky stuff. The crowd didn't know what the fuck I was doing; neither did I. But it won them over in some strange fashion. Dirksen and most of the punks really liked the set. The Avengers had come down to the show, and they invited us to crash at their house.

The next night, D.O.A. were support for Ray Campi and the Rockabilly Rebels. Ray was one of the original cats from the fifties. He had a great young band with him, and they ripped. By the time we went on, at about 10:30, the joint was packed with nearly 300 people. The audience was a real mix, about half of which were punks. Our set was going over okay, but not great. We were getting the "What the fuck are you guys doing here?" look. But then an unexpected incident occurred. I had been drinking beer all day long with Will Shatter and, in the middle of our set, I really had to take a leak. Not an itsy-bitsy one, but a regular Victoria Falls. So I whipped down my zip and proceeded to piss onto the dance floor. At that moment, I knew what Moses must have felt like when the Red Sea parted for him. I got a real arc going, covering about fifteen feet from stem to stern. Needless to say, people were tripping over themselves trying to get out of the way. They were terrified. The funny thing was that immediately afterwards, the dance floor filled up again and people started really getting into our music. I guess I broke the ice, and they must have figured they were safe since I was out of ammo. Now, folks, this is not a stage antic I would necessarily promote, for health reasons alone. But when you're young and out of control, strange things happen. Talk of this incident got around SF quickly, as it turned out, and it really helped create a buzz for D.O.A.

One of the cool things about the Mabuhay Gardens, or the Fab Mab, as it was also known, was that Dirk Dirksen, who was also the emcee, would get into high gear at the end of the night, grabbing the mike and sarcastically making various announcements, like, "Okay, people, the show is over, go home now. Deposit trash in the bins on your way out. Please resist the temptation to throw yourselves in, even though you probably belong there!" or "You are no longer customers, you are trespassers! Now get out!" Some patrons tried to engage Dirk in a battle of wits, but they always lost.

We had no show the next night, but the Dead Kennedys were playing at the Fab Mab, so of course we stuck around to see that. One thing you need to know about the Mab was that the alley beside it was the unofficial punk beer-drinking hangout. It wasn't sanctioned by the club or the cops, but it was tolerated. Everybody would head over to the Filipino grocery across the street and grab as many cans of Old English 800 as they could afford, then down them all in the alley before the show.

That night, just as the Dead Kennedys were about to go on, I decided to smuggle my beer into the Mab. The band started playing, and they were fuckin' great. We were having a good time, that's for sure. But then one of the security guys saw me opening a beer up by the stage. He told me very nicely to get rid of it. Rather than being logical, though, I took my can and shook it as hard as I could, spraying it right in the security guy's face. The next thing I knew, four goons grabbed me and dragged me to the front door. As I was being unceremoniously tossed out, Dirksen started screaming at me, "You're out of here! You're 86ed [banned for life]!" Meanwhile, the Dead Kennedys' Jello Biafra, who had been to both of our shows, was on the mike yelling, "Let Shithead back in for the show, or we don't play any more!" After some negotiation, Dirk relented. Needless to say, this was the start of a long friendship between Biafra and D.O.A. Oddly enough, it was the start of a long friendship with Dirksen as well.

We hung around SF for a few more days, staying with the Avengers and going to shows and parties. After the two shows at the Mab, we actually had some dough. Unfortunately, we had a stack of bills as well. I had meticulously kept track of all the dough I had shelled out for equipment like drumsticks, strings, and the like. So I took that amount out of our stash, then we split up what was left four ways. Rampage understood this as he had actually held a job for a while, but Brad Kunt and Biscuits were a little choked about how little was left. And this wasn't the only source of tension. Rampage had talked us into letting Brad Kunt into the band, but Biscuits and I weren't totally sold on the idea.

Our next show was scheduled for the following weekend in Seattle at a place called the Bird, where we were playing support for a mediocre Seattle band called the Enemy. I took the train and Biscuits and Rampage took the bus, but Brad Kunt was nowhere to be found. He was supposed to have caught the bus with Biscuits and Rampage. I borrowed a guitar, and we got up on stage and played anyway. The place was fairly full, which was good because we were on a percentage deal, but the asshole who ran the joint would only give us twenty-five dollars as our total payment. Brad never did show up.

When we got back to Vancouver, Biscuits and I said Brad had to go. Rampage stuck up for him, but in the end we gave him the boot. Brad was a good guitar player, but the decision was for the best. It really spurred on my own playing too.

Our next show on our home turf was at a place on Homer Street called the Quadra Club (later Club Soda, then the Starfish Room). It was a gay club fallen on bad times, and they had started booking punk bands to try and make some gingwah. *Deep Throat* seemed to be playing on the club's video screen twenty-four hours a day. The bill was good: D.O.A. and the Rabid (Zippy Pinhead on drums, Sid Sick on vocals, Simon Wilde, AKA Stubby Pecker, on bass, and John Doe on guitar). Opening the night were Ernie Dick and the Pointed Sticks (later just the Pointed Sticks), who started out as a fuck band but would go on to become one of the most significant bands of the Vancouver scene. The Sticks had Nick Jones on vocals, Ernie Dick (later replaced by Ian Tiles) on drums, Bill Napier-Hemy on guitar, Colin Griffiths on guitar, Tony Bardach on bass, and Gord Nicholl on keyboards.

In October 1978, D.O.A. had another two nights booked at the Fab Mab, this time with the Mutants, another of the great early Bay Area bands. We drove down with Al Dopeman in his '66 Chevy panel van. A whole pile of punks from Vancouver, including Simon Wilde from the Rabids and our pal Bob Montgomery, also hitchhiked their way down for the weekend.

Just before the first show, Simon encountered a gang of White Power guys in front of the club. Al came in and told us that Simon had been beaten up. He grabbed a tire iron from his van, and the two of us, in a crazy moment, went out to confront the racists. Seems that Simon had "insulted" them with the upside-down swastika on his jacket. "Big fuckin'deal!" I jeered at the leader, who then got this insane look on his face, all contorted and full of hate. He whipped off his jacket and shirt, then turned around so I could see his back. It was entirely covered with a tattoo of an eagle clutching a swastika and, in huge letters, the words WHITE POWER. He swung around, glared at me, and spit out, "I'm proud of this!"

I spit back that everybody is equal, then we cursed at each other.

By this time, all the security from the Mab had come out. I grabbed Simon, and we went back inside. The gang split, but it made for a tense evening.

Before the show on the second night, Zippy Pinhead and I had a few beers in the alley beside the club, then walked over to the parking lot next door. With nothing better to do, we started throwing bags of rotting garbage at each other for kicks. Soon we had the entire parking lot, including cars, covered with crap. This went on until some cops came along and grabbed us by the scruffs of our necks. "What do you jackasses think you're doing?" they asked.

"Um, er, um. . . ." At that moment we were saved. Dirksen came out of the club and vouched for us. He stood there with his arms crossed, while Zippy and I sheepishly picked up the trash. But despite the trash duty, both the shows at the Mab had gone over great; the room was packed both nights. We were really starting to get a solid following in San Francisco.

By the time the show was over, the band had managed to collect an entourage of about fifteen people. We were just walking down the street, with Biafra telling us about some fucked-up shit going down in SF, when we came upon a business that Biafra said was run by a bunch of bastards. Before you could say "a blow for freedom," the plate glass window of this establishment had been turned into tiny pieces by punk boot. Yeah! Eat punk boot, establishment! Then we heard a police siren. Well, we weren't completely daft, so we started to run like fuck, making it around the corner and cramming into Al's small van, all fifteen of us, before high-tailing it out of there. A few of us ended up crashing in the van; others slept in the doorway of the Avengers' apartment building.

That fall back in Vancouver, the owner of Quintessence Records, Ted Thomas, decided to expand his store into a record company. Ted got us into Little Mountain Studios for a midnight session, with Ron Obvious doing the mixing. We recorded our second 7-inch EP, *The Prisoner/13* there, and upon its release it sold like hotcakes. Quintessence also reissued *Disco Sucks*, which was still selling very well, with a new sleeve. We were happy with Quintessence; its staff included Grant McDonagh, Dale Wiese, and Gerry Barad, who for a short time was D.O.A.'s second manager.

We had started playing the Windmill regularly, a real dive on Granville Street in downtown Vancouver, doing a bunch of shows with bands like the

Pointed Sticks. The Sticks had solidified their lineup by this point, with Nick Jones on vocals and Rubber Boot on drums. I remember one big argument we had with Paul, the booking guy for the Windmill. The door charge at the club was always $2.25, and we would get a percentage of that as payment. We said we wouldn't play unless it went up to $2.50. Paul called us fucking capitalists, but he finally raised the price, and it never went back down to $2.25. Getting paid at that dump was always a problem, though, because the owner was never seen without his two Dobermans he kept on a longish chain, not too far from your throat.

Another thing that was always a problem in those days was finding a place to practice. In the latter part of '78, Al Dopeman and Rampage rented a house on Hastings Street in north Burnaby. It was a tiny little dump, but it worked. We practiced in the kitchen. The only drawback was Rampage's little mongrel dog, Gromit. When Al and Rampage were at work, they would leave the little mutt by himself all day long. Of course Gromit would have to relieve himself, and from this trail of evidence it was clear he was not very fond of D.O.A. He crapped in front of the amps and on Chuck's bass drum and hi-hat stand pedals. Neither Rampage nor Al would clean it up in between practices, so it just sat there stankin'.

The Vancouver scene had really grown by this point, so Phil Smith, Grant McDonagh, and Steve Macklam (manager of the Pointed Sticks) began organizing a compilation album to document this wild energy. Bands started recording in late 1978 at Chris Cutress's house in south Burnaby, which was known as Sabre Sound. Chris's mom and dad lived upstairs, so we weren't allowed to smoke or drink inside the house. One of Chris's mom's 50-year-old friends liked our sound, but when she found out our name was D.O.A., she thought we should call ourselves the Bluebirds instead! I burst out laughing and told her we would think about it.

We recorded "I Hate You" and "Kill, Kill, This Is Pop" for that album.

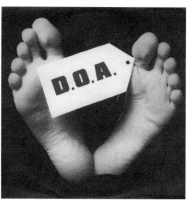
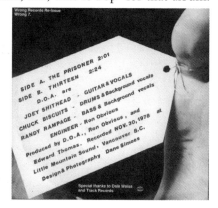

The other bands on the comp were the Pointed Sticks, Exxotone, Wasted Lives, Active Dog, the Subhumans, U-J3RK5 (pronounced U-Jerks), Private School, No Fun, the Dishrags, Young Canadians, the Shades, Tim Ray and AV, and "e." It was a good crosssection ranging from punk to pop to new wave to experimental.

Perryscope Concerts, the big production company in town, had started bringing in the most popular punk and new wave bands of the day to play at the Commodore. Local faves would be put on the bill as support. It was a thrill for everybody to see how they did with the big boys. When Devo played, U-JR3K5 were the support; the Dishrags opened for the Clash. But the night Private School opened for the Police was a real disaster; during their set, P.S.'s drummer broke his bass-drum skin, and their vocalist Ron told some jokes to kill time while they changed the skin. Norman Perry said it was "the most unprofessional piece of shit I have ever seen."

D.O.A.'s turn came on January 6, 1979, when Perryscope asked us to open for the Ramones, one of the bands that most inspired us. Tickets were $6.50, a fucking good deal. It was the biggest crowd we had ever played for – a thousand people – and the pressure was on. We had a great set right up to the end, when the inevitable happened: I broke two strings at the same time on my only guitar. There was no time to change any goddamn strings, so I let Rampage and Biscuits wail away with no guitar on the last two songs. It seemed to work for the audience. The Ramones shone bright that night, as they did on many other occasions. RIP, Joey and Dee Dee.

Meanwhile, a new club called O'Hara's had opened up in Vancouver. It was big, and had a cool location right on the waterfront. D.O.A. were supposed to play there, but we were cancelled after the St Valentine's Day Massacre show during which a huge fight erupted between the punks and the jocks. I didn't give a rat's ass about the club, and the bouncers were dicks, so I didn't really care. But the fighting at that show highlighted the tension around the city between the various factions.

That year, Gerry Useless and Dimwit had a house about eight miles out of Vancouver in the Sapperton area of New Westminister. Saptown, as we liked to call it. The local jocks would pick fights with the punks in their neighbourhood and harass the women in the scene. One night Gerry was walking home when some guys pulled up in a pickup truck. They saw his green hair and starting calling him a fag. One of these geeks swung a motorcycle helmet that broke Gerry's jaw.

We vowed to get even. On weekends, when we knew groups of jocks would be down at the Caribou Pub or over at the local park, getting drunk and looking to kick some punk ass, we would lie in wait at Dimwit and

Gerry's house. One or two people would sit in the front window while everybody else crouched down on the floor. One night the saps from Saptown came calling, and boy, did they get a beating. They were squealing so bad it sounded like a scene out of *Deliverance*. The melee was capped off by Dimwit smashing an acoustic guitar over the last guy's head. EL KABONG!

My girlfriend Cheryl and I got married in February 1979. Her parents hated me so much that they wouldn't come to the ceremony or the reception. Only Cheryl's sister Kelly showed up. The media had a heyday with the story. "Shithead gets married!" one headline read.

D.O.A. was now getting a lot of radio play on college radio stations up and down the west coast, and on February 5, 1979, "The Prisoner" went to #1 at the University of British Columbia's station, CITR. But a big show we had scheduled at UBC in March was cancelled with no explanation. We soon discovered that we couldn't get a show anywhere in Vancouver, not even the Buddha or the Windmill. A series of fire bombings around Vancouver had targeted government buildings. A group calling themselves "Direct Action" was taking some of the responsibility. The Vancouver police were

totally baffled, and the Canadian Bankers Association was offering a $25,000 reward for information. There was never any connection between the bombings and the punks, but we figured the cops must have talked to the venue managers, because we couldn't book any gigs. But after it was certain that nobody had been hurt, a lot of people, and not just punks, laughed at the idea of banks and government buildings getting trashed.

Since the clubs were closed to us, we booked a hall show instead, at the Ukrainian Hall in Burnaby. The support was Wasted Lives, led by Phil Smith and Frank Crass, AKA Colin Griffiths. Punks piled on the buses out to south Burnaby, and the show was going great until there was an attack on the old lady who ran the hall. Two loogans had broken into her place at the back of the hall, and one of them tried to rip her necklace right off her neck. Luckily, her son rushed to her rescue. We stopped the show until we were sure she was all right, and after a short delay she let us finish up. All she said at the end was, "My, my, you boys sure are loud!"

After another quick trip to California where we played in SF with the Dils, one of my all-time favourite bands, Negative Trend, and the Avengers (including their new guitarist Brad Kunt) in Berkeley. Brad had become friends with them after our first trip to San Francisco and when they needed a guitar player, he got the job. When we got back home we did a show at Gambado's in Vancouver with the K-Tels: Art Bergmann on guitar, Barry Taylor on drums, and Jim Bescott on bass. Under threat of a lawsuit by the K-Tel Corporation, the band later changed their name to the Young Canadians. The show was a benefit for Leonard Peltier, a Native American who was on the run from the FBI and had fled to Canada seeking asylum. Peltier was accused of killing an FBI agent in South Dakota at the famous Wounded Knee standoff between the U.S. government and AIM, the American Indian Movement, in 1973. He was eventually deported to the U.S. where he is still doing time for something a lot of us believe he didn't do. A few weeks later we did a Rock Against Racism benefit with a cool reggae band, the Jah Children, and Rude Norton, a great fuck band with Nick Jones on drums, Wimpy on bass, and Dimwit on guitar.

On May 10, we finally played at O'Hara's at a benefit to raise some dough for the compilation album. It was a great evening, and the organizers got the money they needed to release the first thousand LPs. Every compilation album is a huge amount of work, but this one went through some particularly Byzantine twists and turns. Thus its name: *Vancouver Complication*. Jack Rabid, editor of *The Big Takeover* magazine, called it "the finest scene compilation ever put out!"

The Subhumans and the Rabid were set to play a week straight at

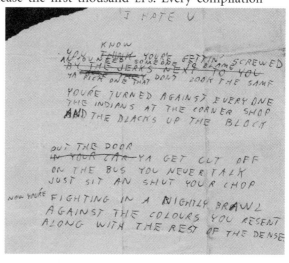

I Hate U (early draft). *Joey Shithead Keithley, Prisoner Publishing*

the Smilin' Buddha, and I was down there on the Friday night, along with about fifty other punks, having a couple of beers. The evening was fairly low-key compared to many nights there. The Subhumans were on stage when, through the front door, in burst ten policemen. I was sitting at a table when one of them tapped me on the shoulder and shouted, "You're under arrest!"

"What for?" I yelled back over the noise of the band.

"For being drunk and disorderly!"

Now, I had been drunk and disorderly before, so I knew what that was like, and this was not one of those times. I stood up, and I don't remember anything after that. According to witnesses, when I stood up I accidentally bowled over two cops. Not a popular move, so I was put in a choke hold and dragged out the front door, with the cops kicking me in the groin and the stomach.

I regained consciousness in the back of the paddy wagon, where there were about ten others. The cops were having their fun with us. We were on a bumpy road beside the train tracks that run alongside Vancouver's waterfront, and the driver of the van kept speeding up to about fifty miles per hour and then slamming on the brakes. We in the back went flying every which way.

We exited the wagon at the elevator entrance to the main police station. We had to go up a couple of floors to get booked, and the guys I was with all eyed each other nervously. In those days, the Vancouver police elevator was infamous for people being booked to be in worse shape when they got off than when they got on. Knowing this, I kept my mouth shut.

All in all, twenty-one punks were thrown into the drunk tank that night. The *Georgia Straight* later reported that the cops had picked up on the lyrics of "Royal Police" and were out to get me. I don't know about that. Whatever the reason, I always thought that the police were "to protect and serve." Sometimes that happens, and sometimes it doesn't. One of the officers involved in the raid was quoted as

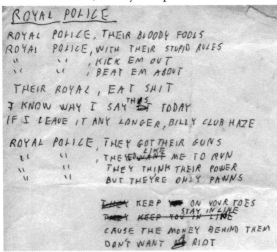

Royal Police (early draft). *Joey Shithead Keithley, Prisoner Publishing*

saying, "We don't like this kind of music." What a surprise.

We did a fair bit of yelling and singing in the cell. Every so often, the door would swing open and a cop would come in and glare at us, which usually shut us up. But when Dave Jacklin, a local photographer, said something the cops didn't like, a cop came in and dragged him out of the cell. Through the tiny window in the door, we could see Dave being punched and kicked. Finally, the cell door reopened and they chucked him back in. Things got pretty silent at that point.

Downstairs in the lobby of the station, we would later learn, it was not so quiet. A bunch of punks and friends who had not been arrested were in there raising shit. John Doe of the Rabid was arrested on the spot, and the Rabid's singer Sid Sick demanded to be arrested too. Our pal Cathy Ghini drove the cops nuts yelling at them. Others, including Gerry Useless, sat on the counter in solidarity. We were finally released at about six the next morning.

Over the next couple of days, a few of us gave the media our side of the story, although I don't think we convinced too many people of our wholesomeness. The police justified their actions by claiming that chairs were being hurled at the Buddha and two plainclothes officers had been attacked by punks. Yeah, right. Dave Jacklin filed a complaint with the police department about his beating, but nothing ever came of it.

After the incident at the Smilin' Buddha, I was quoted in the *Georgia Straight* as saying, "We're not looking for a riot, but we are going to continue playing music and saying what we believe." That's what punk was all about, and we were just getting started.

Wall at Fort Gore. *photo: Bev Davies*

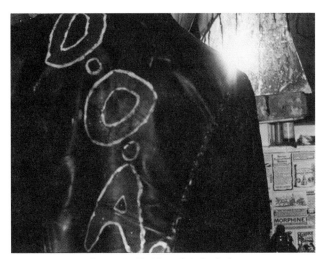

House party at Fort Gore. *photo: Bev Davies*

CHAPTER FIVE

PUNK ROCK PIONEERING

On May 17, 1979, we started our first North American tour. The first show of what we dubbed the White Noise Tour was at O'Hara's, featuring D.O.A., the Dils, and the Shades. The show went well, but the real fun happened the next night.

The night following the O'Hara's show, we were supposed to play out of town with the Dils and the Toiling Midgets, but when that did not work out we went to Dave Gregg's house on Gore Street instead. It was one of a few houses right at the end of the Georgia Viaduct, a block away from Chinatown. They had been abandoned when Dave and Ian Tiles decided to rent one of them and fix it up a bit. There was much fixing to do; the two-storey homes had seen a lot of action. They'd been built in the twenties on what was then Hogan's Alley, once Vancouver's black neighbourhood and at times home to gambling, prostitution, and opium and heroin trade.

Dave Gregg and Ian Tiles used their house, 830 Gore, as their living quarters. It became known as Fort Gore. Dave was the only perpetual resident, with the rest of the gang and I taking our turns living there over the years. It was also D.O.A.'s rehearsal space from 1980 until 1988. A vacant house next door was used as a gig space. One of the bravest acts ever known in the history of Vancouver punk rock was when Ian took on the "shit monster," the toilet upstairs in the second house. Homeless people had been using this shitter, but the house had no running water, so the crap was right up over the brim. Ian donned a pair of gloves and literally started pulling shit out. He was right up to his elbows in it. But he triumphed; it became a working john.

But back to our first impromptu show there. It was a 3D event: D.O.A., the Dils, and the Dishrags. All three bands were three-pieces. The Dils rocked hard and Jade, Scout, and Dale of the Dishrags were now starting to cut a good-sized swath through the local music scene. The house was already way too packed by the time the bands started playing, and only about a third of the people could see what was going on. The punks in the hallway started kicking and smashing holes in the wall, creating much better views of the bands. Hey, cool. Instant renovation.

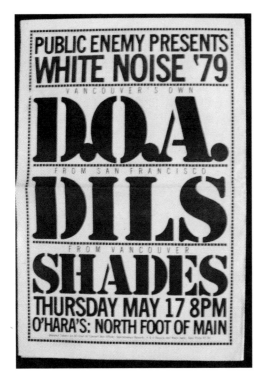

PUBLIC ENEMY PRESENTS
WHITE NOISE '79
VANCOUVER'S OWN
D.O.A.
FROM SAN FRANCISCO
DILS
FROM VANCOUVER
SHADES
THURSDAY MAY 17 8PM
O'HARA'S: NORTH FOOT OF MAIN

The motivation behind our White Noise Tour was an event we'd heard about from Ken Lester and David Spaner, a big Rock Against Racism show in Chicago. The first leg of our tour would take us down the west coast with the Dils. After that we planned to break off on our own, heading east towards Texas, then north to Chicago, then to New York and back into Canada.

We took Dimwit's brother Bob Montgomery along as roadie, and Ian Tiles talked us into letting him be our merch guy. We squeezed the five of us and all the gear into Rampage's tiny 1967 GM panel van. When we got to Seattle for our first U.S. show, however, we realized that Ian had no merch to sell: no T-shirts, no stickers, no hats. Not a fucking thing. Ian set out to rectify the situation. He went out and purchased some blank plastic buttons, then photocopied D.O.A. logos in button size. He coloured in the logos, cut them out, stuck them on the buttons, and snapped the plastic covers over top. Wow! Instant merch. We were impressed.

But a problem with Ian's buttons quickly came to the fore. As soon as an eager fan wearing one of the buttons started to pogo on the dance floor, the top of the badge flew off and the D.O.A. logo dropped to the floor. So the punters left the show unaware that they were wearing nothing more than a clear piece of plastic and a safety pin. Great fuckin' merch!

We played the Washington Hall that night with the Dils, the Dishrags, China Comidas, and Blow Up. It was a good show, and it started a good thing between D.O.A. and Seattle, a great city.

Al Dopeman had joined us for the first part of the trip, this time in a sedan. I rode with him from Seattle to Portland the next morning, guzzling from a case of cheap American swill on the way. When we arrived, I was shocked to find out our Portland show was that night, and not the next day. I was royally fucked up. But the show must go on, as they say, and so it did. By our eighth song I only had three strings left on my guitar. In a punk rage,

I ripped off the rest of the strings, chucked my guitar onto the stage, and charged into the audience to end our set.

We played a big show at the Gay Community Centre in San Francisco with the Dils and the Zeros, then headed down to Los Angeles to visit Bomp Records. I had shipped them a bunch of copies of *Disco Sucks*, and despite repeated phone calls from me, they had refused to buck up for them. We had to occupy their office for three hours to get the lousy ninety-nine dollars they owed.

With fresh dough in our pockets for gas, we hit the I-10 Interstate bound for Texas. It was a long fucking way. And when I phoned ahead to check on the shows I had booked, two of them had been cancelled. That left only Raul's, the CBGB's of Austin. We arrived at the club the night before our show. They were cool, and gave us some free pitchers of beer, but we had nowhere to stay. The only thing to do was to park the van behind the club. The five of us and all our gear were stashed in there, packed like sardines in a smelly can. "Fuck this," I said, and I headed out with my sleeping bag to camp under the beautiful Texas night sky. You can probably guess how this adventure ended. A big ol' Texas thunderstorm passed overhead, totally drenching me. Like a drowned rat I crawled back into that smelly can of sardines.

Early the next morning, Biscuits and I walked to a nearby store to get some junk food and smokes. We were amazed as we looked up at the Lone Star beer sign with its clock and temperature reading. It was only seven AM, and already seventy-five degrees Fahrenheit. Way too bloody hot. That day was my twenty-third birthday. The gig at Raul's went fine, and we had collected enough dough to get us to Chicago.

The next morning when we stopped for gas near Waco, an unfortunate altercation between Rampage and Biscuits occurred. Rampage, the only one of us with money (his parents must have given him some dough before we left), had gone into the store to buy potato chips and dip. We were all feeling some resentment towards Rampage, who wasn't the sharing kind. He'd been eating ham sandwiches along the way while everybody else wolfed down a daily ration of bologna. But I guess seeing the chips pushed Biscuits right over the edge. After an exchange of unpleasantries with Rampage, Biscuits ripped the bag open and chips went flying all over the van. Rampage was pissed off and pulled the lid off the dip and threw the contents in Biscuits' face. A direct hit! Biscuits went wacko in Waco, you might say. He freaked out, jumping out of the van and screaming at all of us. "Fuck it! That's it! I quit! Fuck you guys, you're a bunch of pricks!"

Eventually we all got back in the van. Biscuits demanded a ride to the

Dallas bus station so he could head back home. In front of Biscuits, I asked Ian, who was a drummer himself, to fill in for the rest of the tour. Ian agreed. Next, Biscuits asked me for some dough. I did all the financial shit for the band, but since we had fuck all, he got none. A tense ride into downtown Dallas followed. As Biscuits climbed out at the bus station, he noticed some scuzzy characters eyeballing him. He was fifteen, after all, with freaky dyed-blond hair. He took a few more steps, the scuzzballs moved closer, and in a flash Biscuits turned around and ran back to the van. "Will you guys buy me a milkshake?" he asked in a shaky voice.

"Sure!" I said. Chuck was back in D.O.A., and we were on our way to the Rock Against Racism show.

We got up to Chicago a day early and crashed at the pad of one of the event organizers. We were really looking forward to the show. They were expecting about 5,000 people, and Patti Smith's group (sans Patti Smith), led by Lenny Kaye, Smith's guitarist, were the feature band. When we arrived at Lincoln Park the next morning, though, we discovered that we were scheduled to go on first. That was no biggie, since we were from out of town. The shitty part was that they wanted us to start playing at eleven AM. We moaned and groaned until they moved the start back to one in the afternoon. Our friend Bev Davies, a Vancouver photographer, had flown in for the show and snapped some great photos that day. So that's when things got underway. We pulled off a set that got people talking, with great reactions to songs like "The Prisoner," "Nazi Training Camp," and "The Enemy." People had come from all over the States for the show, and we started some lasting friendships that day.

Kim, the guy we were crashing with in Chicago, had said we could stay as long as we wanted. That was lucky for us, because we didn't have another show for a week. But it was unlucky for Kim, because there wasn't

D.O.A. in Chicago, June 1979. *photo: Bev Davies*

a speck of food or a drop of alcohol left in his house by the time we took off for New York City.

Ken Lester, who had driven down with David Spaner for the Rock Against Racism show, asked if he could hitch a ride with us to New York. We said sure, as long as he bought the food and the beer. He agreed, but trying to get him to live up to his end of the bargain was tough. We would pull into a Kentucky Fried Chicken and ask him to buy some chicken. He'd buy a twenty-piece bucket and eat the first fifteen pieces himself, while we sat by watching like dogs at the dinner table. Then we'd stop at a liquor store and Ken would offer us one dollar for beer. We'd punch him, every punch getting us another dollar, until the amount got up to seven dollars, enough for a case.

We arrived in New York City by way of the General Polaski Skyway. The potholes in the road were so big you could have lost small Toyotas in them. The skyway goes right over Newark, New Jersey. Talk about a beat-up area – I had never ever seen anything like it.

The club we were playing at was at 10 Bleecker Street, half a block from CBGBS. The joint was run by the Yippies, which was an amalgamation of post-hippie culture and anti-establishment politics. The Yippies were almost like professional shit disturbers; they published their own monthly mag and helped organize anti-establishment protests. They lived across the street at 9 Bleecker, and let us us crash in the club which helped finance their activities.

We had two days to go before our show and only twenty dollars to our names. So we did the logical thing: we pissed away the money on beer the first night. Biscuits was mad. He'd wanted to spend the money on Twinkies.

The club was in the Bowery. We fit right in, like transplanted bowery bums. A couple times a day, tourist buses would wing their way through the area, so that folks from Kansas and Iowa could "Ooh" and "Aah" at the Big Apple's decrepit side. The buses always had their windows open because it is so stinkin' hot in New York in the summertime. As they rolled in front of the club, we would jump out from behind the trash cans and douse the tourists with our beer and orange juice. *That* gave them a story to tell the folks back home.

On the day of our first show, the club's sound guy – who would better be described as an unsound guy – got us to help him carry this incredibly huge refrigerator down the stairs at 9 Bleecker and over to the club. He said he needed a big fridge for all the beer he was going to sell that night at two bucks a pop.

There were four bands on the bill: the Cats, the Wild Ones, Mikki Zone

Zoo, and D.O.A. It was a strange bill. There was a strong punk scene in New York, but the bands we played with were rock 'n' roll wanna-bes. They all had tight black pants and greasy hair. In contrast, Biscuits and Rampage had fucked-up dyed-blond hair and we were all wearing ripped jeans, workshirts, and jean vests. I was standing outside yakking as the show got going. After a minute, Bob Montgomery came out. He was rather agitated. "Hey, Joe," he said. "There's a fire inside the club."

I didn't pay much attention, so he said it again: "There's a fire inside the club!"

"Why the fuck didn't you tell me?" I said.

We grabbed Biscuits and Rampage, ran inside, and lugged all of our gear out to the sidewalk. The other bands did the same. It looked like one of those New York midnight sales. A fire sale, you might say.

The fire department showed up to take care of things. It seems that the huge fucking refrigerator we had dragged over had shorted out and caught fire. And not only that: the unsound soundman was running the bar, and when the fire chief asked him, "How about a beer for the boys and me?" the unsound guy had replied, "It's two bucks a beer."

The chief was incredulous, but the unsound guy stood firm.

"Okay, smart guy," said the chief. "Let's see your licence to operate this club."

Well, that was the end of that show. We never got to play. It took a lot of arm-twisting to even get our $100 guarantee. Now we were almost flat broke and 3,000 miles from Vancouver.

The next two nights, the Dils were playing at a club called Hurrah's. Ken Lester phoned up and got D.O.A. on the bill for the second night. We went down on the first night to check the place out. A few people we knew, including Jello Biafra, had also come to see the show, but Hurrah's was kind of an upscale place, so the crowd was a strange mix. When the Dils started playing, most of the New Yorkers just stood there staring at the band like they were from Mars or something. To liven things up, about ten of us started running around the inside perimeter of the club. We were smashing into people, having a bloody great time. Finally, the bouncers corralled us. It seems that Rampage had smashed into some woman wearing an evening gown

The last issue of *Snot Rag* (Sept 1979) with D.O.A. on the cover. (l-r) Roadies Ian Tiles and Bob Montgomery, Rampage, Shithead, and Biscuits on the van.
photo: Lynn Werner

and spilled her drink. She claimed her wrist was broken, and she wanted Rampage arrested and charged with assault. The club freaked out. The first thing they did was kick us off the bill for the following night. They were getting ready to phone the cops when Ken Lester stepped in. I don't know how he did it, but he talked the woman out of pressing charges *and* the club into putting us back on for the next night! We played the show with the Dils, which went over like gangbusters. Then we bid adieu to New York.

Our next destination back in Canada was in Ottawa, where we played a three-night stand at a place called the Rotter's Club. Then it was on to Toronto, where we got a pretty good turnout at the Edge. I guess I *had* made some friends and fans during my stay there. The show ended, and then it was time to head home.

I have no idea why, but we had no shows booked on the way back across the country. It was just 3,000 miles of Canada's vast nothingness, a long haul, but on the bright side it looked like we might make it home with spoils of $100 each. Then, in Regina, I made a wrong turn into the Royal Canadian Mounted Police national training centre. In a bit of a panic, I put the van into reverse and cranked the wheel hard, breaking one of the ball joints. Shit! The van limped along for a bit, but it needed to be fixed. It was about six PM, however, and everything was closed. We found this repair joint, Rudy's Brake and Steering, and parked our van on the lot for the night. The next morning, Rudy took the rest of our cash, fixed the van, and we were on our way. We got back to Vancouver totally broke, with the van running on fumes. It had been a tense trip, with a lot of bitching and fighting. We were all fairly volatile, Biscuits most of all. But it had been one wild adventure. We'd pulled off a continent-wide tour on a fucking shoestring.

We did a few shows at the Buddha that summer, but we were starting to realize we needed a manager. Our friend Tom Harrison arranged a meeting with Bruce Allen, who was managing Bachman Turner Overdrive (BTO) and Loverboy at the time. The first thing Bruce said was, "All right, boys! How much money are you going to make me?" There was a stunned silence on our part. I had gotten into music because it was fun, because it had deep meaning, because I loved the words of Bob Dylan and Woody Guthrie, because of Jimi Hendrix's guitar-playing. Money? What did that have to do with music? That was the last we saw of Bruce for a few years, but our meeting with him awakened us to the evils of the music biz. Like Hunter S. Thompson said, "The music business is a cruel and shallow money trench, a long plastic hallway where thieves and pimps run free, and good men die like dogs. There's also a negative side."

After a bit of thinking, we approached Ken Lester. He had no experience in music, but he was a creative guy, and we got along with him. After much convincing, he agreed. It turned out to be an inspired choice.

Lester had an interesting background. He was a writer and general shit-disturber who had been charged as one of the two organizers of the infamous Gastown Riot in Vancouver in 1971. There had actually been no riot going on until ultra-reactionary, right-wing mayor Tom Campbell ordered the Vancouver police to charge into a peaceful demonstration on horseback with their billyclubs. Lester got off on the charge on the basis that he had only been selling ice cream. He called himself an anarchist, and saw punk as the new way of attacking conservative bullshit. He was also very creative and had a knack for predicting how the media would react to certain things.

In 1979, there was a worldwide movement afoot urging disarmament by the nuclear powers, and some concerned local people (including Ken Lester and David Spaner) were organizing an outdoor Rock Against Radiation concert to be held on September 8. Posters went up all over town, and there was lots of media attention. The show had a great line up of bands: D.O.A., the Subhumans, the Pointed Sticks, Reconstruction (a good local reggae band), and the K-Tels. At the last minute, the city tried to pull our permit, but they relented under pressure and the show went on. Around 3,000 people showed up to make a statement for peace over stupidity. The following year, the Vancouver No Nukes demonstration had 50,000 people marching, led by the mayor himself and backed by church groups. But I guess our combination of punks and free speech had been too much for them.

Lester booked a tour of western Canada for us in October, and right in the middle of it we were offered the chance to open for the Clash

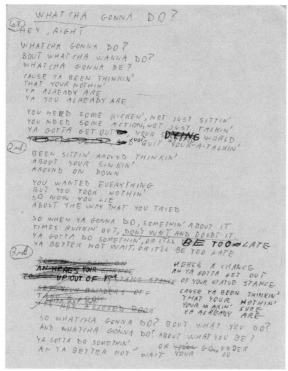

Whatcha Gonna Do? (early draft). *Joey Shithead Keithley, Prisoner Publishing*

in Vancouver at the PNE Gardens. Naturally, we flew home to do it. The show only paid $100, and the airplane tickets were much more than that, but we were really excited. It would be the biggest show we had ever played in our hometown. In February 1979, earlier that year, the Clash had played the Commodore, put on a great show, and the next day hung out with the locals and played soccer. They seemed to be like their music, honest and straightforward.

We got to the PNE Gardens in time for our soundcheck. We waited and waited for the Clash to finish theirs, but when they had, Mick Jones brought out some kid about five years old and started teaching him to play the drums. Now, if there had been the spare time to do it, this would have been cool, but that wasn't the case. Our old pals Ray Campi and the Rockabilly Rebels, who were scheduled to play the middle set that evening, were waiting as well. We never got to do a soundcheck, which pissed us off.

We tried to meet the Clash after soundcheck, but we weren't allowed in their dressing room. Oh well, we were still pretty jazzed. The place was packed, with about 2,200 people in the audience. We got up to play, and things were going great until our set was cut short. I don't know whose fuckin' idea that was. Now we were seriously pissed off. The Clash were supposed to be men of the people, but they were definitely not coming across that way. Ray Campi and his band did a great set; they were a real class act.

Then it was time for the Clash. As they came out of their dressing room to head onto the stage, I blocked each one's path and yelled in their faces, "You guys are bullshit!" There was no security around, so they cowered and scurried away. They started playing, sounding good. (I still think they're one of the best bands of all time!) But in between songs a rancorous discussion was taking place between Mick Jones and some of our fans. It seems word had got around the Gardens that the Clash had been none too gracious to

D.O.A. Lester and a few other people started catcalling Jones, who in turn disparaged Vancouver and D.O.A. Jones challenged Lester to come up on stage and fight him. Lester yelled back for Jones to come down onto the floor. While this was going on, we ran backstage and raided the Clash's dressing room for food and beer.

Later that night, David Spaner, who was covering the show as a writer, phoned up the hotel where the Clash were staying. He got Mick Jones on the phone, and Jones was livid. He said the Clash would never come back to Vancouver. Jones also said what he really hated about the city was that crappy heavy metal band D.O.A. A few of our loyal fans went over there and spraypainted the band's tour bus with "The Clash suck! D.O.A. rule!" I would like to have seen Mick Jones's face when he walked out the next morning!

The Clash did come back to Vancouver, though, three years later. They played the Kerrisdale Arena, and the whole D.O.A. gang worked the show. Our main activity was opening up the side doors of the arena and letting a couple of hundred people in for free. Hey, Joe Strummer, you were a real inspiration, RIP.

We flew back to Regina to continue our tour, which took us across Canada and down into the States again. Just before the tour had begun, we had recorded another single with Ron Obvious at Little Mountain Sound. It was financed by Al Dopeman and included "World War 3" and "Whatcha Gonna Do?" We were really happy with it. We first released it on Sudden Death, and then farmed it out to Quintessence, which is why there are two covers for it.

One highlight of the tour was the Rock Against Racism concert we played in Lexington, Kentucky. Not long before, the Ku Klux Klan had gunned down five people at an anti-racist demonstration in Greensboro, North Carolina. The show in Lexington was electric. It was put on by an

African American, Tony Briggs, and emceed by the head Yippie, Dana Beal. We also played Dayton, Ohio, which was starting to develop a real cool scene. All of the shows on the tour were well-attended, and people were becoming familiar with the songs. Obviously, the three singles were getting around.

On our return, we were booked for a show at UBC's Sub Ballroom with the Female Hands. (The band's Alan Moy and Keith Portius went on to manage 54-40 and to coach our hockey team, the D.O.A. Murder Squad.) UBC had hired some engineering students to do security that night, which turned out to be a bad move. The engineers did not understand punk rock, and when kids came on stage, the engineers went nuts trying to stop them. The punks were feeling their oats that day, and they weren't going to take any shit from the engineers. Complete mayhem ensued, and the engineers pretty much had to run for it. Biscuits' brother, Bob Montgomery, swung Tarzan-style from the huge curtains at the side of the stage; the glass entrance doors to the hall got kicked in. Biscuits shouted into the mike, "Destroy this fucking dump! Destroy it! Anarchy!" then promptly ran back into the

dressing room and hid in one of the bathroom stalls, fearing the engineers might come back to even the score.

When I caught some pukes carting away Biscuits's Ayotte drum set, which I had paid for myself, I said, "Fuck that shit!" I grabbed the three of them and kicked them down the stairs.

Biscuits, Rampage, and I met backstage. We argued and yelled, and all the tension of the first two years of D.O.A. came to a head right there. That was it. We were sick of each other, and D.O.A. broke up on the spot. All of a sudden, it was over.

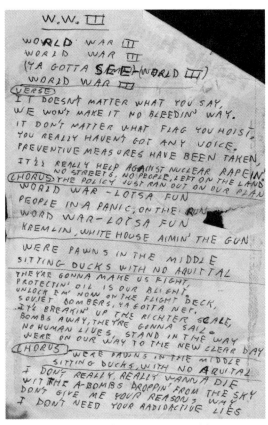

World War 3. _Shithead/Biscuits, Prisoner Publishing_

D.O.A. (l-r Biscuits, Rampage, roadie Bob Montgomery, Shithead) at Cambrian Hall, Vancouver, 1979. *photo: Bev Davies*

CHAPTER SIX

SOMETHING BETTER CHANGE

The breakup at the UBC show pissed me (and a lot of others, including fans) off. D.O.A. had gotten pretty big around town, and people were looking for big things to happen. But we had our enemies, both musicians and otherwise, so someone must have been happy about it. I was undeterred. We had started working on our first album, which was eventually titled *Something Better Change*. We had also entertained the idea of getting a second guitar player. This made for some hilarious auditions. We had guys showing up trying to play jazz, guys with tiny Fender Princeton amps, guys with no fucking idea what punk rock was supposed to be. For the most part, a real plethora of clowns! The auditions sometimes lasted only for one song; then we would stop and turf the offending musician.

We finally got down to two people who we thought might work: Tony Baloney (Real McKenzies) and Dave Gregg. I can't remember why, but somehow Biscuits and I didn't really let Rampage have a vote on this (maybe it was the aftermath of Brad Kunt!). I thought we should get Tony Baloney; he seemed to me to be a better lead player and he was a fast learner. But Biscuits thought Dave was better; after all, he reasoned, Dave had a sound system and a place for us to practice (830 Gore Avenue). I thought about it for a bit, but practicality won out. Dave turned out to be a fine choice.

After that fateful show at UBC, it didn't take me long to get a new lineup for D.O.A. In addition to Dave, I recruited one of my best friends, Simon Wilde, AKA Stubby Pecker from the Rabid, for bass. Dave, Simon, and I got together at Fort Gore and started learning D.O.A.'s songs. We were all plugged into one amp – talk about distortion! After a couple of days, we grabbed a drummer, Andy Graffiti. He was cool, and a good drummer (but not in the power drummer mode of Biscuits or Dimwit). But Graffiti really altered D.O.A.'s sound; he had a lighter touch, so we didn't sound quite so powerful.

Dave Gregg and Simon "Stubby Pecker" Wilde.

D.O.A.'s new lineup played a weekend of shows at the Buddha. It was raucous and rowdy, but not very together. We also carried on with recording the album with the new lineup at Ocean Sound in North Vancouver. This time Dick Drake was the engineer.

The Ocean Sound studio was in the back of owner Ken Morrison's house. He seemed to have an endless supply of beer in his living room, and whenever we needed libations, we would head in there and grab a case of Black Label. At first, we thought this was stupidity on Morrison's part; offering free beer to D.O.A. was like waving a red flag at a fucking bull! But then we realized how devious a plan it was. Every case of beer we guzzled slowed down our studio work, and the studio bill started piling up and up. Roy Atkinson from Friends Records, who had arranged the deal, kept asking Ken Lester what was taking so long. Ken kept assuring him, "Everything's cool, man. Everything's cool."

We had left Quintessence Records just before the band's split when the company got into financial problems. Our three singles had all sold really well, but trying to get our royalties was like trying to pull teeth from the jaws of a sabretooth tiger. Ted Thomas told us IRC had pressed 2,000 copies each of "Disco Sucks" and "The Prisoner," but when we checked at the plant, we found out that 5,000 of each had been manufactured. So Ted owed us for 10,000 singles, plus all the "World War 3" singles we had fronted him. We tried repeatedly to track him down, but to no avail. It was time to take action.

One morning, the four of us, Lester, and Bev Davies got into the "Blue Bullet" (our new tour van) one morning and headed down to Quintessence. It was deserted except for Dale Wiese, the lone employee. As we milled about the store, flipping through the record racks, Dale finally got up the nerve to ask what we were doing. We told him Ted had not paid us for 10,000 records and we were there to collect. We started picking up armloads of 12-inch records, everything from AC/DC to the Rezillos. Quintessence's phone had been cut off, so Dale couldn't call anybody. Once we'd liberated about 1,000 pieces, we loaded them in the van and said, "Adios, amigo!" The next day Roy from Friends took our plunder off our hands and became our new label guy.

D.O.A.'s new lineup played its last show only a few months later. Jim Braineater, an incredible painter who also had a band called I, Braineater, owned a sound system, so I hired him to do the sound. A crowd showed up, but we didn't play well and the sound system fed back all night long. Rampage and Biscuits were there, and we met up after the show. Biscuits and Rampage said the show fuckin' stank, and I agreed. We agreed the three of us had had a strong thing going, and we decided to reunite. The next day, I fired Dave, Andy, and Simon. It was hard on Simon, but we remained strong friends until his death in 1994, RIP.

Ken was unhappy about Dave leaving, though, and he talked the rest of us into taking him back, arguing Dave would be the "George Harrison of the group." Yeah, right, like we were the fucking Beatles! We went back to Ocean Sound and started working on the album again; we ditched all the tracks that had been recorded with the "new" lineup.

In April of 1980, D.O.A. made a two-week trip down the coast, playing Seattle, Portland, Eugene, Sacramento, San Francisco, and then our first show in Los Angeles. The show was at the Stardust Roller Rink in Hollywood. Besides D.O.A., on the bill was a great band called the Alleycats, and the incomparable X, one of my favourite bands of all time. About 1,500 people showed up. The gig looked like a gimme – go out there and play hard, and you'd win the crowd over. That was especially important in a new town. The only problem was that this

burger chain called Carl's Junior right next to the venue had a contest going: correctly answer three musical questions and win a free giant burger. Of course we kept acing the questions, getting the giant burgers, and eating them on the spot. I think I'd eaten four by the time I hit the stage. Our set went well enough, but it was like operating with a giant brick stuck in my gut. I didn't know whether I was going to puke on stage or mercifully die.

Back home, we appeared a few times on a local cable TV show called *Nite Dreems*. It was hosted by J.B. Shayne and John Tanner, both of whom had been blacklisted by the local radio stations for trying to start a union for DJs. There were very few music videos back then, so John, J.B., and their accomplice Susanne Tabata would fill the time by aiming the TV camera at a turntable. Their other tactic was to sit behind a crystal ball and wave their hands around in swami-like fashion while the camera zoomed in and out, with punk rock music blaring in the background. Sometimes they would try to shoot a video for local bands. The video they did for "Thirteen" showed Biscuits and I running around a city park (Rampage missed the shoot), being chased by the six-foot-six John Tanner, who was wearing a giant duck's head.

One show of note early that summer was at the Leonardo Da Vinci Hall in Victoria, on Vancouver Island. (I still don't know what the fuck Leonardo ever had to do with Victoria.) The opening band, the Sick Fucks, were not that good, but they were a Victoria sensation, and later became one of Canada's best-known punk bands, the Dayglo Abortions.

The recording of *Something Better Change* was dragging on and on, but we were close to the finish line. We were scheduled to start a tour of the U.S. midwest on July 9 in Madison, Wisconsin, and by the morning of July 7, all but one of the tracks had been mixed and were ready to go. We were hung up on a song Biscuits had written called "Last Night." Musically I liked it, but lyrically it was making me gag, and I was the one who had to sing it. Chuck and I finally arrived at a compromise, but because of these studio shenanigans we had 2,000 miles to drive and only forty-eight hours to do it. Ken Lester decided to ride his motorcycle behind us, but after a while he was having a hard time with it, saying his guts were getting too shaken up. That goddamn bike caused lots of misery for him. He also claimed that his partial baldness was from wearing a bike helmet. This later led to our standing joke about the two Kennys: Ken Lester was "Half-Roof" and Ken Montgomery, Dimwit, was "Deadweight."

But then who was to ride the bike when Ken couldn't? Well, send forth our champion, Rampage. He refused to wear Lester's helmet, though; "Fuck helmet laws!" he said, but then maybe he also believed Ken about the hair thing. So there we were, flying down the I-90 across the Great Plains. At one point, I was driving the van and lost track of Rampage in my rear-view mirror. I slowed slightly, and then all of a sudden I could see a bike catching up to us at great speed. It was Rampage, of course, but he wasn't doing anything normal with the bike. He was standing on the fucking seat,

with the bike in top gear, reaching down to gun the throttle. Lester starts screaming out the driver's window about his motorcycle and how it might get destroyed, but Rampage zoomed on blithely ahead of us. Eventually he let me catch up and motioned for me to hand him a beer. I got somebody to pass me one. Lester tried to wrestle the bottle away from me, but I won the battle: Rampage pulled the bike in close and I handed him the beer. At the next stop, Lester was screaming at both of us. Talk about a highway to hell!

We pulled into Madison, Wisconsin – America's capital of beers, cows, and cheese – on the evening of July 9, with only an hour to spare. We were bagged, needless to say, but we were booked at a joint called Merlin's for 10: 30 PM, so we headed over there and dragged our gear onto the stage through a sea of people on the dance floor. When we finally start to play, Dave seemed to have forgotten the chords to half the songs. Shit!

But after getting through a couple of songs, the owner of the club sent up some pitchers of beer. The sight of him standing there, admiring his generosity, made me lose my head. I grabbed the pitcher closest to me, took a big glug, and threw the rest of it on the crowd. The owner was outraged that I had repaid his kindness in such a pagan manner, and jumped up onto the stage and grabbed a mike. "I'm going to buy everybody here a free beer," he announced to the crowd, "and I want you all to come up here and throw your beer on this asshole!" People hustled to grab free beer, and I braced myself to get soaked. But I stayed as dry as an Arizona river. The crowd all drank their beer instead.

The next night we played the Starship Club in Milwaukee. The show rocked, but Dave forgot a slew of chords again. Then it was on to Chicago, where we were booked at the original Oz club, which was cool because it was the home of Chicago punk rock. When I went to get a beer before we started playing, I saw Dave knocking back a few on the other side of the circular bar. He looked at me with a drunken smile, and I thought back to how badly he had played in Madison and Milwaukee. I hefted my half-full can of beer and hurled it across the bar at him, nailing him right in the forehead. After that, he smartened up; soon, he became a good guitar player and showman.

We moved on to Detroit for the first Rock Against Reagan concert. The Republican Party was having its convention there to nominate Ronald Reagan for the presidency. Detroit was trying to showcase itself as the "new" Detroit, and not the dirty, run-down, beat-up murder capital of America that everybody had come to know and love. No sirree! It was out with the old and in with the new. The centerpiece of this "revitalization" was the Renaissance Centre, a series of big, black glass towers on the Detroit River.

But there were complications. It was a hot, sticky summer, and Detroit

Fucked Up Ronnie

you're fucked up ronnie, you're not gonna last
you're gonna die too, from a neutron blast
you're fucked up ronnie
I'm lyin' a pool of blood leave me alone
I don't want your help anyways
when you march us off to war
will you be there to save the day
you're fucked up ronnie, leave me alone

Joey Shithead Keithley, Prisoner Publishing

had a garbage strike going on. The trash was piled high in the streets and there were so many rats roaming around you couldn't tell the rats from the Republicans without name tags. A lot of people also hated King Ronnie and what he represented: big business, big military, anti-unionism, big oil. Protestors from all over the U.S., from punks to grandmothers, were in town for the concert. There would be many more over the next eight years of Reagan's reign, but this was the granddaddy of them all.

The afternoon got underway with a lot of energy and speeches. About 2,000 anti-Reagan types were waving placards, chanting, and generally having a good shit-disturbing time. Toxic Reasons, a great band from Dayton, Ohio, had just finished an inspiring set when we noticed a mob of people working their way across Clark Park. As we got on stage, we could see these weren't more of the anti-Reagan people we were playing for. They were pro-Reagan, brandishing signs praising the great de-emancipator and waving American flags. As they drew closer, some fisticuffs broke out.

It looked like total chaos was about to erupt. We kept playing as a phalanx of police vans came roaring up the side streets. Police with shields and riot batons formed a line to separate the two groups. Placards waved above the police line, and fists and boots started flying back and forth. I looked at the rest of the band and said, "Hey, it's time to play 'Fucked Up Ronnie.'" So we launched into it. What a scene!

I was proud to participate in that great event. But by the time we crossed the border back into Canada, we were in a surly mood. Toronto was muggy and hot. During a set at the Turning Point, a divey old club like the Smilin' Buddha, we got into an argument about which songs we were going to play. Biscuits threw his drumsticks at Rampage, who responded by swinging his bass. Then both of them walked off the stage and headed outside while Dave and I stood there looking stupid.

Soon a crowd of people in front of the club were trying to get Rampage and Biscuits back inside and onto the stage. This contingent was led by the club's bouncer, who was called Mr Clean (named aptly for his resemblance to the guy on the cleaning solution bottle). Mr Clean tried to reason with Rampage, then started pleading with him. But Rampage just kept saying, "I'm not going back onstage with that little fucking weiner!" Finally, Mr Clean pulled out all the stops. He said, "What do you want, Rampage? A blowjob? Okay, I'll give you one right now!" Mr Clean got down on his knees, right in front of the club, right in front of the mob on the sidewalk, and started to pull down Rampage's zipper. Rampage turned beat red and said, "Okay! Okay, I'll play!" Finally, everyone got back on stage and we finished the set.

The Toronto heat was really getting to us. Bob Montgomery, who had come with us as a roadie, threw half of Ken Lester's clothes out of a fourth-storey window one day when Ken wouldn't give him his per diem; when Lester, who had recovered his clothes from the sidewalk, was halfway back up the stairs, Montgomery threw out the rest of his clothes. During a show at Larry's Hideaway in Toronto, Biscuit's hi-hat stand stopped working properly. When he couldn't get Bob's attention by hurling drumsticks at him, he picked up the entire stand and chucked it off the stage, hitting Bob in the shoulder. Bob ran onto the stage to beat the fuck out of his brother, but Rampage intercepted him. By this point, the club's bouncers had run down to the stage. They put Rampage in a headlock and were about to pulverize him when I jumped in. Before we knew it, Ken had joined in the fray. Holy fuck! Talk about "Charge of the Light Brigade!"

Over the next few nights, the fist fights among us raged: Ken fought with Rampage, Bob fought with Ken, and Rampage fought with Bob. The Montgomery brothers' fight was the best. One steamy afternoon on the roof of the warehouse where we were staying, Bob and Biscuits started arguing. It escalated until Bob lunged for Biscuits in a menacing manner. Biscuits fell down on his back and started kicking his legs in the air, screaming for mercy, but Bob showed him none. He picked up his brother and carried him, still kicking and screaming, towards the edge of the building. Rampage and I were getting concerned; there was no railing at the edge, just a four-storey drop into a grubby back alley. Suddenly, with a jerk, Bob heaved his brother into the flower box we'd been pissing in for the past four days! We nearly pissed ourselves, we laughed so hard.

One day we were set to play an outdoor Rock Against Radiation concert at Nathan Phillips Square, right in front of Toronto's City Hall, organized by some cool types like my friend Joe College. The bill was a who's who of Ontario's punk scene: the Viletones, the Demics, and the Forgotten Rebels,

The Enemy

you peer through the darkness, billy clubs aimed.
they smash ya once or twice, till ya don't look the same
ya got to know who your enemy is, the enemy
ya got to know who your enemy is, the enemy
they rope ya to a time clock, to keep you on the line
and now your losin', the pieces of your mind
ya got to know who your enemy is, the enemy
ya got to know who your enemy is, the enemy
the newsmen are lying, drawin' lines like black & white
makin' you believe, it's your brother you gotta fight
ya got to know who your enemy is, the enemy
ya got to know who your enemy is, the enemy.

Shithead/Biscuits, Prisoner Publishing

among others. As we pulled our truck into the parking area and started to unload, a guy approached and asked if all the bands that day could use our gear. We scratched our noggins in disbelief. "You mean to tell me that you've got five local bands and nobody has their own gear?"

"That's right," the guy said. "We figured that D.O.A. would have it all here, so we wouldn't have to bother."

This kind of thing happened to us all the time in Europe, and I've never really been able to figure it out. A band on tour is trying to make their cheap gear go the distance. Don't get me wrong; in a pinch, I've even helped out musicians I couldn't stand. That is part of the musician's credo! But how frequently this situation arises has always puzzled me.

When I laid this out for the Toronto guy, he called us a bunch of fucking west-coast jerks. "You better go flag yourself a fucking cab," I said, "or your bands are going to be humming their parts!" He left in a huff to find some other gear.

When we got up to play, most of the crowd was really digging it. But when I said a few words about fighting nuclear proliferation, a few brainless punks started "seig heiling" me, giving the Nazi salute, then chucked a few things at us. When we offered to come down and beat the hell out of them, they slunk to the back of the crowd. The following night, we were playing support for the Forgotten Rebels at a theatre in Hamilton, their hometown, just down the highway from Toronto. Before we left, Bob decided to leave a memento of the gig when he grabbed a can of spraypaint and tagged the Rebel's shiny new rental van: D.O.A. Rules! Forgotten Rebels suck!

We then headed back south into the States; we still had a few more shows scheduled in the Dayton, Cincinnati/Newport, Lexington triangle. The area would become one of our favourite stomping grounds. But that first time we played Cincinnati, we were booked into a rock bar that held "punk nites." As we arrived, they were spraypainting phony punk slogans onto rolled paper, and had some giant safety pins stuck up on the wall. It was dismal. At the end of the night, we knew they'd be taking all this shit down, bringing in bales of hay, and rolling the mechanical bull out of the storeroom. The place was packed, and everything was smooth as the three local bands played. When it was our turn, people went nuts for a song and a half, until the fire alarm went off. The entire club cleared. There was no fire, though, so they let everybody back in and we resumed playing. About a song later, the alarm went off again. Another fucking false alarm! This happened twice more before the club cancelled the show. They were too dumb to post one of the bouncers at the alarm box. The club manager gave us $100 of the $500 we should have received, claiming the club would need to give out refunds. Yeah, right! We got our revenge, though; just as we were about to leave, a delivery truck pulled into the loading area with the club's beer for the next night's cowboy show. The driver stacked the beer on the ground and left. Well, as they say, when opportunity knocks, you had best answer it. We shoved the beer bottles into every empty spot we could find in the van. By the time we drove off, there was barely room to sit down. Yeehaw!

It was back to New York after that. We wanted to play at CBGBS, but we were banned, as Bob Montgomery had defaced a landmark mural of Jesus Christ on Second Avenue the year before. (Over the mural he spraypainted, "Religion sucks, D.O.A. rules!") So instead, we played with Bad Brains at Electric Circus. The band on stage before us was terrible. There was only a curtain separating the stage from the backstage area, and during the shitty performance, Biscuits kept drumming a different beat while the band on stage tried to figure out what to play. Bad Brains, however, were incredible. They were an all-black punk band that smoked like nobody's business. This was in the days before reggae took off, and the very existence of Bad Brains gave punk legitimacy as a truly progressive, inclusive musical movement. Amazing.

After New York, we went back to Ontario to play an outdoor festival called Deep Wave. The promoters were expecting thousands. The headliner was Teenage Head, but the bill had a lot of rock bands from the Toronto scene, some of them really pathetic.

When it was time for us to go on stage, some stoned hippie greaseball named Freewheelin' Frankie Avalanche got up to introduce us: "Ladies and gentlemen, let's have a big hand for Johnny Shithead and the D.O.A.s!" Oh well. There were only about 100 punks there, but they were ready to rock! They went nuts when we started. The rest of the crowd did not, though, including the 300 or so security guys wearing these stupid baseball hats with "Deep Wave" printed on them.

After three songs, Rampage's Fender bass started cutting in and out. He threw it across the stage, where the butt end went sailing into a heavy cable box. Rampage ran over and started trying to smash his bass to bits. I took a turn too. When the sound guy rushed onto the stage and put Rampage in a headlock, I pried him off. The next thing we knew, we were surrounded by security goons who kicked us off the stage.

We were supposed to be paid $300 for the gig. Ken came back with a cheque. We said, "A cheque? What the fuck are you thinking, Lester!" As I said earlier, the promoters had been expecting thousands, but there almost as many security guys as there were fans!

As I was trying to wrestle the cheque away from Ken, it flew out of our hands and fell to the ground, where, not surprisingly, it bounced so hard that it shot up to the moon. Never saw that goddamned thing again!

We worked our way back to western Canada, stopping in Winnipeg for the first time. While on stage, some guy started throwing bottles at us, so we jumped into the crowd and tossed him, violently, out of the hall. Aside from that, we got home without further incident. In August, Friends Records finally released *Triumph of the Ignoroids*, the recording of our set at the 1978 Battle of the Bands. It is so raw I laugh my guts out every time I hear it. The inspiration for the title came from a stop D.O.A. once made at the huge truckadero at the north end of the Grapevine Pass coming out of L.A. We stopped for fuel and just in front of us was a camper. A drunken boob staggered out from behind the wheel with a bottle of Jack Daniels in one hand and a bag of Doritos in the other. A lit cigarette dangled from his lips as he fueled up. The place was jammed with similar idiots. Shit! Those were the days of the Ignoroids.

A nitwit Vancouver DJ, Tom Lucas, used *Triumph of the Ignoroids* on his shows as an example of how terrible he thought punk rock was. He would play a bit, then grab the needle and run it across the record, blurting out in billygoat fashion, "Remember, punk rock is junk rock!"

In early September 1980, we set out for California again. We played the Mabuhay Gardens in San Francisco and then headed to L.A. for a punk rock show at the Hong Kong Café. The bill was fucking excellent: D.O.A., the B-People, and Black Flag. Well, at least the bands thought the bill was good. Apparently nobody else did. Maybe ten people paid to see the show. At the end of the night, a red-faced Chuck Dukowski, bassist for Black Flag,

handed me eight bucks. There wasn't much I could say; I passed math in high school. I knew what was coming. There were more band members than people in the crowd. I said thanks and we headed back north.

Maybe a week after we got back, Ken Lester came over to rehearsal to tell us that Black Flag wanted us to do another show with them at the Whiskey in Hollywood. Rampage said, "Ken! We just played with them and we got eight fucking bucks!"

Lester mumbled something about how it would be a good career move.

I asked the most important question: "How much?"

"One hundred seventy-five dollars. U.S.," said Lester.

So the plan was to drive down for one show and straight back again, a 2,800 mile round trip for one show and $175. Sounded logical to us! We agreed to go.

On October 7, we piled into my vw Rabbit, not the largest of vehicles. We put a bit of Biscuits' drum kit in the trunk along with the guitars. The bass was too long for the trunk, so it went between the front seats and took up a chunk of the back. Now, D.O.A. are not exactly midgets. We were fucking crammed on that ride! But it would all be worth it.

After driving non-stop the entire night, we got to L.A. and headed straight for the Whiskey, the most famous club in L.A.'s storied history of music. We didn't realize that the Hong Kong Café had not been a typical Black Flag gig. They had a strong and growing following in greater L.A. Dukowski and guitarist Greg Ginn thought that maybe there might be enough people to do two shows at the Whiskey that night. By six PM there was a lineup for the first show. The Whiskey staff let everybody in and packed the place. The club's official capacity was about 450 people and there were easily that many jammed in. After D.O.A. and Black Flag played,

they cleared the club for the second show. It was about 9:30.

By now there were 500 people waiting to get in, and 500 people trying to get out. This made for a real mob scene on the sidewalk outside the club. Then something powerful was set into motion. A cop car cruised past the club. Somebody threw a beer bottle at it. Somebody else chucked another. Then a few more bottles flew and nailed the cruiser. The LAPD must have been ready for this; the relationship between the LAPD and the L.A. punks was awfully rocky. Within a few minutes, forty L.A. cop cars raced up to the scene. In each car were three or four cops. Two helicopters hovered overhead. The cops blocked the streets in all directions. Then, out of nowhere, the cop-in-charge walked into the middle of the intersection in front of the club. He held a shotgun up over his head and turned in a slow circle, so everyone could see his firepower. The street got deathly quiet. As the cop finished his circle the other cops sprang into action.

They jumped out of their patrol cars with shields and batons and charged the punks, swinging their batons at anything and everything: heads, legs, arms, whatever got in the way. The street was instant carnage. Blood, chaos, and people running, trying to find a way out.

Our second show at the Whiskey was cancelled. Of course. The club

stiffed us and Black Flag, citing possible damage to the front of the club. The next day the L.A. papers screamed: "Riot on Sunset Strip!" "Punk bands Black Flag and D.O.A. cause mayhem!" "Riot at the Whiskey-A-Go-Go."

So we crammed back into the Rabbit and drove back to Canada. We never had any problem getting a crowd in L.A. after that. The Whiskey show, and its aftermath, would be the template for Southern California punk for the next ten years or more.

Black Flag joined us in Vancouver a month later for three nights at Gary Taylor's Rock Room. Some of the patrons didn't know what to make of the unorthodox musical combo of Ron Reyes on vocals, Chuck Dukowski on bass, Greg Ginn on lead guitar, and Robo on drums. Black Flag was totally original; none of the musicians played in the "normal" rock style at all. Over the years, D.O.A. gigged with Black Flag with all their various lead singers: Keith Morris, Ron Reyes, Dez Cadena, and Henry Rollins. They all fit the bill and all did a great job.

Late November of 1980 saw us on the road to California yet again. We played support for Siouxie and the Banshees at the California Hall in San Francisco before a crowd of 2,000, then drove to L.A. to play support for X for three nights at the Starwood. Every show was a soldout, raucous affair. People were going nuts for X, and we were glad to get to know them. Bonebrake, Exene, and John Doe are excellent people. Billy Zoom was a tough guy to figure out, but what a killer guitar player.

The last show was the most memorable of the bunch. We were backstage after a set when who should show up but David Lee Roth from Van Halen. He bullshitted a bit, then said to Biscuits, "You guys are doing the same thing as us, man! You just package it differently!"

Biscuits looked at him half in amazement, half in disgust. "I don't think so, man!" he said.

Also in the audience that night were Gene Simmons of Kiss and Danny Bonaduce, who played Danny Partridge in *The Partridge Family*. Having grown up wearing lumberjack shirts and toques, we were impressed.

After the show, as we were out back loading the van, we were joined again by a completely fucking drunk David Lee Roth, accompanied by an equally drunk female companion and someone who turned out to be Van Halen's bassist, Michael Anthony. Our roadie Bob started yelling, "Hey, Dave, give us one of your screams!" There is no other scream in the world quite like Roth's "Ow-Ow!" It's a classic. "I'm busy, man!" Dave shot back. This went back and forth a few times. Finally, Bob walked over, grabbed Roth, and put him in a headlock. "All right now," said Bob. "Give us one of those screams."

David tried to scream, but fuck all came out. He tried again and managed a feeble "Ow!"

"Thanks very much, my friend," Bob said, and let Roth go.

On December 8, 1980, something happened that shook me and millions of others around the world: John Lennon was shot outside his home in New York City. Lennon's songwriting and his political stances had had a big effect on me when I was younger, and his death was a tragedy. In a small tribute to him, on a rainy day when the sky was black and merciless, D.O.A. played a few Beatles songs at a tiny clothing store in Gastown. We opened up the windows and door so people could hear us play. The crowd got soaked, but they stood patiently outside, listening. *Georgia Straight* editor Bob Mercer, our friend (and a fine musician in his own right) who had organized the tribute, joined us on "Working Class Hero." It was a stirrng moment. Yeah, a working class hero *is* something to be.

D.O.A. (l-r Shithead, Rampage, Biscuits, Dave), 1981. *photo: Edward C. Colver*

CHAPTER SEVEN

HARDCORE 81

The punk scene in Vancouver had grown considerably by the early '80s. There were bigger crowds, more venues to play, and more bands. It was endless fun. D.O.A. had the best of both worlds: we gigged a lot at home, and there always seemed to be more places to play around the continent.

In the fall of 1980, we had done some demos for our next album at Skid Rowcording in Burnaby. The recording studio and house was run by the tireless and ever-witty Bill Barker, who would throw completely out-of-control parties there. It was common for people in a hammered state to jump off of Barker's ten-foot-high porch and grab the rope hanging from a tree in the front yard. The idea was then to kick off from the porch, use your momentum to swing around the side of the house, kick off from the side wall, and make it back to the porch again. Few could accomplish this feat in one pass; most either missed the rope and plunged into the front yard or made it around the corner of the house, then smashed into the house and crumpled to the ground. And if you wanted to pet Barker's cat, you had to take it out of the kitchen freezer first. It had died, but this way Barker could still play with it when he liked.

The rough tapes we made on Barker's 8-track turned out to be pretty good. These were the songs that eventually formed our second LP, *Hardcore 81*. We went back to Ocean Sound to record it, but this time we were determined not to let the session drag on and on. The engineer this time around was Tracy Marks. The stash of Black Label beer was gone, and the whole recording, fourteen tracks in all, took only a week. Ken Lester came up with two different ideas: *Hardcore Plus* or *Hardcore 81*.

The previous fall we had seen an article in a music mag from San Francisco that talked about the west-coast punk scene: the Avengers, the Circle Jerks, Black Flag, the Dead Kennedys, the Dils, X, D.O.A., and a pile of other bands. The title of the article was "Hardcore," and we thought that was an apt description for our kind of punk rock, which was different from the New York and London scenes. It was a fresh new sound that spanned from Vancouver to San Diego. It was faster and more aggressive than New York or London punk, and nobody tried to sing with phony English accents. Before long, the world of punk rock would be imitating us.

The term "hardcore" seemed to encapsulate the spontaneity, energy, and rebellion of the scene. The ideals we took from it were these:

- Think for yourself
- Don't back down
- Change your world
- Be free

In celebration of the hardcore ethic, we organized a Hardcore Festival to run for two nights at a big Vancouver club called the Laundromat. On the bill with us were Black Flag, Seven Seconds, Bludgeoned Pigs, the Rock 'n' Roll Bitches, the Butchers, and Insex. Both nights were packed. This worked for the cops as well. It seemed like they were still investigating the whole anarchist-punk connection, as they set up a video camera across the street and taped everybody going in or out of the club, figuring that they had a lot of the hoodlums in one place at one time. Things were going along well the first night until something flew off the balcony and hit Dim Borghino, the lead singer for Seven Seconds, in the leg. Snotface, a local troublemaker, had crapped into a paper towel and thrown it off the balcony. Bullseye! Once Dim realized it was shit, he started doing the most amazing dance – I dubbed it the "Shake the shit off your jeans while still trying to fucking sing" dance. I guess that was the only pair of jeans Dim had brought with him on the long drive from Reno, because the next night he

was wearing them again, with a square cut out of one leg. What a great event. Hardcore was here to stay.

D.O.A. (l-r Biscuits, Rampage, Dave, Shithead) at the Laundromat, 1981. *photo: Bev Davies*

In April, we started the Hardcore 81 tour in Seattle at the Gorilla Room, which was run by Bryan Runnings. The show went well, but on the last song of our encore, I slipped off the stage and fucked up my ankle. A couple of punks gave me some painkillers, but the next morning I woke up screaming. I made my way to a hospital, was diagnosed with a bad sprain, and somehow managed to get a walking cast put on for free. For our next five shows, the sound guys got me a goose-neck mike stand and I sat with it on the side of the stage. Shit, all I needed was a harmonica and I could have done my Bob Dylan impression. We put Rampage in the middle of the stage and got him to dance around for visual effect.

We picked up our buddy Dream in L.A., who became our roadie/driver. Cheryl and I had my vw Rabbit, and Dream helped drive it. This was the first time she had come on tour. The rest of the band thought having an extra vehicle was almost as much of a pain in the ass as having Cheryl along on the trip.

We did a nutso show at the Cuckoo's Nest in Costa Mesa, California. The punks were out of control inside the club, and even worse outside when they tangled with the crowd from the cowboy bar next door.

We then headed east to Texas, and from there to the east coast, then played our way back home through Canada. We met a lot of great bands on that trip: Really Red, Agent Orange, Hüsker Dü, and the Crowd, to name a few. On April 22, *Hardcore 81* was released on Friends Records. Between that and our tour, we helped the expression "hardcore" become vernacular.

Later that month, we played a show in Bloomington, Indiana, at a dump called Bullwinkles. All the locals seemed to talk about was basketball. Finally, I said "Did you guys know basketball was invented by a Canadian? Why don't you get into another sport we invented? This one is actually exciting – it's called hockey." After the Bloomington show, Dream, Cheryl, and I drove to Dayton, Ohio, to stay with my pal Jim Carter; the rest of the gang was to catch up the next day. But in the morning I got a weird phone call from Ken Lester. All I could get out of him was that I had to patch up some big crisis.

Ken kept saying over and over again that Biscuits was a fucking asshole, so I asked Ken to put Biscuits on the phone. But I couldn't get a straight answer out of him, either. Later in the day, the gang arrived at the club in Dayton for soundcheck, but Biscuits was refusing to play that night. He hated the rest of the band, he said, and they said they hated him.

I finally pieced together what had happened the previous night. It seems they had all gone to a house party in Bloomington, where Biscuits and Rampage both tried to pick up the same girl. That scenario played out like it usually did: Rampage won out. Biscuits went into a rage, breaking the passenger seat of the Blue Bullet, our brand-new Dodge van, the one we were making payments on every fucking month. A short while later, Biscuits went back into the van and snatched up all the cash from our tour. He ran into the front yard of the party house, throwing bills up in the air like a fucking madman. The other band members ran after him, while Lester ran

The Montgomery brothers, Bob and Chuck (Biscuits), at the Laundromat, 1981. *photo: Bev Davies*

after the money. His brother Bob cornered Biscuits in the kitchen, where Biscuits had armed himself with a large butcher knife. The gang converged on him as Bob knocked the knife out of Biscuits' hand. The show in Dayton went on after I had a talk with Biscuits, but it was very strange. Biscuits would not speak a word to the others for a couple of days.

We had a big show booked on May 8 at the Peppermint Lounge in New York. That evening was out of control. We had agreed to play two shows in one night, but our rider was overpowering: 100 bottles of beer and three bottles of spirits and wine. We got wasted before the first show. Biscuits chucked an empty beer pitcher and it bounced off the stage and nailed some poor woman in the head. Rampage and I told Biscuits to fuckin' smarten up. None of this seemed to matter to the New York fans; they loved it. We straightened out by the time the second show rolled around, though, and played our second sold-out show of the day.

A funny thing happened when we arrived for our show in Boston. The club thought we were an Irish folk group, for some reason, and when they found out we were a punk rock band, they paid us the guarantee and cancelled the show. The kids who had showed up that night told us about a place called the Underground, so we went over and got on the bill there and got paid again. The audience went completely nuts for D.O.A., and they did something we had never seen at a punk rock show – they got up on stage and started crawling around. Between our legs, around the mike stands, the drumset, and the monitors. After the show, we asked them what the fuck it was all about. They replied, in unison, "The Worm!" The incredibly fun and entertaining worm. Later on we copped it into our "Taking Care of Business" video.

We played Woodlawn High School in Arlington, Virginia. It was one of those shows we couldn't believe we were booked for. A fucking high school auditorium! It turned out to be a great show. The support was Minor Threat and Henry Rollins' first punk band S.O.A. (State of Alert). The next show was at the Marble Bar in Baltimore, where the stage collapsed after fifty kids jumped on it while we were playing Black Flag's "Nervous Breakdown." The Subhumans, who were two weeks behind us on their own tour, had their show at the Marble Bar cancelled due to D.O.A.'s antics. The promoter called us "asshole Canadians." This happened four times to the Subhumans. Hey, it's hard to follow in D.O.A.'s footsteps.

After the show, Cheryl, Dream, and me headed to New York in the Rabbit, and Montgomery drove the Blue Bullet. Rampage was sitting in the back seat of the van with a woman on each arm. During the ride, Montgomery and Rampage let the bullshit fly at each other. Montgomery would say something like, "Rampage, you're so full of shit, your eyes are brown!" Rampage would fire back with, "Hey Bob, ya fuckin' knob, lick me!" and would laugh, the gals laughing with him. This went on for a bit until Montgomery had had enough. He pulled the van over. They were going to have it out. Rampage was really loaded, and when he got out of the van, he could barely stand. But this did not deter either of them. Rampage said, with his usual bravado, "Fuck off! I'm gonna kill ya!" Montgomery countered with

one punch to Rampage's noggin. It dropped Rampage into a garbage-filled ditch, his girlfriends howling. Montgomery got back in the Blue Bullet and waited. The girls managed to get Rampage in the van, and they carried on to New York without further incident.

We played another great show in New York at a little club called the A7, right across from Tompkins Park. We were booked for two sets there, the first one starting at one AM. When we got off stage an hour later, somebody said, "Hey, why don't you guys come down and do a set at the 171A?" It was a tiny club just down the street, but not connected to the A7, in the bowels of the Lower East Side. Bad Brains were also playing the 171A that night, as was Jack Rabid's band, Even Worse. The members of Black Flag and Circle Jerks were there hanging out. We wanted to show Bad Brains that we could play reggae too, so we played our version of the Bob Marley reggae classic "Johnny Was." Then we headed back to the A7 for our second set. By the time we'd finished it was about 5:30 AM. The sun was up, birds were singing and regular folks were on their way to work.

On our way back through Canada, we were booked in Winnipeg for two nights at a joint called the Marion Hotel. On the second day, Cheryl and I went to visit some of her relatives and got back to the club a little late. I could hear D.O.A. playing as I got out of the car. I was furious. The rest of the band glared at me as I ran onstage, so I gave them my "I'll kill ya later" look. Once I'd grabbed my guitar and plugged in, I started changing all the lyrics to stuff like, "I will fucking kill you after this show is over!" In those days I was always breaking strings on stage, and Bob would hand me my back-up guitar when that happened. That night I didn't break one, which was a lucky thing. After the show, Bob showed me my back-up guitar. Part-way through the show, he had cut all six strings in half.

It had been a long tour, and we were sick of each other. I threatened to quit, but Lester talked me out of it, and we managed to finish the trip. By early June, the Hardcore 81 tour was over.

At the beginning of July we headed down to California again. We opened for Stiff Little Fingers at the Old Waldorf in San Francisco, another two-shows-in-one-night deal. It was great. The next night we were on a triple bill at Perkin's Palace in Pasadena. I was surprised that they didn't arrange a parade, the lineup was so cool: Stiff Little Fingers, the Adolescents, and D.O.A.

Back in Vancouver, our next show was at the Commodore with the Dead Kennedys and Toxic Reasons. Ken Lester had booked the biggest show that we had ever tried to pull off in Vancouver, and the place was completely jammed. Toxic Reasons were totally fucking great; they had grown into a full-on, barnstorming punk rock band. And the Dead Kennedys showed why they were easily one of the top bands of the era. They played their hard-hitting punk with catchy, crunchy riffs accompanying topical lyrics, and Jello had his unique, crazed, politically aware madman aura finely tuned. All in all, a great night.

The next night there was a secret show at the Smilin' Buddha with the Dead Kennedys and the Toxics. It was fun for us to just go and listen. The Dead Kennedys took the stage, and the crowd started going mad. I saw my buddy Ed Pittman at the back, and I got the idea to charge him and force him onto the dance floor. Pittman weighed about 280 pounds and had been an all-state linebacker in high school in Texas. So even though I hit him as hard as I could with my shoulder, I bounced right off. Then Pittman picked me up wrestling-style, spun me over his head a few times, and threw me onto the dance floor. Yikes!

The next day a few of us were over at Ken Lester's place. Cheryl and I were crashing in his basement at the time, being too broke to get a place of our own. Pittman and the Toxics' drummer, Mark Patterson, got to arguing in the kitchen. Patterson kept saying he was sick of the tour and wanted to go home. Lester got in between them to try to break it up. Finally, Patterson spit in Pittman's face, and in an instant, Pittman took his huge right paw and, over top of Lester, nailed Patterson right in the forehead. Patterson went down hard, and ended up with a lump on his head the size of a fucking baseball. That was it for him. I drove Patterson to the bus station with his drums and he caught a hound back to Dayton.

Now one of our favourite bands was on tour, 2,000 miles from home, with no drummer. Enter Jimmy Joe, a sixteen-year-old drummer from North Vancouver. He was a Chuck Biscuits clone, real young and real good. Jimmy Joe got permission from his parents to go on tour with the Toxics. He ended up drumming with them for close to twenty years and never came back to Vancouver.

At the end of July 1981, we set off down the west coast again. California was becoming our home away from home, and we had developed a strong network of friends and contacts there. Wes Robinson, a promoter from East

EASTERN FRONT

SATURDAY JULY 25	11 AM to 6 PM	SUNDAY JULY 26

D.O.A.	THE SLITS
FLIPPER	SNAKEFINGER
T.S.O.L.	THE OFFS
THE LEWD	EARL ZERO
WAR ZONE	MIDDLE CLASS
THE FIX	THE WOUNDS
7 SECONDS	TOILING MIDGETS
SIC PLEASURE	TANKS
ANTI-L.A.	

AQUATIC PARK BERKELEY   3' St & BANCROFT WAY

tickets available at boss

Bay, was staging a two-day outdoor festival in Berkeley called Eastern Front, and he invited D.O.A. to headline. On the first day, the punk rock day, we shared the bill with Flipper, T.S.O.L., the Lewd, War Zone, the Fix, Seven Seconds, Sic Pleasure, and Anti-L.A.

The show was held in a park right on San Francisco Bay. It was really hot, but the ocean breeze kept the temperature down. The stage was a flatbed trailer, and in front of it was a big field of dirt, which was surrounded by an orange fence. Robinson had hired a bunch of his East Bay bros as security. Unfortunately for him, many of them were older, heavier, and slower than the crowd. Whenever a group of skinny punks breached the perimeter of the fence, it was a lost battle: the punks were in. I have no idea how many people actually paid, but Robinson probably left wearing a barrel.

You could tell how much the punks liked each band by the size of the dust storm kicked up in front of the stage. By now this area had been officially named the mosh pit. People were choking on the dust, which probably led to even more beer than usual being consumed. When Flipper came on, the dust was almost unbearable. They were being their great noisy selves. Flipper were the antithesis of punk in a way, a lot slower and weirder, but they were totally punk in that they didn't seem to give a shit about anything except causing trouble. In other words, they were my kind of band.

By the time D.O.A. got on, it was very late in the afternoon. Before you knew it, there was a Texas-size twister in front of the stage. The punks had gotten a little smarter by this time. Back then, punks wore bandannas around their necks, on their belts, or around their bloody legs to look cool. That day, the bandannas were being used as they were intended; like cowboys of old, punks tied them over their noses and mouths to keep out the dust. From my perspective, it looked like a gang of spike-headed Jesse James and Billy the Kids out there moshing around.

The next day of the festival was a bit more artsy, with the Slits as the headliners, and Snakefinger, the Offs, Earl Zero, Middle Class, the Wounds, Toiling Midgets, and Tanks as support. We weren't scheduled to play, but we hung out and caused our share of trouble. After umpteen beers, Peligro, drummer for the Dead Kennedys, and I decided we'd had enough of that particular dust-up. We got into his van, planning to head for a show at the Mabuhay. But Peligro drove in such a fucked-up manner that he hit a curb in the parking lot and blew a front tire. We changed the flat and took off, but he again hit something he shouldn't have and blew another tire. That time we didn't have a spare, so we were forced to abandon ship.

A few days later, we drove to Reno for a Hardcore 81 show. My pal Cliff Varnell, one of the Rend Crew, was the promoter. There was a strong mix of bands on the bill: Toxic Reasons, Section 8 (a new band formed by Dim Borghino, formerly lead singer of Seven Seconds), and Who Screwed You? Ken Lester had told Varnell the name of the last band over the phone, but Varnell had never heard of them, so he spelled their name phonetically. When Hüsker Dü arrived and saw the poster, they just laughed.

We had met Hüsker Dü the year before when they opened for us at the 7th Street Entry in Minneapolis. They played their entire *Land Speed Record* LP non-stop, and it was fuckin' brutally cool. It was so fucking fast we couldn't believe it. We asked drummer Grant Hart where he had learned to play drums like that, and he said with a straight face, "From Frankie Yankovich, the polka king [who also hailed from Minnesota]. Where do ya think?" They were a great band and a good bunch of guys. A few years later, I was at a show of theirs in Seattle at the Showbox. They invited me on stage for their rendition of BTO's "Takin' Care of Business." Bob Mould handed me his Flying v guitar and said, "Hey, we need a fucking Canadian to play this song!" So that's what they got.

From Reno we headed to L.A. to play at the Vex, the second incarnation. We had played two nights at the original Vex in East L.A. a year earlier, and that was the first time we'd ever seen a search for weapons at a punk rock show. (Back in Canada, beefs were settled with hockey sticks at twenty paces.) Our show at the second Vex was with China White and Legal Weapon. The show went all right, but afterwards we couldn't find Joe, the promoter, and nobody had been paid. In lieu of a cash settlement, we helped ourselves to the microphones from the sound system. When it turned out there was a misunderstanding, everything was made right. We gave the mikes back.

The following night we played our first show in San Diego, a gig at the Fairmont Hall with the Hated, No Age Limit, Violation 5, and Moral Majority. Talk about a bloody sweatbox; you couldn't breathe in there. Up to this point we'd thought Orange County punks were the most outta control, but San Diego's might have been tops. Throw in a few marines from Camp Pendleton, and you've got trouble with a capital T. Fuck! I even got one of my SG guitars broken by three drunk girls who ran through the dressing room and knocked it over. But most of the gang down there were great. Marc Rude was the local wildman, and Tim Mays promoted the early shows there. As far as that gig went, they should have had an ambulance on standby. Some punks would go against the flow of the pit, while others would jump from the tops of speakers and land on their heads. Holy pain central, Batman!

After two nights at the Hong Kong Café in L.A.'s Chinatown, we headed north, stopping for a few shows along the I-5 strip on our way to Seattle, where we played a joint called Danceland USA. By the time we got onstage, the temperature in the club must have been 105°F. We'd done some sightseeing in Tijuana after our show in San Diego, and our little Mexican visit was catching up with me now. I had Montezuma's revenge. Let's just say my Danceland experience was something I would wish only upon my mortal enemies. We put on a good show and I didn't crap my pants. Not bad.

Our tour had been gruelling, and once we were back in Vancouver we took a bit of time off. A bunch of our friends, including Dimwit, were working at a downtown steakhouse called Mr Mike's. Biscuits got a job there as well. Imagine those punks doing your cooking! It was cool, for a while. Biscuits even threw the restaurant's phone in the deep fryer for fun. But it was good for free food. I didn't work there, but Cheryl did. After a while, she hooked up with the greasy manager of this greasy eatery, and left me. That ended up being just fine with me.

One day someone was leafing through a U.K. music weekly and got a shock. It said that D.O.A. would be supporting the Dead Kennedys at the Lyceum in London on October 4. We hadn't heard anything about this, but it sounded like a damn good idea!

Ken Lester got on the phone. It turned out we weren't actually on the bill, but he changed that through some fast talking. We then got hold of Bill Gilliam at Alternative Tentacles Records in London, who agreed to put out a 7-inch. We prepared an EP at Ocean Sound, re-recording the vocals for "Fucked Up Baby" as "Fucked Up Ronnie" and doing a new version of "Disco Sucks" called "New Wave Sucks." We added "World War 3," "The Enemy," and "My Old Man's A Bum." Presto – an instant new release entitled *Positively D.O.A.*

Bill from Alternative Tentacles released *Positively D.O.A.* about two weeks before we arrived in London, and one of the big music papers there made it record of the week. It started selling really well, but there was one big hitch in our plans: we didn't have any dough for the airplane tickets. We were only earning enough at our gigs to pay for gas and make the van payments. Somehow, each of us begged, borrowed, and worked enough to come up with $700 each. Before we left, we had a big sendoff at the Smilin' Buddha.

There were free cocktails on the plane ride over, and several of us got a little carried away. When we were about to land at Heathrow, we noticed Biscuits was missing from his seat. I went to the back of the

D.O.A. invades London, England, 1981. *photos: Bev Davies*

plane and banged on the toilet doors. I heard a groan from one of them, and finally Biscuits opened the door. I got him to his feet, then grabbed his passport, which was lying on the bathroom floor.

We found a place to stay in London with Jonathan Werner and Lynn McDonagh. We'd be playing the big show at the Lyceum, then three smaller shows around London. When we arrived at the Lyceum, the Dead Kennedys were already there; it was nice to see some familiar faces. But then we found out that we were opening the show and the Anti-Nowhere League was playing the middle slot. That sucked. As much as half the crowd would miss us because we were on so early. We tried to appeal to John Curd, the promoter, to switch spots, but he was having none of it. After finally seeing the League (nothing against the band), we still didn't agree with the order.

The Anti-Nowhere League had a whole gang of bikers hanging out at the show. Before the gig started, a couple of them came to our dressing room. They didn't say a whole lot, but we were friendly and they listened to us for a bit. Then, apparently having heard enough, one of the bikers turned to the other and said, "You're right, mate. They do sound like Yanks!" Later on we found out that East Bay Ray had intervened on our behalf, as there was some talk amongst the League crew of giving us a good old-fashioned boot-fucking for our insolence. I guess they didn't like that we had tried to get the League's middle slot. The show went pretty well for us; there were about 3,000 people there that night. The Dead Kennedys were sterling.

The three gigs that followed were all at places with tiny stages. But the crowds were okay, and reasonably responsive. The bands that did support for us were amazed at our Canadian politeness. For example, we would move

our drums off the stage so another band actually had some room to play. People would say stuff like, "I've never seen a headliner do that before!" The music scene there seemed so dog-eat-dog compared to ours. Old blighty!

When we got back to Canada, I felt we needed to stir things up. We'd been playing the same twenty songs for over three years now. Biscuits and I had both written a bunch of new songs, so we started learning them. Dave, Biscuits, and I did, anyways; Rampage started going AWOL from rehearsals, and even when he did show, he would be too fucked up to learn much.

We booked six nights at the Smilin' Buddha, hoping to hone the new songs into something good. We had different opening bands each night, including Rude Norton (Dimwit on guitar, Wimpy on bass, and Nick Jones on drums), Contraband, the Scissors, Tim Ray and AV, the Insex, the Butchers, the Fastbacks (a smokin' band from Seattle), Dale Hickey and the Hickoids, and 54-40. As it turned out, those six nights were a pain in the bloody arse. I kept having to turn my guitar neck towards Rampage so he could see what the fuck we were playing. It wasn't working out with him any more. The machine-like precision we had been building up in D.O.A. was dissipating. If you're doing what you love, you should take pride in it, and not being 100 percent every time you're on stage sucks.

We did two more shows that year in Vancouver, one at the Arcadian Hall with the Fastbacks and the Silly Killers, the other a New Year's Eve show at the Buddha to welcome 1982. That night we started playing at about 11: 20, but after a few songs we had to stop because Rampage took off, saying he forgot something. We sat there waiting for him until the clock struck midnight and then started on "Auld Lang Syne" without him. Rampage finally came back at about 12:15. He was really fucked up. When we finished our set and looked outside, it was snowing like fuck, and the whole downtown was closed. Lachman locked the doors of the club and everybody hung out till about five in the morning.

Rampage and Shithead, 1981. *photo: Bev Davies*

That was the last time Rampage would play in D.O.A. until 2001. It was too bad. I love the guy like a brother, but nothing ever stays the same. That's the way it has to be – revolution is constant.

Crazed fans at a D.O.A. show, 1984. *photo: Bev Davies*

CHAPTER EIGHT

WAR ON 45

With Rampage gone, we needed a bass player. Dimwit, besides being one Canada's greatest drummers, also had a passion for playing the bass, and he was living at Fort Gore at the time. So it was an obvious decision: Dimwit was the man. Now all three Montgomery brothers were involved with D.O.A. We started rehearsing some new songs, and during the next few months of

the spring of 1982 D.O.A. appeared on three record compilations. The first was the studio version of "The Prisoner," on *Let Them Eat Jellybeans*. This compilation had almost all of the top North American punk bands on it; it was a significant release that became known around the world. We also had some live tracks on *Live At The Eastern Front* and *Rat Music For Rat People*, which included "America the Beautiful," a new song I had written. Both were recorded in the Bay Area.

We set off on another tour, playing five shows with T.S.O.L. (from L.A.) around California. Sharing the stage with Dimwit and Dave was a formidable task at times. We must have been fucking comical to watch. Dave was long and gangly, though no pencil neck. I was well over 200 pounds, and Dimwit had a few on me, making him about 100 pounds heavier than Rampage. Whenever Dave or I made full, stage-smash contact with Dimwit, it was like running into the Chicago Bears of old.

We took a few days off to record

America the Beautiful

Lock your doors, lock it tight
It's the new immoral right
They wanna cleanse the home of the brave
For the master race of the USA

It's so beautiful

On the street you won't know them
Like a pack of wolves in sheeps' clothing
Spreading wide, spreading far
Not just another false alarm

It's so beautiful

America – I got my Bible
America – I got my handgun
America – now I'm ready
America – home of the brave
America – and the home of the slaves
America – now I'm ready

But are you?

Joey Shithead Keithley, Prisoner Publishing

some of our new songs at Mystic Studios in L.A., but we weren't too crazy about the sounds. We scrapped the session, although a few tracks resurfaced later when some scum weasel grabbed the tapes without our authorization and put out a 7-inch single called *The Menace Lives*. The real unfortunate thing is that it sounds like it was dubbed from a cassette tape that was sped up; my voice sounds like I am sixteen years old. Some cuts from this session appear on *The Lost Tapes*.

Back in Vancouver, we kept working on the new material, trying to add some different elements. I had loved reggae since my trip to Jamaica as a kid, and Lester came up with the idea that I should do a rewrite of the Ranking Trevor song, "War in the East." We were working on the reggae groove one day at Fort Gore when an argument erupted. Dimwit suggested that Biscuits try something a little more sparse. Biscuits was never good at taking advice; he would always ignore suggestions from Rampage, Dave, and me. Now, a critique from his older brother, who was also his equal behind the kit, was too much for him. After a heated exchange, Biscuits finally blustered, "We'll add the sparseness in the mix!" When the rest of us burst out laughing, Biscuits stomped out of the room and right out of D.O.A. For a while, we thought he was an asshole, but in fact he helped us make a lot of good D.O.A. records, and I always hoped the best for him in life.

It didn't take us long to find a replacement; Dimwit volunteered right away. That part was easy. Now we were back to needing a bass player. After considering all the available candidates around town, we decided to ask our longtime friend Wimpy. He had been singing with the Subhumans, who, it was rumoured, were on the verge of splitting. He hemmed and hawed about it before Lester convinced him to join us. So there we were, with three quarters of the Skulls back together again.

About a week after Biscuits quit the band, Black Flag pulled into town. They stayed at the Plaza, a gigantic old house in East Vancouver that we were now living in. Lester had moved out of his digs in East Van, so he, Gary

Failure (our good pal and Guy Fawkes' number one fan), and I decided to get together to find a place. The Plaza, as we called it, was a huge, old house with eight bedrooms. We wanted it to be a place where bands could stay and party. Every punk party seemed to end up there. Shortly after they arrived, Chuck and Greg from Black Flag told Lester and me that they weren't happy with their drummer. They asked us about Biscuits. Would we be mad if he joined Black Flag?

D.O.A. (l-r Shithead, Dimwit, Biscuits, Dave) in the van touring California, 1982. *photo: Bev Davies*

Not a problem, I said, but Chuck still owed us a grand for his drum kit. They conferred for a minute, then said they would pay it off for him. We got the dough, and then Lester and I phoned Dave to tell him the hilarious news. We equated it to a sports trade; we had sold off the young hotshot for futures and cash. Biscuits would end up leaving Black Flag after about six months, but over the years he went on to drum for a succession of fine bands: the Circle Jerks, Danzig, and Social Distortion.

D.O.A. just before Biscuits quit. He's not "one of us." *photo: Bev Davies*

The new D.O.A. lineup (l-r Dave, Shithead, Dimwit, Wimpy). *photo: Bev Davies*

Just before Mother's Day of 1982, we were having another one of our parties at the Plaza. That night I met the most wonderful person I have ever known. Her name was Laura Walters and she was from my hometown of Burnaby, too. Laura and her sister Cindy were hanging out at the Plaza, and we got to talking. That night

I felt very lucky to meet somebody so smart and cute. We started going out together soon after that.

On a Thursday in mid-July we set off again for California, beginning one of the most insane weekends I have ever experienced. Lester had booked us a three-day cross-continental tour. The first night we played on a great bill at the On Broadway in San Francisco. The Undead opened the show, and then MDC, Millions of Dead Cops, charged onto the stage. MDC, who had recently relocated to San Francisco from Texas, were one of the standard bearers for political punk in those days. Their songs confronted mainstream American life, and like D.O.A., they played shows for many different causes. I hate it when people say you shouldn't mix politics with music. How the hell can you not? If an actor can become the president of the United States, why can't a musician be an activist?

We got up the morning after the On Broadway show and caught a plane to New York City for a show at the Paramount Theatre on Staten Island with the Dead Kennedys, Kraut, and SS Decontrol. About 3,000 people crammed into the place. Kraut were the opening band, and we would become pretty good pals with Doug Holland, the guitar player. He and Jack Rabid were roommates, and we stayed at their place in New York sometimes after that.

When the Dead Kennedys came on, the place went berserk. The band, tight as ever, rocked on. But on certain songs they would just vamp on a riff while Jello spewed out a political rant. The times were changing. Ronald Reagan was the U.S. president now, and the powers that be in the U.S., Canada, and Western Europe were instituting more and more reactionary policies. The environment was coming under greater attack as James Watt, Secretary of the Interior, was busy paying back Reagan's well-heeled backers. Right-wing religious fervor was in lock-step with a number of administrations, a routine that really bothers me to this day. Religion is what stops the poor from murdering the rich! In the meantime, the number of homeless people was increasing; some things never change. Jello's rants referred to all of these issues, as did songs by MDC, Minor Threat, and a host of other bands of that era.

When the Paramount show was over, we caught the Staten Island ferry back to Manhattan, along with lots of the punks who were at the show. When we arrived we had to catch a cab. That sounds like a simple thing, but all the other punks were trying to catch one as well, and the hacks wouldn't stop for any of us. We ended up walking three miles with our guitars to the grubby Lower East Side pad where we were going to crash. After only about an hour of sleep, it was time to get up and catch a plane to L.A.

We'd left the Blue Bullet in San Francisco in the hands of our new roadie, Bristlehead, who had driven down from Vancouver with us, and he was in L.A. to meet us. We headed straight for the Olympic Auditorium, a huge venue built for the 1932 Olympics. It held 5,000 in the balcony alone, and more than that in the lower section. It was a fucking great bill: Black Flag, 45 Grave, D.O.A.,

the Descendants, Hüsker Dü, and UXB. The Punk Rock Olympics were on.

There was tension in the air, a sense of potential confrontation between the LAPD and the punks from L.A. and Orange County (and every other fucking town around the area). To have a show like this was kind of like making a declaration to the LAPD and the rest of the city: "Look out! There's a lot of us."

When we got up to play, the place was a sea of leather jackets, spikes, mohawks, and Doc Martens. There were three different pits going at the same time. It was completely out of control; there were even some geeks throwing quarter sticks of dynamite around. Every once in a while, Big Frank, the friendly head stage guy, and his punk-rock crew would have to run out and grab the punks who'd run up on stage. Even the metal fans who claimed to have invented moshing – after copying the punks – would have been scared shitless. But all of the bands rose to the occasion, slaying the audience with a forcible display of sound and power. After the show, I felt like rubber!

PARTICIPATION NOT DECIMATION!!!

To Whom It May Concern:

In front of the stage is a free frame of reference. It's physical, it's fun, it's for everyone who wants to take a risk.

It is not for the strong to smash the weak, the big to muscle the little, or men to mash women. It is not a combat zone for any one person or group of people to control.

Everyone, should be able to participate. Together we can create and expand the bounds of freedom.

FOR THE BEST: **D.O.A.**

A day later we headed out to the desert to play Phoenix with Jody Foster's Army and Hüsker Dü. Cool show. Then it was back to California to appear on some bills with the likes of the Vandals, China White, and Channel 3, all good rockin' outfits. We had also booked five midnight sessions at Perspective Sound with a producer named Thom Wilson (who produced a number of great records, including the Offspring's first three albums, one of which was *Smash*, and T.S.O.L.'s *Beneath the Shadows*). On an earlier trip, we had invited Thom to hear us jam at a rehersal studio in L.A., and he liked what he heard. This all came about because Alternative Tentacles Records really liked how *Positively D.O.A.* had sold and the fact that Jello Biafra was a fan of D.O.A. People had also responded well to "The Prisoner" track on the *Let Them Eat Jellybeans* compilation.

Alternative Tentacles USA had just gotten a distribution deal and money from an L.A. company called Faulty Products, which was owned by Miles Copeland, brother of Stewart Copeland, drummer for the Police (their father had been in the CIA and the third Copeland brother, Ian, ran a booking agency in New York called FBI). So Faulty Products and Alternative Tentacles forked over the princely sum of US$2,500 (it was princely to us!) to make a record.

An all-night session in the studio was half the price of a regular one. It started at midnight and went on until you couldn't stay awake any more, which was usually about seven in the morning. As producer, Wilson had a good feel for what we were doing, and we didn't waste any time. We were becoming punk rock veterans, too, which led to great coordination as a band. Even though our new lineup had been going for only a few months, it had really jelled, thanks to the incredible rhythm section of Wimpy and Dimwit. And Wilson had a calming effect on the whole process.

After three nights, we had nailed "Liar For Hire," "I'm Right, You're Wrong," "America the Beautiful," "Let's Fuck," "War," the Dils' classic "Class War," and a new version of our *Vancouver Complication* song "I Hate You,"

which has vocal support from the Bar-B-Que Choir including Heather Haley from the Zealots and Jughead from the Modernettes. Then we attempted the biggest departure we had ever recorded: we laid down the beds for "War in the East." Once we had a solid drum

Shithead and Dave at Vancouver's Commodore Ballroom, 1982. *photo: Bev Davies* take, we sat down and listened. Dimwit and I thought it didn't sound right. Dimwit redid the bass, which was cool with Wimpy, then added piano, percussion, and drummed on a beer bottle for one of the dub effects. That all worked well. But Dimwit kept beefing about Dave's rhythm guitar track, saying it was off time. Dave told him he was full of shit, so the guitar track stayed.

On our fifth and final night of recording, we again worked into the wee hours of the morning. Finally, Wimpy and Dave passed out from exhaustion, which gave Dimwit the chance he had been waiting for. Before you could say, "Holy fuck! That was Darby Crash!" Dimwit was in the recording room redoing the guitar track for "War in the East." Thom got the entire session mixed and completed that night. I have worked on too many sessions to count, as both a musician and a producer, but I have never seen anybody mix eight songs so crystal clear that quickly. We said our goodbyes and hit the road, back to California. Somewhere south of  Sacramento, we were playing "War in the East" on the tape deck when Dave bolted upright and said, "Hey! Where's my guitar track?" Finally, somebody admitted that we'd erased it, and Dimwit had played the new part. Fuck, was Dave mad!

We played our way back up the coast and gigged with some great bands, including Code of Honour, Hüsker Dü, Rebel Truth, the Wrecks, the Authorities, Young Pioneers, and in Portland we did a great show with Poison Idea and the Fartz (whose Duff McKagan later formed Guns N' Roses).

We hired Shawn Kerri, an artist friend from L.A., to do the cover for our new album, and she really pulled it off. We called it *War On 45*. The title was a play on *Stars on 45*, these crappy greatest-hit singles that were coming out at the time. One group performed snippets of Beatles tunes and put a putrid drum machine behind it. Well, we surmised, we had a bunch of songs about war, power, and struggle – *War on 45*.

At the same time that Faulty Products and Alternative Tentacles USA released the record, Alternative Tentacles in the U.K. did as well, but with a different front cover. We had seen a piece of art by Clay Sampson, a Native American friend of ours from Reno, which depicted the famous General Custer full of arrows. Lester added two older tracks on the U.K. release, which was cool by us, as they gave the collectors something else to buy.

At the end of September, we headed off on our War on 45 tour. The idea was to play forty-five shows in forty-five days. It was fucking crazy, but we almost made it – I think it took fifty days in the end. Nobody could call us lazy! We played a killer show at the Oakland Auditorium, with Discharge, Bad Brains, the Lewd, and the Fartz, and then it was on to Reno, to play the National Guard Armory. (We escaped before they were called out.)

Then came a long, long drive to Denver. We learned two important lessons on that trip. At about three o'clock in the morning, fifty miles east of Salt Lake City on 1-80, the guys in the back asked Dave, who was driving, to pull over so they could take a piss. (A phrase that's always bugged me. Why would you want to "take" a piss? I'd rather drain my bladder, "leaving" the piss. Take it a step further. Would you want to "take" a shit?) Dave pulled the van over and everybody got out. But when we jumped back into the van, it wouldn't start. Nothing. Not a fucking sound. The engine was more silent than a boneyard. That was lesson number one: DON'T TURN YOUR FUCKING VEHICLE OFF IN THE MIDDLE OF NOWHERE!

Of course, this was bloody years before the advent of the cell phone, so we couldn't call for help. Wimpy and Dave started walking down the freeway towards the previous exit. It was about five miles back, we figured. Two hours later, the search party returned with the news that they had secured a tow truck, which was on the way. There was only one problem: the tow-truck driver would only be able to carry three passengers, and there were seven of us. So we rigged up a blanket inside the van, just behind the driver's seat, so that you couldn't see in the back. That's where the rest of the gang hid.

The tow truck arrived, greeted by Wimpy, Dave, and me. The driver lifted up the back end for the tow and then reached inside the open driver's window to rope the steering wheel into position. So far, so good. The blanket held; he didn't see our hidden cargo. But after we'd driven about fifty feet, the driver stopped. "Wheel's not straight, goddamn it!" Yes, folks, he said "goddamn it" right in the middle of god-fearing Mormon Utah, and got away with it. So did I, when the driver stopped the truck about eight more

UK release

times to adjust the Blue Bullet's wheel. I thought for sure the little D.O.A. mice would be discovered and left to walk fifty miles across the fucking salt flats. But we all made it safely to a garage in Salt Lake City, where they charged us a bloody fortune to repair the timing chain.

It was noon before we got underway to Denver, where we had a show that night. We were making pretty good time until we bought some beer at a gas station. It was the usual sort of thing for a road trip, but after a while there was the usual whining about making a piss stop. "Naaaaah! There ain't no time for that!" Lester said, looking at the clock.

Somebody yelled, "Watch it, Lester, or we'll piss into your mouth!"

"Piss into a bottle!" said Lester, tossing an empty back.

This was no easy feat, considering that the van was ripping down a bumpy highway at seventy-five miles an hour. But I got the job done, and we had learned the second important lesson of the journey: PISSING INTO AN EMPTY VESSEL IS A FUCKING WONDERFUL TIME-SAVING TECHNIQUE.

We made it to Denver just in time. Bad Brains were there on a day off, hanging out, so we thought we would play "War in the East." It was only our second time playing it live, and it really stunk. That was embarassing, being in front of the Brains.

The next night we pulled into Lawrence, Kansas, to play at a joint called the Off the Wall Hall. There were only about forty people there; I guess we weren't exactly household names in the heartland. (One of them was a fourteen-year-old kid named Bob Cutler who got in with fake ID. It was his first punk show. D.O.A. was corrupting youth once again! Cutler would become a punk stalwart who, fourteen years later, would become our soundman.) Not only was the attendance pitiful, but everybody seemed to be sitting on their hands. So in between songs we would make up horrible jokes about *The Wizard of Oz*. "Hey, whatever happened to Toto?" "Ah, he got run over by a semi on the I-70." "Hey, whatever happened to Dorothy?"

US release

"Oh, her! She's working as a hooker on Los Palmas in Hollywood!" A couple of people chuckled.

After the show, Lester was furious at us. He called us the biggest bunch of lamebrains he had ever met. He even called us Epsilon semi minuses! D.O.A.? Epsilon semi minuses? They were the least intelligent people in *Brave New World*. We got pissed off right back, and he stormed out of the room. I mean, what were we supposed to be? Journey?

The next night Bob Mould of Hüsker Dü put on a show for us in Minneapolis at a place called Goofy's Upper Deck. The name pleased Lester; he thought we fit right in. The show was cool. After that, we went back to Canada, into Ontario and Quebec for a week. In the middle of the Canadian leg we shuffled off to Buffalo to play a Sunday night at the Continental, where it was "Canadian Night." Fuck, it was bad. They were selling shitty swill at twenty-five cents a glass. Talk about a bunch of drunk Canucks – both the fans and the band. Our soundman was puking out the window by the time we arrived back at the Canadian border that night. In Montreal, we played at a place called Le Foie. Montreal was cool, but strange, a completely different atmosphere from the rest of Canada.

Boston was our next stop and another scene altogether. Our gig there was at a tiny place called Cantrone's. The stage took up about a quarter of the room. Cantrone's probably held about sixty people comfortably, but when they opened the doors at eight PM for Kil Slug's performance, about 200 kids jammed in. They were standing on tables, on chairs, even on each other, for Christ's sake. The owner sold booze as fast as he could. We wormed our way up to the stage, tuned up, grabbed a drink, and got ready to go. It was packed like sardines, and hotter than a sauna.

As soon as we started, the place got out of hand. People started dancing wherever they happened to be, and those up high enough pulled all the acoustic tiles out of Cantrone's ceiling. All the tables and chairs were broken

Shithead, 1982. *photo: Bev Davies*

by the time we got to our second song. People were falling everywhere, and the dust from the tiles was choking out what little air there was in the place. But none of this destruction slowed the crowd down. Halfway into our third song, about forty Boston cops burst into the club, or at least tried to. They had to throw people out to make room for themselves. One of them cut the power to the sound system, which marked the end of the show. The cops charged the owner for exceeding his club's legal capacity and, in a relatively friendly way, told us to split. We tried to get some money out of the owner before we left, but no go. He accused us of provoking the fans into wrecking his club. Shit! The Boston newspapers carried features on the punk rock riot.

We'd been on the War on 45 tour for almost a month, but our days on the road weren't over yet. Over the next few weeks we played shows across the midwest and in New York City. While there we had a wild drunken jam at the A7 with Steve Jones of the Sex Pistols and with Jack Rabid drumming. Then it was on to Virginia, then Washington, where we played with Minor Threat. Next was Texas, and we finished up with a couple of shows in L.A. and San Francisco.

Before we left southern California, Faulty Products arranged for us to do a video for "War," which was getting a reasonable amount of airplay, at A&M Records in Hollywood. This impressed me for a couple of reasons. First off, almost no punk bands had videos in those days. Secondly, I have always been a huge Herb Alpert and the Tijuana Brass fan, and Alpert is the "A" in A&M. I also knew that Alpert and Jerry Moss, the "M" in A&M, had started their label in a garage around 1962. By 1966, they had sold 13 million Tijuana Brass records. Wow!

Once we had convinced the A&M security guard that we weren't there to pull off a robbery, we had to find a parking spot for the Blue Bullet. I pointed out an empty one to Dave. "Nope," he said, "that one's marked Herb Alpert."

The video was shot on a big old-time Hollywood soundstage, the very one where Charlie Chaplin had made most of his movies. What an honour. Not only because Chaplin was one of the funniest guys ever, but because his movies said a lot about the world. The record company had set up four videos to be shot that day. We watched Sparks do theirs first, and then we were on. We mimed to a recording of "War," standing amongst some sandbags and camouflage netting they'd placed around our amps and drums. The Go-Go's were up next. I can't remember who the fourth group was that day, but the video shoot was a real production line. *Modern Times*.

That was it for the War on 45 tour. It was really just the first big battle of the second phase of our bigger war on the mainstream.

Shithead douses the fans while Biscuits and Dimwit play on at Vancouver's Cambrian Hall, 1982.

CHAPTER NINE

POLITICS, PROTEST, UPHEAVAL

On New Year's Eve 1982, D.O.A. was booked for another end-of-year show, but this time the venue wasn't the Smilin' Buddha – it was Irving Plaza in New York City. We were pretty excited about it. I had a big Christmas dinner with Laura and all my relatives, then the band and I set off in the Blue Bullet on Boxing Day, deadheading it 3,000 miles (4,860 kilometers) east.

As we drove through the American heartland, we got bored really fast with the music we were hearing on the radio. As they say in them thar parts, "Only two types of music around here, boy: country and western." The music was intercut with farm reports and a show called "The Prophecies of the Bible," hosted by Hubert W. Armstrong. To make matters worse, we had very little dough, and the Blue Bullet was sucking back gas faster than Alice Cooper could drink beer.

About halfway across the U.S., in South Dakota, we started hearing radio reports about a huge storm approaching. It was dark by the time snow really started falling. The road was flat, so we weren't having much trouble driving, but we did notice snowdrifts building up along the roadside. Some of them were already four feet high.

A lot of cars had slipped off the highway and into the ditch. The radio jocks were now saying that the state police would close the I-90. Fuck that! On we went. But it was pure whiteout, and Dave had to slow down to about twenty miles an hour, and had to stick his head out the driver's window to see where we were going. I stuck mine out on the passenger's side, warning Dave, "Back to the left! Quick!" whenever he came too close to the edge of the road.

We were the only vehicle on the highway at this point. It was fucking nuts! We pulled off a good deed, though. There was a car by the side of the road with a guy slumped over the steering wheel. Dave stopped the van and I ran out and banged on the guy's window, waking him up. We offered to give him a ride to the next town. It turned out he was in the U.S. Navy, and he was one grateful sailor that night.

We travelled for about another hour. The radio station in Sioux Falls, South Dakota said that absolutely nobody had gotten through the stretch of the I-90 that we were on and the cops had the road blocked at the Minnesota state line. We had another problem: we were almost out of gas! Finally we saw that the exit for Sioux Falls was just a mile ahead. We all cheered as if we were at a hockey game!

But when we got to the exit our cheers quickly turned to cursing. There were two semi's with their trailers stuck on the off-ramp. Fuck! There was no way around into town, short of driving through an eight-foot snowdrift. So we stopped the van right on the interstate. The radio DJ again said that nobody – and he meant *nobody* – had gotten through to Sioux Falls on the I-90. We rolled down the windows and started yelling, "We made it! D.O.A. fucking made it through your stinkin' snowstorm!"

We had to get out of there. After all, we were D.O.A and we had a *big, big* show to do in New York City! We had to dig a track in the snow for each front wheel so we could get the van moving again through the four feet of snow that was in front of us. We had no shovel, so we grabbed the cooler lid and a crib board. Wimpy and I started digging a couple of tracks as best we could. When we did about fifty feet, we jumped back in the van. Dave looked at our pitiful path and was rather skeptical, but he went for it. We started moving, and all of our spirits were lifted. Yeah, for only about ten seconds, though. Then the van got grounded again. Fuck! Well, we thought, that was a shitty plan, unless we felt like digging our way to Minnesota with a damn crib board!

We crashed out right there in the middle of the highway. Finally, a snowplow came by to help us, and we were on our way. They called that the "Blizzard of '82."

We got into New York the afternoon of December 31. We found the Irving Plaza and started dragging our frozen gear out of the van. Unbeknownst to us, however, while we were making our hellacious cross-country trek, some of the punks in New York had been saying that the D.O.A. show was a rip-

Dimwit, 1983. *photo: Bev Davies*

off at fifteen bucks a ticket. So the False Prophets, a band from New York, had organized a competing show down the street, featuring nine bands for five bucks. Those bands weren't even close in quality to our show's lineup, but it was still a super deal. Our promoter was worried. We were worried, too; this show's guarantee of $1,500 was the biggest of the tour we'd planned, the fucking centre of the wheel.

As our show opened, there weren't that many people, and after the second band was finished, the soundman came up to me and said, "Sorry, dude, I ain't been paid. I have to pull the sound." Dave and I confronted the promoter. He weasled around for a while, then said, "Here's a hundred and fifty bucks, man. That's all I got." Ten cents on the dollar. It was like a bloody bankruptcy proceeding. We grabbed our gear before even playing a note, and headed down to the competing show. They invited us to get up and play, but we decided to sit around glumly and have a beer. Wimpy said something about finding a bridge to jump from, but we agreed the Hudson and the East Rivers would be too fucking cold at that time of year.

After having our asses kicked so severely in New York, we hoped North Carolina would be better. But that wasn't to be when we found that our first venue, the Pier, was in the middle of a shopping mall. Still, we had driven down with nothing but fumes in the gas tank, so we played anyway. The cover was two bucks, and Dimwit, ever the grumbler, said, "Wow! We're gonna strike it rich!" About forty people showed up, and we ended up with $60. We did meet some cool people, though, including a couple of guys from the very first version of Corrosion of Conformity.

Ken Lester, who thought we didn't have a proper plan for this tour, had stayed in Vancouver. For the past few years, we had been operating on a $10 per diem while we were on tour. That was supposed to cover food, beer, smokes, and laundry, and even rent when we got back home. (Of course, there was never any left over for rent.) Given our current financial situation, it was up to me to come up with a new plan. Amidst much grumbling, I announced the new per diem, the princely sum of two bucks a day. "Look at it this way," I said. "Down here in the Carolinas, smokes are seventy-nine cents a pack and a six-pack of generic beer is $1.09. The beer will sub for food, so you're all set!"

Over the next few days we played through the southern U.S.: Chapel Hill, Louisville, Charlotte, Atlanta. The tour wasn't shaping up too well. We weren't getting the crowds; there were more rednecks than punks in the south. The next show was back

Dave, 1983. *photo: Bev Davies*

in New York at the Mudd Club with the Sluts from New Orleans. The organizers hadn't done anything to promote the show, though, so as we were getting a percentage of the door, we made our own posters and stuck them up around the Lower East Side. We couldn't afford that show to be a dud too. The night of the gig, the club had nobody assigned to the door, so I did that as well. When it was time to get up and play, I got the singer from the Sluts to take people's three-dollar covers. After a gig in Philadelphia at the Eastside Club, we were set to play a show at Casablanca's in Richmond, Virginia, with Channel Three, White Cross, and Graven Image. Along the way, we decided to stop in Atlantic City, the gambling capital of the east. We hung out there till the afternoon, becoming even poorer, if that was possible, then hit the road to Richmond. When we arrived at the venue, we could see quite a crowd outside. Wow, we said to ourselves; this should be good. There were a lot of people there and it was still early! But just as we were parking the Blue Bullet, the promoter ran out and started yelling. "Where the fuck have you guys been? I just refunded the door money because you guys never showed up!" It turned out our show was scheduled for Sunday afternoon, but nobody had bothered to tell us. That's when I learned the hard way that you should "advance the show" – phone ahead to see what's shakin'.

In the third week of January 1983, we played the Jockey Club in Newport, Kentucky. A great crew ran the place: Bill Leist, Clem, and Jughead, punk fans turned promoters. The club itself had an incredibly rich history. Back in the fifties and sixties, Newport had been *the* gambling town of the midwest, and the Jockey Club was at the centre of it. All sorts of cats had graced its stage, from Little Richard to Fats Domino. Frank Sinatra, Elvis, and Marilyn Monroe had been among its patrons. People had even been gunned down on the sidewalk out front. I don't think any maintenance had been done on the club since the glory days, though. The wallpaper was peeling off, the ceiling was falling in, and the bathroom smelled like it hadn't been cleaned in twenty years. The show went over great. We had a real loyal following in that area. It was also cool to hit the same stage that had been graced by early rock 'n' roll greats.

Ed Pitman came down to the Jockey Club with a crew from Dayton. After the show, he offered to take us to what he called the finest eatery in the midwest: it was White Castle, the burger joint chain. The burgers were tiny, square, and full of holes, for some unknown reason. But here was the best part: they were only twenty-five cents each! The price was right. With our budget, we yelled out, "Holy fuckin' Bob Barker!" and ordered about six each. Ed said he'd once eaten seventy-six White Castle burgers in one sitting on a bet.

Our next show was January 21, 1983, at the City Club in Detroit, where we were support for the Angelic Upstarts. Around dinnertime, sitting around in the dressing room, we started to speculate about what had happened to Gerry Useless. None of us had heard hide nor hair of him in over a year. That seemed strange to us, since we'd been pretty tight as the gang of four.

As we were talking, somebody came into the dressing room and said, "Hey, your manager is on the phone." What Lester had to say was shocking. Gerry and four others had been arrested by an RCMP SWAT team on Highway 99, near Squamish, a little town halfway between Vancouver and Whistler. The cops had posed as a highway crew to stop the van Gerry and his friends were in. They were dragged out at gunpoint, arrested, and booked. The charges were staggering. The five were charged with the bombings of the Litton plant in Toronto, two adult video stores called Red Hot Video in Vancouver, and a BC Hydro power plant on Vancouver Island, as well as various weapons offences. Charged along with Gerry were Brent Taylor, Ann Hansen, Doug Stewart, and Julie Belmas. It was uncanny that we had been talking about Gerry just a few minutes earlier.

We were stunned by the news and very concerned for Gerry's well-being. D.O.A. was committed to changing the system. We believed that injustice and inequality could be dealt with through words, ideas, and people power, not through violence and bombs. But one of our best friends was now in bad trouble. We knew right then we wanted to help him and the others.

In October the year before, we had heard about an explosion at Litton Systems in Toronto, the company contracted to build the guidance system for the U.S. cruise missiles that were being built at the Boeing plant in Seattle. The police attributed the action to would-be terrorists. Apparently there had been a phone warning which the guards at Litton had chosen to ignore. Nobody was killed, but one person was seriously hurt. We had no idea back then that this kind of protest action would end up becoming so personal.

As soon as we got back to Vancouver, we met with Ken Lester and mulled over what to do about the "Squamish Five," as they were being called by the press. We didn't know whether Gerry and the others were guilty or not. But we figured they would need some money to get a fair trial. This was the biggest "underground" action in Canada since the FLQ crisis in Quebec in 1970. The communiqués issued at the time of the bombings stated that the targets were companies that were anti-women, anti-environmental, and pro-war. Whether you agreed with their tactics or not, they made some strong points.

The Squamish Five's supporters had already set up a defence fund, and

we came up with the idea of doing some benefit concerts to help. Lester also suggested the brilliant idea of doing a benefit record. Thus began a D.O.A. tradition: the emergency single. We picked out the two songs we wanted to record: my song "Burn It Down," which was inspired by a poem written by U.S. prisoner Assata Shakur, member of the Black Liberation Army, and Gerry's own "Fuck You." We had a trip to L.A. coming up in a few weeks, so we got hold of Thom Wilson and he agreed to produce it.

We called the record *The Right To Be Wild*. The package included a letter Gerry had written after his incarceration.

The single came out on Sudden Death Records in Canada in March 1983 with a simple black-and-white cover. Ken Lester's brother Dave came up with a full-colour cover for the American single. Faulty Products was going out of business, so Lester made a deal with CD Presents to put out the single. (Shit! We were already on our fourth record company and we had been going for only five years!)

As winter turned into spring, the band had a few gigs scattered here and there, including two shows at the Commodore in Vancouver, opening

US release

Canadian release

for Iggy Pop. Now there was a thrill. Iggy was easily one of the giants of rock music. He never had a number-one record, but he's influenced at least three generations of musicians and fans. We busted our balls to play as well as we could. Iggy was sensational, as usual. He was also gracious. We saw him at the side of the stage watching us, and as far as we could tell, he dug it.

In April, D.O.A. ended up on the cover of *Boston Rock*. They used a great photo by my buddy, the excellent photographer Ed Colver; it was a takeoff on the photo of the Go-Go's in their underwear that had appeared on the cover of *Rolling Stone*.

Our next U.S. tour started in May. Among the highlights were a show in Montreal with the Dead Kennedys and Scum at the Spectrum, and one at the Channel in Boston with the F.U.s and Toxic Reasons. In Richmond, Virginia, we played with Minor Threat, Iron Cross, and Judicial Fear at Benny's, previously Casablanca's. The bands were really intense that night. But the funniest thing was watching people go in and out of the men's bathroom. Somebody had crapped in the sink in there, so the guys left the can either laughing their guts out or with looks of horror on their faces.

Many people at our shows were asking about the Squamish Five, and we talked a lot about the issues from the stage. The *Right To Be Wild* record grew in notoriety, helping to raise awareness of their plight. This led to many fine people and great bands participating in benefits for the Five, including the Dead Kennedys, Really Red, and Red Tide.

On Canada Day, July 1, 1983, we put on a big benefit concert for the Five at the New York Theatre in Vancouver. It was a great show with Shanghai Dog, the Dreadbeats, and No Exit, all excellent bands with their hearts in the right place. The security for the show were all women: our friends Gail and the Iverson sisters – Connie and Phyllis – were all prisoners' rights activists and took care of the ruffians better than any ex-football player could. The show raised about $2,000 for the defence fund.

Another gig that sticks out was at West Richmond High, a school in a Vancouver suburb, with Contraband and No Exit. The promoters had hired the local weightlifting club to do security. Our buddy Ron Allan had set up the sound equipment and was mixing away, but when we started playing, some of the rival factions of local hoodlums and punks decided that this was their cue to cause trouble. They started throwing stuff at the weighlifters, taunting them, and trying to start a fight. This worked pretty well, as the weightlifters were spoiling for one. But the weightlifters were vastly outnumbered, and as soon as they jumped off the stage they were swarmed. Rampage, who had come to see the show with some of his biker buddies, jumped up on the stage and started yelling about "raising some shit," which was no help at all. The amps got knocked over as fighting spread through the dance floor and onto the stage. Somehow, we finished the show. It was like the opposing groups had all decided to meet at the D.O.A. show to settle some scores.

Shortly after, Dimwit decided to quit the band. He was dissatisfied with his paycheques, which were still pretty well non-existent, and he had an offer from the Pointed Sticks to drum for them. I could understand the guy wanting to make a living. I had a proper taxi-driving licence by now, and that's how I fed myself and helped keep the Plaza going. I would work a sixteen-hour shift, three days a week; when I went on tour, the company had a hundred other jerks to take my place.

Ken Lester had been working out a deal with David Ferguson and CD Presents to release a D.O.A. album. The idea was to head down to San Francisco and do a remix of some of the songs from *Something Better Change* and *Hardcore 81*. And with Dimwit gone, we also needed a new drummer. So Dave, Laura, and I hopped into the Blue Bullet and headed south to Fantasy Studios in Berkeley. Fantasy Studios was where one of the greatest American rock bands of all time made their records. I am talking about Credence Clearwater Revival. Wow! They rule. The only hitch with the studios was the big lawsuit that had gone down between John Fogarty, CCR's leader, and Sol Zantz, owner of the studios and Fantasy Records. I felt bad about that. Fogarty had written some of the greatest rock anthems ever, and then was ripped off. Typical music-biz bullshit.

The engineer, Gary Hobish, was all right. The coolest thing was that he had worked with George Horn, probably the best mastering engineer on the west coast. George also developed the technique of baking analog recording tape in a convection oven to help preserve it. Very handy trick.

The mixing took about four days. Gary wasn't crazy about the snare sound on some of the tracks, so he worked to augment it. At the time I was trying to quit smoking, and I was very antsy until Dave and I discovered something about the vending machines in the foyer of the Fantasy complex: if you tipped the machines towards you, the contents would pour out. Before we knew it, we had more gum and chocolate bars than you could shake a school lunchbox at. If I had paid for all the gum I chewed that weekend, the Wrigley family might have had enough dough to buy a decent team for Chicago years ago.

The finished album was called *Bloodied but Unbowed*. The tracks were slightly different for the U.S. and U.K. versions. This would be our best-selling album over the years, though through a myriad of circumstances, we didn't always get paid for it. Like I said before, typical music-business bullshit.

We were staying with soundman Ian "Warp 9" Stein (Ken Lester gave Ian the nickname for his propensity to turn sound systems up to warp nine – a *Star Trek* reference – which made audience ears bleed) in San Francisco. Ian told us about a drummer Dave and I should try out. His name was Greg James and he was drumming for Verbal Abuse, a fine South Bay band, at the time. Greg was good, and he was interested in coming to Vancouver, so we had ourselves a new drummer. We renamed him Ned Peckerwood.

By the fall of 1983, there was a very serious situation brewing in British Columbia. Our not-so-esteemed premier Bill Bennett had recently been elected to a third consecutive term, and he was spoiling for a fight with his natural enemies. At the top of his list were the unions and anybody who was perceived as being even slightly left-wing. On Bennett's side were the people with lots of money and anybody else the mainstream media could con into believing his bullshit. The animosity between these opposing factions was long-standing. Bill's dad, W.A.C Bennett, along with his gang of cutthroats, the Social Credit Party, had won seven elections in a row between 1953 and 1972. After three years of a left-wing government under Dave Barrett and the New Democratic Party, the younger Bennett had led the Social Credit hordes back to victory in 1975.

Shortly after his election victory, Bennett the younger instituted a

US release   UK release

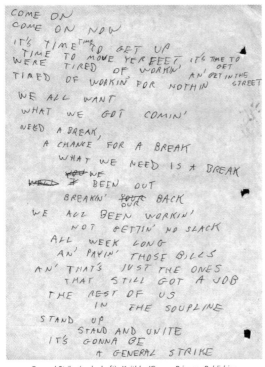

COME ON
COME ON NOW
IT'S TIME TO GET UP
TIME TO MOVE YER FEET, IT'S TIME TO
WERE TIRED OF WORKIN' GET
TIRED OF WORKIN' FOR NOTHIN AN' GET IN THE STREET

WE ALL WANT
WHAT WE GOT COMIN'
NEED A BREAK,
A CHANCE FOR A BREAK
WHAT WE NEED IS A BREAK
WE
WE'D I BEEN OUT
BREAKIN' YOUR BACK
WE ALL BEEN WORKIN'
NOT GETTIN' NO SLACK
ALL WEEK LONG
AN' PAYIN' THOSE BILLS
AN' THAT'S JUST THE ONES
THAT STILL GOT A JOB
THE REST OF US
IN THE SOUPLINE
STAND UP
STAND AND UNITE
IT'S GONNA BE
A GENERAL STRIKE

General Strike (early draft). *Keithley/Gregg, Prisoner Publishing*

series of harsh economic measures that adversely affected the working poor, the unemployed, and most middle-class people in B.C.

The opposition struck back in a very organized fashion. Two organizations sprang up: Operation Solidarity, which represented the unions, and the Solidarity Coalition, which represented women's groups, the working poor, people on social assistance, and others in the grassroots. The Solidarity name was inspired by the uprising Lech Walesa had recently led in Poland. The Solidarity groups asked Billy Boy to back off. But Bennett, being an experienced buccaneer not used to sharing the spoils, thumbed his nose at what he perceived to be a ragtag collection of mutineers. Outraged, people started planning a province-wide general strike. Ken Lester proposed that D.O.A. record another emergency single, so Dave and I sat down one afternoon at Fort Gore and started writing. In about an hour we came up with "General Strike."

Now it was just a matter of showing the song to Wimpy and Ned,

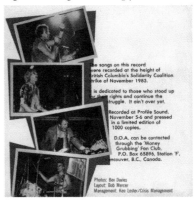

our new drummer, now in Vancouver. There was a rumour going around Peckerwood's old stomping ground of South Bay that D.O.A. had provided him with a penthouse apartment, a Corvette, and $1,000 spending money per month. In reality, Peckerwood would join Dave down at the soupline for free sandwiches. I had a few of these too. I didn't know that you could spread peanut butter that thin!

We went into Profile Studios to record "General Strike" with Billy Barker as engineer. For the flipside we recorded a version of Frank Sinatra's immortal "That's Life." We had been using the song for a while as a show stopper: when we didn't want to play any more encores, we would play that, and for sure, it would stop the show! Talk about an instant single; "General Strike" had been written and was on the streets within a week.

Things were heating up on the political front. There was a huge Solidarity rally at Vancouver's Empire Stadium in November, 50,000 strong. Bill Bennett knew that we meant business. The general strike was going to happen! But as the big day neared, Jack Munro, head of the local International Woodworkers' Union, struck a bargain with Bennett: Billy would retreat on some of his restraint measures in return for labour peace. Some people hailed the deal as a victory, but many, many assailed it as a sellout. Whatever the case, Solidarity was probably the biggest display of people-power British Columbia had ever seen. It really scared the shit out of the government, big business, and their mouthpieces, the mainstream press.

We played two more Free fhe Five benefits that year, one in Seattle and one in Vancouver. Our close-out gig for 1983 was New Year's Eve at Stalag 13 with I Braineater, Industrial Waste Banned, First Aid, and Death Sentence. Stalag 13 was a cool place, a former Boy's Club rented and run by our old roadie, Bob Montgomery, and Arnold the Dutchman.

That was it. The year was over, and a tumultuous one it had been. But, as always, we were ready for more.

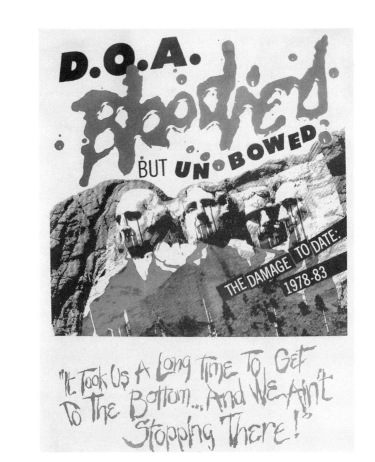

CHAPTER TEN

1984

As 1984 began, Ken Lester was busy putting together a game plan, trying to get us a foothold in Europe. On February 13, after a two-week tour across Canada, the band and our roadie, Bristlehead, flew from Toronto to London to begin a European tour. Woo-hoo! Big-time excitement. Laura had flown to Gatwick Airport earlier and met us there. It was great to have Laura along; she fit in well with the gang. Also waiting at the airport was our Vancouver buddy Scary Failure. Ken Lester and Ian "Warp 9" Stein came in on a later flight. Ian's dad worked for McDonnell Douglas and sold airplanes to the Pentagon, I believe. Lester had let Warp 9 come along as soundman because Warp 9 got him a free airplane ticket.

Bill Gilliam of Alternative Tentacles lined up gear and a van for the U.K. part of our tour. Lester had been in contact with a number of promoters who made the various bookings; each promoter handled a different territory. Our first show was at the famous 100 Club in London, the original home of U.K. punk. It went well. We played with Amebix, one of the bands that spawned the whole "crusty" movement (crusties were half-hippies, half-punks). The U.K. punk scene was quite big at this point in time, though. It had a few splits: at one end were the political anarcho-activists, and at the other were the punks who only seemed interested in drinking as much beer as they could while shouting about how British they were.

The next day we headed north to Yorkshire. As we were driving up the M1, a truck labelled "Keighley Moving" passed us. I knew I was headed for the homeland. Half of my family was from Ilkley, West Yorkshire, out on the moors, not far from the town of Keighley. (If you're wondering about the spelling difference, in 1990 I changed my name from Keighley to Keithley. All my life I was sick of people mispronouncing my name; it was spelled with a "gh" but was supposed to be pronounced "th." At least Shithead is simple; I kept that.)

We had a show scheduled in a little town called Colne, not far from Ilkley. It wasn't a typical ground-floor British pub, though; this place was a dingy sort of nightclub on an upper floor. When we arrived at the venue and walked up onto the stage, we noticed that the small speaker columns were stacked on their side instead of upright. Warp 9, ever the bull in a china shop, even on his best behaviour, spewed to the local soundman, "What – is everybody around here three-foot fucking tall?"

The soundman protested, "We always put the columns on their side at punk shows!"

Warp 9 shot back, "Well, you won't be doing it at this one! Now turn them right side up!" Ian was right, of course. Having them on their side would fuck up the sound. He pissed that guy off in a hurry.

Once we had set up our gear, we had some time to kill, but nowhere to go. The people who ran the venue didn't offer us anything in the way of food or drink, so we just sat around until they left for a bit. As soon as they were gone, I ran behind the bar to see if there were any beers for the taking. Hallelujah! A dozy barman or barwoman had forgotten to turn off one of the taps. We rushed in and glugged as much as we could. 'Ere by gum, that's what I call a lovely bargoon! Lucky for us too, because we'd soon discover that English hospitality was pretty well non-existent in the rock world.

The stage in that venue was ridiculous: it was a 4x8-foot piece of plywood set on top of four milk crates. So Peckerwood set his drums on the floor behind the plywood and Wimpy stood on the floor beside it. Dave and I jumped around on the plywood until it collapsed, as we knew it would. All in all, the crowd was into it, and it was a cool show.

Our next show was at the Assassins Club in Leeds. Only about 100 people showed up, but there is a pretty good video of it called *D.O.A. Live at the Assassins Club*. It also features a few cuts from the other acts playing that night: Benjamin Zephiniah, Mensi from the Angelic Upstarts.

That night we stayed with our friend Nick Toxic and his roommate. We asked if they had a map so we could figure out the route to our show the next day. They brought out a very large map of the U.K. When they unfolded it, Warp 9 burst out laughing, "Look at the size of the map, will ya! And this place ain't even as big as Alberta!" (Alberta was his home province; he had been an oil roughneck there in his youth until he moved to San Francisco to get into the music business. At that moment, I would have liked to cap a well with his severed head!) Our English hosts were cool, but they did not find this bit of redneck ridicule funny.

We went down to Swindon to play at Level 3, then on to Bristol. The show there was at a church in the Old Market area. Toxic Shock and the English Subhumans also played. At first, we were a little resentful that these guys had taken the name of Wimpy's old band, but I learned over the years what a great band they were. The show itself was one stop short of anarchy. The kids who came were getting fucked up on this weird homemade cider from a local grocer. (Too weird for me, man.) Afterwards we stayed at a joint called the Peace House, which was so jammed with punks and crusties you couldn't even lie down in the hallway.

While we were in the U.K., we did as much sightseeing as we could: Cardiff Castle, the Tower of London, the old Roman town of Bath, Stonehenge, and, of course, Nottingham Castle (we were big fans of Robin Hood, the guy who stole from the rich to give to the poor). Our last show in England was at the Ambulance Centre in Brixton. It was a Free the Five benefit, among other things, and a good crowd showed up: ex-Vancouverites who were now Londoners, Lynn McDonagh,

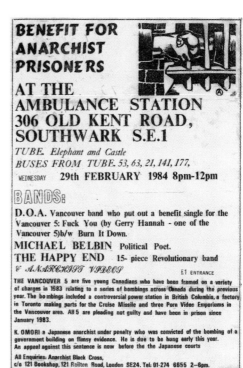

BENEFIT FOR ANARCHIST PRISONERS

AT THE AMBULANCE STATION 306 OLD KENT ROAD, SOUTHWARK S.E.1

TUBE. Elephant and Castle
BUSES FROM TUBE. 53, 63, 21, 141, 177,
WEDNESDAY **29th FEBRUARY 1984 8pm-12pm**

BANDS:

D.O.A. Vancouver band who put out a benefit single for the Vancouver 5: Fuck You (by Gerry Hannah - one of the Vancouver 5)b/w Burn It Down.

MICHAEL BELBIN Political Poet.

THE HAPPY END 15- piece Revolutionary band

& ANARCHIST VIDEOS   £1 ENTRANCE

THE VANCOUVER 5 are five young Canadians who have been framed on a variety of charges in 1983 relating to a series of bombings across Canada during the previous year. The bombings included a controversial power station in British Columbia, a factory in Toronto making parts for the Cruise Missile and three Porn Video Emporiums in the Vancouver area. All 5 are pleading not guilty and have been in prison since January 1983.

K. OMORI a Japanese anarchist under penalty who was convicted of the bombing of a government building on flimsy evidence. He is due to be hung early this year. An appeal against this sentence is now before the the Japanese courts

All Enquiries: Anarchist Black Cross, c/o 121 Bookshop, 121 Railton Road, London SE24. Tel: 01-274 6655 2—6pm.

John Werner, and Simon Werner (the old Skulls guitar player), as well as staff from the "171a" anarchist bookstore, just a brick's throw from Electric Avenue where the famous Brixton riot had taken place in 1981. There was a socialist band called the Happy End that played before us that featured tubas, trombones, trumpets, the whole shootin' match. It was good fun.

On March 1 we took a slow tub of a ferry from England to Hoek van Holland, a four-hour trip. On the way, Peckerwood asked me where we were going. He wasn't quite sure. When I said "The Netherlands," he replied, "Oh, I thought we were going to Amsterdam." Yikes. What do they teach 'em in the U.S. school system?

We had left the van in the U.K., so in Amsterdam we picked up a twelve-seater bus and headed north to Groningen, to a venue called the Simplon. We marvelled at the windmills and the dykes and the endless stream of bicycles. The guy who ran the place was known simply as the Wildman. He seemed a reasonably normal guy when we got there, but that night we saw how he got his name. You see, the Dutch have a peculiar system for selling beer: you stand in line for a while, then they give you a small glass which holds only about six ounces of beer after they level off the foam. You gulp that down, then get back in line for another. It didn't take us long to figure out that it was better to order a tray. The Wildman, though, had an even more efficient idea: he would just go behind the bar to get a tray of beer for himself. If any of the staff got in his way, he would smash a couple dozen glasses.

Our next few shows in Holland went pretty well. We were joined by a guy who became our Dutch roadie. We called him Ron the Dutchman. Ron would take our first-aid kit, stick a couple of beers inside, and relabel it "Thirst Aid." He was also a kick boxer, so that was handy, not that we ever ran into the level of aggro that we did in the States at times. The Dutch punks were quite enthusiastic; they seemed into having a good time, not like the U.K. punks, a lot of whom seemed bent only on taking the piss out of you.

From Holland we headed up towards Denmark. During the bus ride, we had a four-hour argument with Lester about whether Canadian hockey or Russian hockey was better. To complicate matters, Wimpy discovered he had lost his fucking passport, so we had to drive all the way back to recover it. We were all mad as shit as we finally approached the German border; we stopped at the first "haus" we could find and ordered a round of Schnapps.

Copenhagen in Denmark is a great city. The architecture is amazing, and so were the people we met. We were scheduled to play a place called the Ungdomshuset. It was a youth centre, but not of the YMCA variety. The building was a squat, and that was where we got introduced to what I consider one of the best things ever to go on in Europe. Sadly, squatting has never really taken root in North America. It grew from the tradition of absentee aristocratic landlords in Europe, when some rich fucker from one country would marry into the family of a rich fucker from another country. (You know, the political, "let's-make-a-deal-and-protect-our-asses" type of marriage, which led to inbreeding, an explanation for why some of those fuckheads are so stupid.) These dukes, earls, lords, and princes acquired more and more land they didn't give a rat's fuck about and never even visited. At the same

D.O.A. (l-r Wimpy, Peckerwood, Shithead, Dave) in Holland, 1984. *photo: Peter Kers*

time, a whole lot of poor people needed places to live. So they would bust their way in to these empty quarters; eventually the courts gave some legal rights to the squatters. The phenomenon got really big in western Europe in the sixties, and the squatters movement is still a force that governments there can't ignore.

Over the years, D.O.A. has done hundreds of shows in squats and former squats – unused buildings turned into camps for refugees, workshops, living quarters, concert halls, bookstores, and, best of all, gathering places for shit disturbers. We've played in squats in Italy, Holland, the U.K., Norway, France, Slovenia, Austria, Denmark, and Germany. In many places the local governments gave up trying to evict the squatters and instead just gave them the buildings. A noble movement indeed.

But back to Copenhagen. Our new friend Feyong took us first to the squat where we would be staying. There were businesses on the bottom floor: a garage and a grocery store. The six-floor apartment building above was the squat. You couldn't enter from the front, so we walked down an alley, climbed over a five-foot wall, and then crossed a courtyard to the entrance. To get in, you had to climb up a ten-foot ladder. Somebody inside would take the steel bar off the solid steel door and you could enter. I asked Feyong about the big pile of bricks and rocks in the courtyard. "If the police come to evict the people," he said, "people throw these at them from behind the wall. By the time the police are over the wall, the squatters have climbed up the ladder and pulled it inside the steel door. As the police cross the courtyard, the squatters can throw bricks and rocks down on them from the windows." Well, we thought, an old-time bloody European castle defense system. The only thing missing was the boiling oil!

Inside the squat it was all quite normal, with running water, electricity, and the other comforts of modern life. I asked one of the squatters, "If the city hates the squatters so much, why they don't cut off the water and electricity?" The city had done this previously, he said, but people in the squat had dug up the street and cemented-in the shut-off devices for water and power. The plan was perfect. Now the city could not disconnect water or power without turning off the entire city block. Fucking brilliant!

The people at the squat fed and took care of us. One woman even liberated a whole stack of "Little Mermaid" postcards for us to send back home so we wouldn't waste money on "stupid" tourist items.

Our show that night at the Ungomshuset went really well. The next day we were taken on a tour of Christiania, the world's biggest squat. It is an old army base built for the defense of Copenhagen. At the time, there were 1,000 people living there. It was a town within a town. There were workshops, a concert hall, living quarters, a library, and a main street for pedestrians. And – this is the part we couldn't believe – there were metal tables set up in the middle of the street where people were selling blocks of hash, whatever size you wanted. A large part of this trade was apparently controlled by the local bike gang, the Bullshit. As we were hanging out there, a buzz suddenly went through the crowd, and the street quickly emptied. Next thing we knew, four cops came walking down the main street. After they left, the market reopened, business as usual.

We drove back to Amsterdam, where we had a show at the famous club the Paradiso. The Dutch punks weren't concerned about punk fashion; they came to listen to music and get the message. The show went really well. While we were there, we made friends with one of Holland's best bands, B.G.K. They had been trying to organize a gig for us at a squat called Wyers, but the squatters had recently been kicked out by the cops. Apparently, the squat was making way for a Holiday Inn. The local punks promised lots of trouble. Activists in Europe were always ready to take on big corporate chains, whether it was Holiday Inn or McDonald's. In Europe, people are generally more politicized than the docile, sheep-like North American public.

After that show, Scary took off to visit some relatives. The next part of our trip was going to be in Germany; a couple of German guys in a vw van came to Amsterdam to pick us up. The driver, whose nickname, Animal, said it all, was fucking obnoxious. He drove around Amsterdam like an

idiot, muttering constantly in a mixture of broken English and Deutsch, "I'll show these Dutchies how to drive. I am the Animal of Hanover!" We weren't sure if we needed a work permit to play in Germany, so the Animal told the German border guards that we were Dutch farmworkers. The old vw was unheated, so we froze our asses in the back, huddled up with blankets pulled over our heads, pretending to be "farm workers."

Our first German show was in Hanover, with the Beton Combo, a good German band. At the time I thought the show was just okay, but years later, punks would say that that show was a big thing in Germany. It was the first time most of them had seen a North American punk band. It was the same for almost all the shows on the tour. The thing we remembered best was the German tour poster, which featured a big illustration of Charles Manson that Raymond Pettibone had done for Black Flag. A minor case of copyright theft, but the poster looked good, and tons of people came to our shows.

Dimitri, the guy who had arranged our German tour, sent a van and a driver with the rental gear for the German part of the tour to meet us in Hanover. The driver's name was Charlie, and he would turn out to be a good friend. We nicknamed him Checkpoint Charlie when we found out he was from Berlin. Charlie's van had no paint, just primer, and I'm sure it was the most fucked-up vehicle in all of the Fatherland. In North America you can buy a beater of a car for a couple hundred bucks and drive it for years if you're mechanically inclined, but in Europe the cops stop you constantly if you're missing a little paint or your fenders are close to falling off. So while travelling with Checkpoint Charlie, we were always getting pulled over.

We were on our way to Berlin, which took us to the East German frontier. We were allowed to enter the corridor only after a close inspection of our passports. The border guards, wearing very silly uniforms, looked us carefully in the eye, I guess to see if we were secretly American spies bent on destroying their superior way of life. They made us laugh.

The corridor itself, the A30, was a highway crammed with cars and trucks. You could get off it for gas and food, but you weren't allowed to go into the countryside. The Cold War meant that things were still very frozen. History has travelled this highway, which runs from Berlin west to Amsterdam, and east to Warsaw and Moscow.

The East German cops had these tiny cars that my old dog could probably outrun. But it was their job to collect Western currency, because the East German mark wasn't worth fuck all. At one of the autobahn stops, Charlie even got a ticket for making a wrong turn in the parking lot. We had to pay with West German Deutschmarks.

When we got to the outskirts of Berlin, there was this huge pedestal displaying the first Russian Tiger tank to enter Berlin in 1945. (After reunification in 1990, the tank was replaced by a pink, graffitied Volkswagen Beetle.) At the checkpoint, a set of guards studiously checked our passports and travel visas, then the passports were put into a 200-metre long vacuum tube that sucked the documents up to the next set of border guards. When we got through that gang, we were finally in Berlin.

Berlin was so fascinating it was unreal. There were viewing stands on the wall that let you look right into the no-man's-land between west and east. It was filled with large cement structures that turned out to be anti-tank barricades. Strange to be seeing this place where so many people had been shot to death while trying to escape to the West.

The first of our two shows in Berlin was at the Pankehallen, a building that looked like an old factory, with glass skylights in the angled ceiling above. There were four bands on the bill, and tickets were ten Deutschmarks (about US$5), which seemed reasonable to us and to the five or six hundred people who had already paid to get in. But there were a bunch of drunks outside who weren't happy with the price of the show. They didn't want to pony up even after the door charge was dropped to five Deutschmarks after the first band played.

There were still about 100 of these geeks hanging around outside, grumbling and threatening. As D.O.A. took the stage, these jerks started throwing bricks and rocks onto the roof, where they crashed through the skylights and rained glass, bricks, and rocks on the crowd inside. It was chaos. Next, the malcontents rushed the door, smashing aside the ticket takers.

The punks inside the club were overwhelmed at first, but they quickly regrouped and launched a counterattack. The geeks were driven back outside. The cool punks then grabbed pieces of fence and old boards and

chased the assholes down the street. The rout was complete. We finished the show, but boy oh boy, did we ever get an "impression" of Berlin. So that's how they had fun there! After the show, we crashed at a punk rock apartment in a district of Berlin called Kreuzberg.

Our gig the next day was a "secret" show at Kob. About 150 people jammed the place, which was only big enough for 100. We'd agreed to be paid in alcohol rather than money, part of which we cashed in before the show started. Yikes! There's a faulty

D.O.A. (l-r Dave, Peckerwood, Wimpy, Shithead) at the Berlin Wall, 1984.

plan. We all had our share of the spoils that night, but I think Wimpy was the victor. The stage was small, and about four feet high, and right beside where Wimpy was standing was the passageway to the bathrooms – a long, deep trough for him to fall into, should he manage to lose his balance. And manage he did. The crowd caught him a few times, but he tumbled into the abyss at least three times. Thanks to his inebriated condition, he didn't break anything.

Our German date in Freiburg was lively. We played in the basement of the old university library, about four floors underground. Freiburg is close to both the French and the Swiss borders, so the crowd was a mix of languages and nationalities that night. Unfortunately, that caused some tension. Right up by the stage, one fucking git pulled out a huge knife and started waving it around at his perceived enemies. Dave pleaded with the guy to give him the weapon, but I don't think he understood a single word Dave was saying. Fortunately the show ended without anybody bleeding to death.

This venue was memorable for another reason. It was so far underground that it stank. To make matters worse, even though there were bathrooms, most of the male punks ignored them and simply pissed against a wall when they had to. When we emerged above ground where Charlie's van was parked, tons of people were hanging out drinking. We slept in the upstairs part of the venue, and when we left the next morning, the whole driveway was soaked in piss. We had to scrape our boots before getting into the van so we didn't coat the floor with urine. Lovely.

The next day, Ken Lester announced that he was quitting. I guess he figured we weren't taking his advice. He didn't really explain himself, he just got grumpy and wouldn't talk: it wasn't the first time he would act like this, nor would it be the last. He just sat in the van, fuming, and then left. Not knowing how long this would last, I took over handling the money and doing the road managing, with help from Checkpoint Charlie, until Lester returned to duty a few days later.

We did about a dozen German shows in total, including a great one in Bielefeld at the AJZ, the youth centre. It used to be a squat and it always has one of the liveliest crowds going. That town and that venue have remained among my favourite places to play. Our show in Bremen at the Schlachthof was much less fun. *Schlachthof* means "slaughterhouse" in English, as all of you Kurt Vonnegut fans will know from *Schlachthof Fünf*. The old building was squatted, and it was a fine venue that continues today. The support band was a very good German band called Blut und Eisen (Blood and Iron). The problem was these big guys with huge mohawks who were standing on the dance floor and smashing anyone else who went out there. You know the type: "I'm more punk than you and I'm going to smash your face!" Fucking idiots.

We finished off the German part of the tour in a beautiful little town at the foot of the Alps called Kempten. If you're ever there, look up my buddy Hans Peter, who runs a cool bar called the Star Club.

We had one show scheduled in Vienna, Austria. We were a bit sad, because it was Checkpoint Charlie's last day. He was amazing. He could find any venue without making a single wrong turn, even in towns he had never been to. He also had a distinctive way of waking us up in the morning. He would march into the room, shouting, "Come on, you babies, vee must go! Come on, you Canadian babies! Vee must go!" We were going to miss him when we left for Yugoslavia the next day.

The venue in Vienna was called the Arena, another former slaughterhouse that had been squatted. (D.O.A. at a bunch of slaughterhouses? Go figure!) The show was well-attended and things were going fine until a big Austrian punk geek with dyed black hair came up to the front of the stage. We'd been playing for years now, and we'd seen plenty of ways shows could get fucked up. But as the immortal wrestler Freddie Blassie said, "Every time I pull into one of these new hick towns, there's always some loudmouth geek hanging around!"

So there we were playing away when this guy started spitting beer on us. I told him to fuck off. Next, he pulled the time-honoured "turning the monitors around on the band so they can't hear fuck all" routine. Bristlehead flips the monitor around and yells at the guy. The geek's next hackneyed trick was to shake the mike stand. I continued playing as I went over and kicked the asshole in the chest with the sole of my boot. He got pissed off and withdrew into the crowd.

The audience was hanging back, waiting to see what would happen next. Dyed black hair man returned, this time pulling out trick #113 from Punk Rock 101: he took a full mug of beer and hurled it at Dave, hitting him in the face. Snap! I lost it. Bristlehead was standing ten feet away from me. I threw him my guitar, then jumped off the stage and put the moron in a headlock. I dragged him to the front door, threw him out, and told the people at the door not to let him back in.

I guess he wanted to show us how to be punk rock. Listen, geek, we wrote the book on it.

We finished the set, but you could tell there was quite a murmur going through the crowd. "These lumberjacks from Canada, they not only chop wood, play music, and play hockey, they act as bouncers too!" After the show, when Lester (who had now returned as our manager) and I went to collect our pay, we discovered that the promoter's face was a mess of cuts and gashes; turned out the geek I had thrown out had come back and punched him out. The promoter said that that would be the last punk rock show at the Arena, and as far as I know, it was for some time.

The next morning Charlie came in and started yelling, "Wake up, you babies! Wake up, you Canadian babies!" It was seven AM, and the only train to Ljubijana, Yugoslavia that day left at eight AM. Everybody hustled and quickly piled into Charlie's van.

I've mentioned Charlie's ability to navigate without a map in any German town. This was not a German town, though, although Hitler had tried to make it one, and that morning he was driving in bloody circles. At 7:45 AM, Ian "Warp 9" Stein and I started bugging Lester to hire a cab to guide us there. Even Checkpoint was agreeing with us. Lester hummed and hawed about spending the money, so Warp 9 and I jumped out and hailed a cab ourselves. The driver charged us a whole $4 to guide us to the station! We grabbed the gear while Lester ran to buy the tickets. We said a quick goodbye to Checkpoint, then raced through the station trying to find the right platform. There it was! The Ljubiljana Express! We were on for only thirty seconds when the train started to chug out of the station. It was that close. This was another valuable lesson for the road. A crowd may wait for you get on the stage, but TRAINS, PLANES, AND FERRIES DON'T GIVE A FUCK WHAT BAND YOU'RE IN!

We were excited as we crossed the frontier into the Slovenian republic. The countryside was beautiful. None of us had been to a communist country before. The train was packed with soldiers. Later, we discovered all the trains there were packed with soldiers, although I never figured out why. It was like the same troop was trying to guard every town. We tried talking to a couple of people in our train compartment, but they spoke no English. As a way of letting them know where we were from, we pulled out our Canadian passports. Immediately, one guy said, "Kapitalistas!" D.O.A., capitalists? We had to laugh.

Ljubiljana was a beautiful town with incredible architecture, and we were amazed at how prosperous it looked for being in a communist country. The cars seemed to be in good shape, and the shops were full of things to buy. About 800 people showed up for the gig at an old community hall. The gear was good, but there was no real bathroom, just a place to piss. Before the show, Dave had to take a crap, so he went out behind the hall. Only thing was, he didn't have any toilet paper. So he took this stupid hat he had been wearing for the whole tour and wiped his ass with that! I could just see some poor Slovenian sod finding it the next morning: "Hey, a free hat! What luck." Anyway, the crowd went nuts that night. The guys from the opening band were the biggest troublemakers. They kept running across the stage and knocking over the mike stands and the monitors. I don't think they had seen too much punk rock, especially from North America, but they knew what to do.

The two Slovenian guys organizing our show, Igor and Marion, had arranged for us to stay at the main tourist hotel in Ljubiljana. Laura and I had our own room in this elegant old building. From our window, we had a perfect view of the castle on the hill. The medieval architecture of the east was different from anything else we'd seen. It looked like Count Dracula's castle. Spooky. The night before, Marion had ordered us a wonderful baked cheese dish in the hotel restaurant, and the next day Laura, Warp 9, and I tried to order it again. The menu was in Slovenian, but I thought I could interpret it. We ended up with one of the worst concoctions I had ever seen – a huge platter of saltines and some chunks of blue cheese. I made myself eat some of it because I didn't want to insult the locals. I'm sure the waiter was standing in the back laughing at the stupid punk rock westerners forcing down blue cheese and crackers.

We caught the train to Zagreb with Igor and Marion and a host of new D.O.A. fans. Along the way, we had a good gab about how punk rock went down with the authorities in Yugoslavia. Hey, it was nice to be involved in something so universally unpopular. Igor told us he'd been sent to jail for two months for wearing a Dead Kennedys badge that said "Nazi punks fuck off!" The local magistrate had interpreted the badge as being pro-Nazi!

The venue in Zagreb was a giant sports hall. The room we were set to perform in had a great sound system and brand-new Marshall amps. What a relief. The majority of the gear we'd been using on our tour had been second rate, to put it kindly. About 1,000 people showed up, and it was pretty much like the show in Ljubiljana. Berserk!

After the show it was back to the train station, this time for an eighteen-hour journey to Milan, Italy. The Yugoslavian train was packed with soldiers, as usual, but we had a fine time on the way back to Ljubiljana, sharing bottles of the local vintage with our hosts and the fans who had come up to Zagreb with us. Our companions got off in Ljubiljana at about four AM and the train resumed rolling. We were very tired by this point, so we started looking for a compartment to crash in. Lester, the cheapskate, had purchased second-class tickets for us. In first class you got a seat, but in second class you had to stand out in the bloody hallway. (I'd hate to see where they put you with third-class tickets.) First of all, though, we needed to find somewhere to put the guitars.

We tried the baggage compartment, but the conductor reacted in a very unfriendly manner to that idea and screamed at us in Croatian. Our next move was to put all the guitars into a bathroom, then stand outside to guard it. This was definitely on the grotty side of things. The train was winding its way through some very mountainous countryside, and there was about two inches of urine on the floor, slopping back and forth every time the train turned a bloody corner. Anyway, it didn't take too long until the same conductor chased us out of there. We ended up leaning the guitars against the wall in a passageway. After the piss had dried off, I tried to use them as a bed in the aisle, but that was useless. As the train wound through the mountains, I would roll off into the passageway.

Warp 9 and I went in search of seats, and after a short while we spotted an empty compartment. It was locked, though, and there was a note in the window that we obviously couldn't read. I asked Warp 9, who was really drunk, "What do you think that note says?"

"It probably says 'Fuck off and stay out of this compartment!'" he said. "But I don't fucking care!" So he grabbed the door handle and wrenched it with all his might, snapping the lock. Holy shit. The door was open.

Lester, Dave, and Wimpy were, wisely, still standing in another car.

Warp 9, Bristlehead, Peckerwood, Laura, and I each took a seat, and we piled the guitars on the remaining one. It was nirvana, heaven. I had never felt so comfortable in all my life. I could just . . . zzzzz, zzzzz, zzzzzz.

It probably wasn't more than half an hour after that that the same old grumpy conductor came around to check the tickets. Bristlehead woke up and showed his, which of course was still second-class. The conductor started screaming. Bristlehead told him to fuck off and fell back asleep. A few minutes later, the train ominously lurched to a stop. The next thing we knew, our compartment door flew open. Standing there were the conductor and five policemen wearing big blue overcoats and blue hats with red stars on the front. We were all awake by now, and not very happy at this turn of events.

The biggest cop entered the compartment and backhanded Peckerwood across the face. Next he slapped Warp 9, who swung back, so the cop slapped him harder, then dragged him out of the compartment. Following that, all five of us were thrown off the train. The cop seized our passports as we stood on the platform freezing. Lester, Dave, and Wimpy had grabbed the guitars by this time, and Lester got off to help negotiate our fate.

By this point I was thinking that a Yugoslavian jail was probably not very comfortable. Warp 9 was still drunk from the night before, and he was causing more trouble on the ground. Remember that his father had helped sell planes to the Pentagon, so he started spouting gibberish at the cops,

"Call in an air strike! Let's nuke this place! Call in an air strike!" The head cop couldn't understand what he was saying, but I could tell he didn't like the tone of it. I told Warp 9 to shut up several times, then finally grabbed him by the collar and screamed in his face, "Shut up! Shut up! Shut up!" He hung his head like a beaten dog who'd been caught in the garbage.

Finally it was worked out that we had to pay the difference between first- and second-class tickets. The cops returned our passports, and we got back on the train. But by then, our seats had filled up with people. Fuck! We were back out in the passageway.

Soon afterwards, the train stopped for customs and passport inspection at the Italian border. We nabbed some seats as it emptied out a bit. We were just sitting there minding our own business when a plainclothes cop came in. He looked a lot like Robert Blake in the cop show *Baretta*. He was wearing a leather coat, and he hadn't shaved for three days or so. He started yelling, "Passports! Passports!" We pulled out our passports to comply, but Peckerwood was a little slow with his. Baretta grabbed Peckerwood's U.S. passport, spat on it, and threw it on the ground. He threw ours back in our faces, then began searching our bags. My guess was that the Yugoslavian cops had called ahead to describe us and tell the Italians to look for drugs. The Yugoslavian jails must have been too full already. Baretta was disgusted to find nothing, and he left with a surly grunt.

We changed trains in Venice, and the rest of the gang were all asleep before we left the station. When Lester and I double-checked the train schedule we discovered that the back half of the train would be disconnected and go to Germany. So we woke everybody up before we accidentally took Von Ryan's Express to Stuttgart.

When we pulled into Milan at about four in the afternoon, we had another setback: the main station was closed, and the train was diverted. Fortunately, the promoters had dispatched two cars to each of the suburban stations, and they found us at one of them. Mission accomplished.

001

I HATE YOU   2 ND
SINISTER SEASON
FUCKED UP RONNIE
THE FRONTIER
SINGING IN THE RAIN
     WWIII
WAITING FOR YOU
WHATCHA GONNA DO?
I'M RITE YER WRONG
AMERICA
     GENERAL STRIKE
DOA.
     RICH BITCH
LET'S FUCK
PRISONER
     WAR IN THE EAST
     WAR
13
     SCUMLORD

- LIAR FOR HIRE
BURN IT DOWN
-CLASS WAR
     FUCK YOU
THAT'S LIFE.

The place we were scheduled to play in Milan was one of the most historic squats in Europe, Leon Cavallo Sociale Centrale. It was an old factory and at one point, the cops, on orders from the city, eventually attacked it with bulldozers. But the squatters had built another structure inside and counterattacked with bricks and rocks as the cops tried to enter. Leon Cavallo still exists, in its third incarnation.

The place was incredible. We marvelled at its size and all the different activities that had been set up there. Like most squats, though, there was one thing they didn't have together, and that was a proper toilet. But hallelujah, brothers and sisters, there was a toilet backstage. A rarity, I must say. There was one problem, though: it didn't flush. That didn't stop the D.O.A. entourage from using it. By the time the last man, Dave, got there, the pile was up over the seat.

The sound system, as far as Warp 9 could figure, was wired completely backwards. But he eventually got it working, and good thing too. It was a historic gig, the first time a band of our ilk had played in Northern Italy, and people had come from all over to see the show. On the bill with D.O.A. were two great early Italian hardcore punk bands: Crashbox and Rappresaglia.

The promoters had enough money to cover the show expenses after the first 1,500 people had showed up, so once they had that they opened the doors to everybody else. The crowd swelled to about 3,000. There were three separate pits swilling around as we played. It was insanity on a level such as can only be experienced in Italy, and turned out to be one of those shows that they still talk about there. The deal for us involved no lire, but the squat paid for our airplane tickets back to London.

The next day was a sad one for me and the love of my life: Laura was going to backpack around southern Europe for a few months, and I was staying with the band. The Leon Cavallo people had sent around a guy to drive us to the airport. He had this beat-up vw van, and we all piled into it. But our collective weight was too much for the old beater; it wouldn't go more than ten miles an hour, and it died about five miles out of Milan.

Laura and I said our tearful goodbye on the side of the highway.

We sent Peckerwood to a nearby service station, and he came back with two taxis. The cab drivers ripped us off royally, charging us $160 in total, but they did get us to the airport on time. We hopped on the plane and were on our way back to London.

CHAPTER ELEVEN

LET'S WRECK THE PARTY

When we got to London, we stayed with Simon Werner, who had played with us in the Skulls, in his Brixton squat. Then we found a rehearsal spot so we could work on some tunes. Bill Gilliam had got us booked into the main BBC building in London to record a "John Peel" session. It was a good break for us. John Peel was, and still is, one the best-known DJs in the U.K.; he would take the recorded session and play it on national radio. But we had to come up with four songs that we hadn't yet released on an album. This was a little tough. We had been touring a lot and we'd changed drummers, so we hadn't been writing many songs. We decided to re-record "General Strike" as well as "Burn It Down," which had only been released as singles. Luckily, we had two songs that we hadn't recorded: "Race Riot" and Wimpy's "Season in Hell."

Steel Pulse were recording in the BBC studio when we got there the next day. They ran a little overtime, but that was cool. They were Steel Pulse. And it gave us a chance to look around a bit. What a bloody great facility. The recording room for orchestras was huge and fabulous. It was a thrill to be recording there.

Our session was orderly and smooth. We just played the songs once or maybe twice. When the bed tracks were done, we went back and added the vocals. The producer and the engineer worked fast. The session was four songs, top to bottom, and we had from three PM till midnight to finish. At

11:58 PM, as an old janitor headed into the studio for the nightly cleanup, the engineer finished the last mix of "Race Riot" and the producer grabbed the master tape.

The BBC gave us £500 to do the session, and a short while later we bought the master tape back so that Bill Gilliam could release it as an EP. It was called *Don't Turn Yer Back (On Desperate Times)*, and it was dedicated to miners around the world. Britain's Iron Lady, Prime Minister Margaret Thatcher, was engaged at the time in a vicious battle with U.K. miners, and there were also big miners' strikes going on in Chile, South Africa, and Poland.

On April 4, after an action-packed seven weeks abroad, the band and Bristlehead flew back to Toronto. Lester and Warp 9 carried on to San Francisco, but the rest of us headed over to Bristlehead's mom's place. We enjoyed her home cooking, and on TV the National Hockey League playoffs were just starting: the Montreal Canadians versus the Boston Bruins. Fuckin' great! I loved the Bruins and hated the Canadiens! But in between periods, as I looked at a map of Canada, I started to get worried. Our next set of gigs was in Canada's east-coast provinces, and we had to be in St John's, Newfoundland, to play in a little over two days. None of us were aware until then just how far St John's was from Toronto.

It was 1,300 miles from Toronto to Sydney, Nova Scotia, where we were to catch the ferry to Port Au Basque, Newfoundland. When we got there, we were amazed to see icebergs in the harbour. As we drove onto the ferry, we knew we were in for serious business. This was no ship made for mild crossings between islands like we were used to back home. No sir; this was an ocean-going vessel. The deckhands tied down every vehicle on board with thick steel cable. The ship started rolling almost as soon as we left the harbour. It was no picnic out there. I was sitting with Wimpy, who was looking rather green. We were staring at this little steel ball attached to a chain and fastened to the wall. At the top of the chain was a red line, which indicated the ferry was going to tip. The steel ball was swinging ever closer to that red line. It was a full-on gale. The ride took a harrowing ten hours. Wimpy asked one of the old deck hands what the ball was for. With his Newfie accent he cooly replied, "Well, I'll tell ya, boy. If that ball gets past the red line, we're in the drink fer sure, boy."

We arrived on the Rock in a full-blown rain storm, with a long drive to St John's ahead of us. When we finally got there, it had been fifty hours since the time we had left Toronto. Whew! Who'd booked this fuckin' thing, anyway? Our equipment started steaming as we plugged it in. It had been sitting in the back of the Blue Bullet, in an Ontario winter, for almost two months. About 200 people turned out for the gig, and it went great. The people were really warm and friendly, and they were amazed that we'd actually shown up all the way out there.

We took the return ferry back to Sydney, and drove to Moncton, New Brunswick, through blizzard conditions. A huge storm was crashing down on the east coast. We'd played St John's just in time. An ice storm hit the city hard soon after we left and knocked out most of the power in the city.

The gig in Moncton was on the outskirts of town, the promoter told us, so we were to follow his car. Follow we did, way out into the boonies. It was snowing harder and harder. Finally the promoter pulled off onto a forest road with no sign of any stinkin' hall. Where the hell was this place? Somebody started whistling the tune from *Deliverance*.

Finally, though, there it was, a tiny community hall out in the woods. We dragged our gear inside and set up the equally tiny sound gear on a couple of tables. Then we sat down to wait for a crowd. About seventy-five people, from all over the Maritimes, finally showed up. How they found the place I haven't a clue. It was such horrible weather that we didn't dare turn off the Blue Bullet; we locked it up and left it running while we played. But it turned out to be a great evening. Funny how the weird little shows can be the most fun.

The next day we played in Halifax, Nova Scotia, at a fourth-floor dance studio. There was no elevator, though, so we humped the gear up the stairs. But the gig was well organized and well attended. It was put on by promoter Greg Clark, who has organized all of our Halifax shows over the years. Hats off to him. It's hard to stay in this biz without losing your mind.

We then played a few shows along the east coast of the U.S., including one in New York at the original Rock Hotel on Jane Street with Iron Cross and Agnostic Front, then a few more on our trip back across Canada. The trial of the Squamish Five was drawing closer, and the prosecutors were asking for lengthy sentences for them all. Over that summer, all five pleaded guilty, and were sentenced to between six and twenty-two years.

D.O.A. then headed back south and played to about 4,000 people at the Olympic Auditorium in L.A. on June 1 with the Exploited and Kraut. The Exploited had to borrow our gear to pull off their set. We did a fabulous show the next day at the On Broadway in San Francisco. What a bill: D.O.A, T.S.O.L, MDC, Fang, and Tales of Terror. The room was full of raw energy.

When we got back to Vancouver, I called a meeting with Dave and Wimpy. Peckerwood was becoming a problem. He'd been with us for a year, but his work ethic was lousy and his drumming was not improving. We'd had to can a session we'd recorded in L.A. with Thom Wilson; he didn't like

the drumming. Later that day, Peckerwood arrived at Fort Gore and we continued a D.O.A. tradition. Dave put on the theme song from *The Good, the Bad, and the Ugly*, then we called Peckerwood into the kitchen and sacked him.

At a follow-up meeting, we talked about a replacement. Wimpy and I leaned towards Dimwit. His Pointed Sticks gig had run out, since the band had crashed and burned. Dave started improvising some lyrics to the tune of a Van Halen song: "I think you're headed for a whole lot of trouble! If you get that drummer back in the band!" But Wimpy and I ignored him. Dimwit rejoined, and so three of the gang of four were back together. But it was a funny thing. We'd known each other a long time, and as it turned out, we all knew the things about the others that bugged us.

I was living at Fort Gore (although Dave would later boot me out for being too loud and obnoxious after shows), and Dimwit joined us there. We'd meet at the Fort to practice, and then proceed to do everything but. We would play ball hockey across the street in the food warehouse parking lot. We would play football or baseball at the east end of the Georgia Viaduct, before it was full of junkies and needles. We would play table top hockey in Fort Gore's kitchen and slap pucks at the front door to see who could

make the deepest dent. Dave had a canoe suspended from the kitchen ceiling that we would sometimes take out to Sasamat Lake. It was like our own boy's club. But eventually we got around to practicing, and we started working on a few new songs.

We had another tour to California booked, and just before the tour, we covered our guitars and the sides of the cabs in shiny silver mylar to match Dimwit's drums. When light hit the stuff, it blinded the audience. We started billing ourselves as "the band that put the metal back in metal."

The first show of the tour was in Olympia, Washington with the He-Sluts and the Melvins. The next night we were set to play an all-ages show at the Lincoln Art Center in Seattle with the Unwanted, Green River, Dismal, and Immoral Roberts. But too many people showed up, and the fire marshal cancelled the show. A mini riot ensued, during which three Seattle cop cars were spray-painted with "D.O.A." in big letters. Around this time the band had taken to wearing thick flannel shirts we called mac jackets. Back home there was almost a code to wearing these things depending on where you

Mr. Shithead incites fans and fuzz alike.

were from. Guys from Surrey wore green ones, guys from North Van wore purple ones, and guys from East Van and Burnaby wore red. Some years later a few pundits spouted the theory that the flannel look of the Seattle "grunge" scene was an offshoot of all the local musicians who'd seen D.O.A. wearing mac jackets at shows when they were kids. All I know is that I wore the Burnaby colours.

The tour continued with four shows in Texas, where we played with Die Kreuzen, Shanghai Dog, the Offenders, and the Unwanted. One memorable gig featured D.O.A., Dr Know, and the Rhythm Pigs at the Coke House in El Paso. It was a great show, despite the fact that there were only thirty-three people there – including all of the band members, the club staff, and the promoter. We played with the Dicks in San Francisco and did four shows with Abrasive Wheels, a U.K. pop punk band, including one at the Olympic Auditorium.

Back in Vancouver, we opened for PiL (Public Image Ltd), Johnny Rotten's post-Sex Pistols band, at the UBC War Memorial Gym. We played well, but some people were critical of us afterwards, accusing us of acting like rock stars because of our "expensive" new silver guitars and amps. It had cost us $30 to cover everything with that shit! PiL were good, but like ninety-nine percent of the audience, I would have far rather heard the Sex Pistols that night. At one point in their show, Johnny Rotten (who was now back to his real name, John Lydon) took off his shirt and threw it into

D.O.A. (l-r Wimpy, Dave, Shithead, Dimwit), 1985. *photo: Bev Davies*

the audience. Six guys did a Tasmanian Devil imitation trying to get sole possession of that souvenir and tore it to pieces.

That fall, Laura arived back from living in Greece. I was a much happier man.

The band was ready to embark on some recording, so we got hold of our old buddy Billy Barker, who had done the demos for *Hardcore 81*. I wrote most of the songs for the album, but Wimpy's songwriting really helped fill it out. We started recording at a warehouse rented by Luxury Bob, our new roadie. Soon afterwards we got a call from Sam Feldman, a local music mogul, telling us that Brian "Too Loud" McLeod was interested in producing our new album. Too Loud played in a famous Canadian hard-rock band called the Headpins. He was an accomplished musician and a good producer, so we met with him to see what he had to say.

It was a tough decision. Some of us thought Too Loud's approach was too commercial for D.O.A. Dimwit argued it was an opportunity we'd be fucking stupid to pass up. Dave and Wimpy were on the other side of the fence. Lester was more or less in Dimwit's camp. I cast the deciding vote, and we went with Too Loud McLeod, working out a deal to record at the new Ocean Sound. Too Loud brought his silly little poodle, Sailor, to all of the sessions. The work he did was very thorough. Although that album is far from my favourite, I learned an incredible amount about producing from him.

While this was going on, D.O.A. got into a lawsuit with David Ferguson and CD Presents over who owned the copyright of certain songs, and about future D.O.A. releases. A lawyer friend of ours, Pat Nichols, negotiated an out-of-court settlement after about a year.

Lester arranged for a Montreal company called Just in Time to release the new album in Canada, and lined up Alternative Tentacles for both the U.K. and the U.S. This would be our most "rock 'n' roll" release to date, and we wanted a funny title for it. Dimwit had come up with a metal/rock piece

US release

of headbanging music, and it was up to me to put some words to it. Once I wrote the words, we had the album title: _Let's Wreck the Party_. On one level it reflected the sheer fucked-up-ness of D.O.A., but on the political side it referred to the "party" of conservatives who were running most of the western world, figureheads like Prime Minister Brian Mulroney in Canada, Prime Minister Margaret Thatcher in the U.K., President Ronald Raygun in the U.S., and Chancellor Helmut Kohl in West Germany.

The cover concept was D.O.A. wrecking a party. With help from our friends, we laid out a big Thanksgiving-type dinner for the cover shoot and had our friends fill the roles. Ken Lester posed as the father, Cathy Cleghorn (who now runs the Anthill merch company in New York City) was the mother, and the young lad was played by Keif Davies, the son of Bev Davies. Lester didn't think the image worked for the U.K. release, though, so again we ended up with two different covers for the same album.

Our release party, in March of 1985, was billed as "The Night D.O.A. Played Club Soda." Club Soda, formerly the Quadra and later the Starfish Room, was a Vancouver club considered too "hoity-toity" for D.O.A. They rarely featured any really rocking acts there, so we made an event of our appearance there, producing T-shirts to commemorate the occasion. The place was jammed beyond belief. We called up our special guest Too Loud McLeod to join us on our encore, "Takin' Care Of Business." He grabbed one of my guitars on his way up. Too Loud usually played with a whammy bar – I did not – and while trying to get a wild downwards note, he bent the neck of the guitar so hard that he broke it. He grabbed another guitar, then went nuts with the solo. The crowd roared, and we hadn't even hit the first verse yet. It was a great night of rock 'n' roll. (Too Loud died of cancer in 1989, RIP.)

A few weeks later, the band flew up to Anchorage, Alaska. The theme for the gig was that, being so close to the U.S.S.R., Alaska might become part of Russia again any day. The show was at the National Guard Armory, and we played with Skatedeath, featuring Mike of Fuckemos, and Psychedelic Skeletons. The whole show was hyped by this cool video show hosted by Mr Frank the Clown. Mr Frank later made the video for "Dance o' Death," a song on _Let's Wreck the Party_. We had a great time in Alaska, and even got a ride over the wilderness in a four-seater

l-r Johnny Ferreira, Too Loud McLeod, and Shithead
at Club Soda, 1985. _photo: Bev Davies_

Cesna plane. Dimwit missed most of the fun, since he took some sort of strange pill after the show and was passed out for about forty hours. We kept checking on him to make sure he was still alive.

We didn't know it at the time, but we were about to start the longest tour D.O.A. would ever make. It was eight months long in all, covering North America and Europe, and by the end of it we'd be nearly dead. It was called the Let's Wreck the Party Tour to begin with, but we later renamed it the Endless Tour, Parts 1 and 2.

Our opening show was in Seattle at the Rock Gardens, in a cool two-room setup with the Fastbacks and No Means No, one of my all-time favourite bands. In Portland, we were billed as "the Hardest-Working Band in Show Business!" That was a new one. But if James Brown could be billed as the Hardest-Working Man in Show Business, we would gladly accept the new moniker. The East Bay promoter Wes Robinson, in fact, wanted to do a big show in Oakland at the Auditorium, with a bill featuring James Brown, D.O.A., and Flipper. There's an idea that didn't stand a chance!

The next few months were a bit of a blur, as we circled around Canada and the States. Things were helped by the fact that we had a decent crew. There was our new soundman, Patrick Hutchinson. Hutch was a good guy and ever dependable. Leslie Jambor came along to sell the merch. Our roadie, Luxury Bob, was a hard partier, which sadly led later to his untimely demise. But he got the job done. I was the road manager, since Lester wouldn't be joining us until the fall. To pass the time while we drove, we ate sunflower seeds, which we called spits. Dave sometimes popped so many of them while driving at night that he left a stack of empty shells a foot high in the space between the driver's seat and the door.

At the end of May, Chris Williamson from Rock Hotel arranged to fly us out to New York to play a big show with the Dead Kennedys. It was a two-night event at a place on the Lower East Side called The World. D.O.A. opened the first night, and the Butthole Surfers opened the next night.

On the bill that night were the Dead Kennedys, D.O.A., Reagan Youth, Live Skull, and the False Prophets. By the time we got on at around eleven PM, the place was stuffed with about 2,000 people. We played a good set and when we left the stage, somebody from the production company announced that they had oversold the show. The venue, on the second floor and only built to hold 1,000 people, was in danger of collapsing from the extra weight. It was an old building, and it did seem a little shakey to me. They asked for people to voluntarily leave. Of course, not a person budged. The Dead Kennedys were about to go on! So the organizers stopped anybody else from coming up the stairs from the main bar, which meant a lot of people who had paid couldn't actually get upstairs to see the DKs. I got away from the dance floor and stayed by the stairs, just in case.

Successful tours depend on the smooth interaction of the participants. We kept it going pretty well during this time, even with seven of us jammed into the Blue Bullet. The one person who sometimes made it tough was my old buddy Dimwit. Dimwit was always looking for a deal, an easy way to improve his lot in life. One morning after a show in Denver, he came running into the motel room where we had all crashed out, begging somebody to lend him $300. When we asked what the hell for, he replied, excitedly, "There's this guy down in the parking lot selling gold and diamond rings at a tenth of their value! One of you fuckin' guys has to give me some money. I want to buy one as an engagement ring for Naomi."

Finally Wimpy, who had managed to squirrel away a little dough out of his $10 per diems, spoke up. "Dimwit, I've got $90 that I can *lend* you. It's all the money I have in the world. This is a loan, not a gift!"

Dimwit was almost frothing at the mouth by this point. "Sure, sure, I'll get it back to you. Give me the money. Give me the money!" He snatched the cash from Wimpy and flew out the door.

We were on the second floor and some of us looked over the railing to see Dimwit handing the $90 to a shady-looking character in a beat-up Detroit tank. I looked to see if the name of his jewellery company was on the side of his car, "A-One Mobile Jewellers" or something like that. Dimwit ran back up to the room to show off his fabulous purchase, and a few minutes later we saw some cop cars patrolling the parking lot. I guess the independent businessman had another appointment.

The ring was a gold-coloured band with a reasonable-sized rock on it. Tied to it was a little paper tag, with a handwritten price: "$2,500." Dimwit, wearing the biggest shit-eating grin I had ever seen, was parading around with this thing like he had just won the Stanley Cup. He wouldn't let anybody except Wimpy touch it.

Finally, we had to burst his sad balloon by questioning whether the ring was real. Dimwit called us every name in the book, and a few we hadn't heard before. So we laid off, at least for a while.

We were driving along a boring stretch east of Denver on the I-70 when Dave started humming a familiar tune. After a few minutes, he added some words. With apologies to Gary Lewis and the Playboys, they went like this:

> Who wants to buy this diamond ring?
> Paid ninety bucks, ain't worth a goddamn thing.
> This diamond ring doesn't shine for Dimwit any more.
> This diamond ring's a piece of shit, that's for sure.
> He got burned, ha ha ha, ha ha ha!

Before you knew it, the rest of us were singing along as loudly as possible. You could see the steam coming out of Dimwit's ears! Finally we knocked it off. We were all pals after all. We were merciful. We only sang it for an hour.

Dimwit also had a horrible pinball habit that would bankrupt him almost every day. Then one afternoon at a shopping centre he demanded all the money he had coming for that leg of the tour. He said he wanted to make an investment. After a quick look at the books, I gave him ten bucks. He snatched it out of my hand angrily and stomped off.

I took a short walk to kill some time, and when I got back to the van, Dimwit was there with his investment. He had bought a loaf of white bread, a jar of mustard, and a pack of chickaloni. Now if you don't know what chickaloni is, I'll tell you: it's all the stuff from the slaughterhouse that's been left lying on the floor – eyeballs, guts, everything except the chicken's squawk! Balancing his purchases on his knees, he started mass-producing sandwiches, yelling at me when I asked to squeeze by to get into the van. I stood outside and lit a smoke,

Dangerman (early draft). *Joey Shithead Keithley, Prisoner Publishing* then told him politely I wanted to get in. I explained it was rather cold outside. Again he told me to fuck off. So I squeezed by anyway, and waved my ass over the sandwiches as I passed by, laughing as I go.

Dimwit snapped. He threw everything, including all the sandwiches and an unopened pack of chickaloni out the van door, then jumped out of the van and stomped on them. The chickaloni shoots out of the pack and onto another car's door like a giant cum shot.

A while later, as we were driving to our next show, Dave started humming another tune. This time, the lyrics went:

> Hurray!
> We're having chickaloni
> Chickaloni's really neat
> Ground-up chicken's heads and feet
> But be careful when I eat
> Or I'll stomp it in the street!
> Hurray! For chickaloni.

Of course we all joined in, singing as loudly as possible. But Dimwit was our pal, so we were merciful. We stopped singing along after about an hour and a half.

A lot of people think the music biz is nothing but fame, glory, and money. I'm not sure about the fame and glory part, but I do know the money part sucks. We rarely stayed at hotels or motels when we were on tour; mostly, we tried to find a place to stay through someone connected to the show. The person who offered us the accommodations would usually promise us that their place was going to be clean and quiet. But some of them would instantly tell all of their friends. "Hey, man. I've got D.O.A. coming over! Call up everybody and bring as much beer as you can carry. It's gonna be an all-nighter." We would arrive at the house completely exhausted to find a full-on raging party. Those of us who wanted to crash would often be directed to a room where the resident kept three or four kitty-litter boxes that hadn't been cleaned in months.

D.O.A. (l-r Dave, Wimpy, Dimwit, Shithead), 1985. *illustration: Ken F.*

"Hey, man. Is this all right?" Sure, if I rearrange the litter over the cat turds and use one pile for a pillow.

Whenever this happened, we would often revert back to the Blue Bullet. We would drive as far as we could after a show, and then Dave would pull into our favourite hotel chain: McDonald's. What? You've never heard of this chain? Where have you been? Dave would park the van in a McDonald's parking lot and *voilà* – instant punk rock accommodations. Three or four people would crash in the van, one guy would crash on the roof of the van, and a couple of us would grab sleeping bags and stretch out in the parking lot. The guys in the lot would be wakened at six AM by a kick in the ribs from the McDonald's manager, who would say something like, "What the fuck are you idiots doing here?" To which one of us would reply, "We're waiting for you to open, man. How come you're late?" We'd head into the restaurant and pay a buck for a coffee, then use the sink in the bathroom to shave, brush our teeth, and have a "shower." After six guys had done this, there was usually an inch of water on the floor. The manager would sneer at us as we left. (In 2001, on tour in Switzerland, we saw an actual McDonald's hotel on the autobahn. Yikes! Is that the future? You spend your entire life living, working, eating, and sleeping all within the same corporate walls.)

Once in the Boston area we parked the Blue Bullet in a suburban neighbourhood. Four of us grabbed our sleeping bags and headed into this little forested section. It was nice and peaceful . . . for about half an hour. Next thing we knew, there were a couple of cops shining flashlights in our eyes. I explained the situation; it was a long weekend, and there was nowhere else for us to go. The cops nodded sympathetically, or so it seemed, and told us to follow them. After about fifteen minutes, they pulled off the road – into a graveyard! "You can crash here," they told us. Before they left, they asked us a question we'd heard a number of times in the U.S. "Where's British Columbia? In South America?"

Another time, in the mountains of West Virginia, we were supposed to stay with the singer from the Inbred. We pulled into Morganstown at about two AM and found the Inbred's house, but there was a note on the door: "Sorry, D.O.A. Have gone to play a show in Hurricane, West Virginia. See you tomorrow." Well, shit on a stick. I went around to the back of the house and rattled the door to see if we could get in that way. But with all this racket, lights in the neighbourhood started coming on, and dogs started barking. We figured a West Virginia jail cell would probably not be that comfortable, so we skedaddled out of there.

I drove us around until I spied the perfect accommodations.

"Here we go!" I said in a merry tone.

The group groaned when they saw what I had picked out. "It's a parking lot!"

"Yes," I replied, "but not just any parking lot. It's a *gravel* parking lot. So it should be way more comfortable than a regular old asphalt one!" After all, hadn't the great Bob Marley sung, "Cold ground was my bed last night, and rock was my pillow too."

The next morning, I awoke to sunlight and two women staring at me in horror. When I sat up, one of them said, "What are you guys doing here?"

"We're big-time rock stars," I replied, "and this is our hotel room at the Hilton."

Dimwit rolled over and spotted a large waste disposal bin on the other side of the parking lot. "Hey, Joe, I'm going to crawl over to that trash container and grab some breakfast! Care to join me?"

"No, thanks," I said. "I've got some stale Cheezies in the van."

The two women scurried off.

On August 9, 1985, we played a big show in L.A. billed as the Nagasaki Nightmare. It was the fortieth anniversary of the U.S. Air Force dropping the atomic bomb on Nagasaki, Japan. The bands were Conflict (U.K.), the Upright Citizens (Germany), the Asexuals (Canada), and D.O.A. – an all-foreign bill. The crowd of about 4,000 people was rowdy. People constantly charged the stage as we were playing, knocking things over, and running into us. One huge guy who looked like he had swallowed several shopping carts full of steroids was dancing off on the side. He wasn't a punk, but he was watching what the punks were doing, and imitating the knocking-over-shit part. I motioned to Big Frank, the security guy, to give this jerk the boot. Big Frank shook his head: no way! Next, this giant made as if he was going to do a stage dive, but he couldn't quite get off the stage because of the crush of people up front. He stood there hunched over, looking at the crowd, with his ass sticking out at us, so I thought I would give him a helping hand, or foot. I got ready to kick him square in the ass, but somehow I missed, did an undercut, and caught him square in the balls. What was worse, my kick hadn't propelled him off the stage. He turned around and looked at me with a "I'm going to rip you apart limb from limb" look. Should I try to avoid total annihilation by smashing him over the head with my guitar? Fortunately, Big Frank had been watching this unfold. Thank Hades for that. It was like the U.S. punk cavalry riding to my rescue. Big Frank and five other guys ran on stage all at once and heaved the monster into the pit. Whew! I think I owe my life to them.

On the way down to San Diego from L.A., the Blue Bullet blew a front tire in seventy-miles-an-hour, bumper-to-bumper traffic. It took all the

composure I had to hang onto that fuckin' driver's wheel and bring the van to a standstill on the inside lane. When we got out the spare tire, we realized we had no tire jack. We were fucked. There was no way to cross that freeway without getting killed.

At that moment, the Upright Citizens, who'd been travelling in the slow lane, spotted us in trouble, and pulled over. We could hardly communicate across the four lanes of rush-hour traffic, but finally they understood we needed a jack. How to get theirs to us, though? The solution was Mario – let's call him Super Mario – the band's gangly drummer. Super Mario dodged hundreds of speeding commuters to deliver the jack to us. It was like Mario was playing Frogger on the I-5. We took Mario with us. We were not going to take a chance on the bravest man in all of Germany being squished like a bug on that freeway trying to get back across. We bought Super Mario many beers that night.

We worked our way east towards New York; we'd be flying out from there in early September to start our European tour. In Minneapolis, we played the Cedar Riverside Center, with Soul Asylum, Process Blue, and the Upright Citizens, a fine, fine bill. While we were getting ready for soundcheck, Dave, Bob, and Hutch unloaded our big black D.O.A. backdrop. But instead of hanging it behind the stage as usual, they hung it from the edge of the roof so it covered the top floor of the four-storey building. You could see it for miles.

After admiring their handiwork, I went over to the local Circle K for coffee. As I walked back towards the Center, I noticed something looked different. The backdrop was gone. Some scumbag had gotten themselves a nice souvenir. We searched the entire building and eventually I found the banner stashed at the bottom of a large waste container. Fuckin' lucky! (In 1990, on what I thought was our farewell tour, I sold that backdrop to the Cactus Club in San Jose for $250, with the proviso that I could buy it back anytime for the same price. In 1993, I retrieved that dust-and-nicotine-soaked piece of D.O.A. history from their ceiling and started using it again.)

Our last American show of the tour was in Washington, D.C., at the WUST Radio Hall. The support that time was Government Issue and Dagnasty. A big crowd showed up, and in the middle of our set the guy who ran the hall motioned me over. "Now, don't panic," he said, "but we think somebody just came into the hall with a gun. We are trying to figure out who." Great, I thought to myself. Some nut has got a gun in here, and D.O.A. might be the target. We finished our set with a bunch of short-hairs and no-hairs giving us the old "Seig Heil" salute, but nobody got shot that night. Somebody had stolen our license plates, though. We needed to get to New York City, so we drove there without the plates. Hey, we were outlaws. We didn't need no stinkin' plates.

While we were in New York, we got the bad news that Wimpy's dad had died. He was a hard-working family guy, and only in his sixties. Shortly after that, Wimpy got a call from his girlfriend, Jan Berman, telling him that he was going to be a dad. I don't know how he'd found time to get that accomplished; we had only been at home for a total of five days since the Endless tour had started. After talking to his mom, Wimpy decided to continue with us rather than fly home. Jan would come over to Europe and meet him partway through the tour.

So it was time to head off to Europe again. We left the Blue Bullet with some friends in the Bronx, Big Todd and Cyd (Faulty Products), who we'd been staying with while in the area, and headed for the airport.

D.O.A. (l-r Wimpy, Shithead, Dimwit, Dave), 1985. *photo: Edward C. Colver*

CHAPTER TWELVE

THE ENDLESS TOUR, PART TWO

When we arrived in London, Ken Lester and Bill Gilliam of Alternative Tentacles picked us up at the airport. Before we were ready to go on tour, we needed to find some gear and a van. On our last European tour we had paid way too much dough to rent amps; we didn't like being ripped off with rental prices, so this time we would buy them. The van was another matter. We looked around at used car lots, and almost got an old ambulance – which we thought was fitting for D.O.A. – but settled on a bluish Ford nine-seater for £1,750. We named it Gertie. Gilliam bought the cabs for us as an advance on royalties.

We got a dreadful shock when the U.K. version of *Let's Wreck the Party* arrived at the Alternative Tentacles office. They were all fucked up. Gilliam had sent the cover art to a music publication to be reduced in size for an ad. The ad came out fine, but nobody had thought to take off the "reduce to 17%" sticker off the art before it went to the company that printed the LP jackets. So here were all the albums with little tiny images on the cover. It was a Spinal Tapism all the way. Gilliam declared he would do another run of the album, and gave us some free copies of the fucked LP, to calm Lester down. At least we had the tour to look forward to; since our last visit, we had sold a lot more records and our reputation was growing.

When we were loaded up, we drove north out of London to Bletchley, Milton Keynes, Buckinghamshire, and stopped at the Marshall factory. It was like dream come true. This was where all those great amps were made. They gave us a real deal on the heads, and I still use mine to this day.

Our first show, at Adam and Eve's in Leeds, was packed and raucous. It

UK release   UK release misprinted front cover

looked like we were on an upswing, and the rest of our British dates proved that to be true. The door charge at our show in Brighton was three pounds (US$5), which we thought quite reasonable. After we'd finished playing, though, Dimwit and I were backstage when some punter came up and yelled at us, "Get back up there and apologize!" Dimwit, already in a bad mood, snarled, "Apologize for what?" The punk replied, "For charging more than two quid at the door! That's what!" Lucky for that fuckwit I was there; Dimwit was ready to run him down the back stairs head first. U.K. punk shows always had their share of characters.

Laura and her sister Cindy met us in Holland. In Amsterdam, we played a great new squat called Emma. The place had huge, heavy rubber swinging doors; if you were a little drunk and not paying attention, those things could knock you flat on your ass. After the show, some of the Dutchies "borrowed" bicycles and doubled Laura, Cindy, and me over to where we were crashing. It was a funny thing about bicycle-stealing there, as bikes were never locked up. If you left your bike outside a club and somebody took it, you'd just take the next one in line. There always seemed to be enough bikes to go around. (When a Dutch person wanted to make fun of a German, he or she would say, "Bring back my grandfather's bicycle!" At the end of the Second World War, when the Canadian Army was helping to liberate Holland from Hitler's armies, German soldiers used any form of transpo they could to escape, including bicycles.)

Our support for almost the entire European tour was Frightwig, a good,

really funny group from San Francisco made up of three women: Deanna Barker on bass, Susan Miller on guitar, and Cecilia Lynch on drums. They hired two Dutch guys, Dirty Dick and Nick, to drive them around in an old, beat-up Mercedes delivery van.

After Holland, the next leg of the tour was Germany. We played Munich on October 3, while Oktoberfest was going on. Talk about a beer-drinker's paradise. There were about eight separate beer gardens, and the one we went into was as big as a medium-sized hockey arena. It was packed with more than 4,000 people. There was an oom-pah-pah band on stage at the far end, and a horse track that ran right up the centre. We ordered beer and roasted chicken. The beer glasses were gigantic, and so were the chickens. As we settled down with our grub, the band sounded a fanfare, and the gates at the end of the horse track sprang open. Out raced two fine-looking horses, each with a rider standing on its back. The crowd roared its approval! Michel, our German tour manager, told us Oktoberfest wasn't all a bed of roses, however, especially if you were a punk or a person of colour, since the beer halls were frequented by a lot of German rednecks. Luckily, though, nobody bothered us. After that experience, we played a great show at the Alabama Hall. The support that night was Sonic Youth and Frightwig.

The biggest problem we had on our German tour was the sheer size of our entourage. Between D.O.A and Frightwig and all the associated people, there were seventeen of us. Michel, who did most of the road managing, was patient with everybody, a challenge considering he also did all the interpreting. He would go through an entire restaurant menu as thoroughly as he could for us, and then be forced to repeat large parts of it due to a couple of people who hadn't been listening. By the time our two weeks in Germany were over, Michel looked as if he'd aged ten years.

Our show in Berlin was good, but nowhere near as eventful as our first time there; there was no riot this time. Before we left for Frankfurt, we heard about a big anti-fascist rally that had gone on in Frankfurt the night before. This was an active time in Germany; squatters and other politically-motivated people on the left were working hard to stem the rising tide of racism and fascism, two ugly movements making a comeback in western Europe. A protestor had been killed in Frankfurt when a police truck carrying a water cannon ran over him. So tensions were running high, and another big protest was brewing.

When we got to the West German side of the border (remember, at that time, Berlin was in the middle of East Germany), we were promptly ordered out of Gertie. "Mach schnell! Mach schnell!" they yelled. Apparently German border guards and cops were on alert for anarchist and leftist troublemakers, and I guess we fit the description. The guards ripped the van apart from top to bottom, looking for weapons, propaganda, and drugs. They even sent in a drug dog. Of course, they found nothing.

By the time we reached the hall in Frankfurt, apprehension filled the air. Jan Berman, Wimpy's girlfriend, was arriving that night, and Dave and Wimpy went to the train station to pick her up. But they couldn't even get close. A riot had broken out between the police and the protestors. Wimpy and Dave did find Jan, almost by accident, and they all made it back to the hall safely. Our show that night had an electric atmosphere.

In Switzerland, we played at the incredible Rotefabrik in Zurich. It was an old factory that had been squatted some years before, and about 700 people turned out for the show.

At every show, during Frightwig's set, a D.O.A. member would fill in for Cecilia on the drums while she came out front and sang one song. While she was singing, Cecilia would make semi-lewd motions with the mike stand, all the while telling the punks in the audience to fuck off. This always got people worked up, in both a good and a bad way, as you can imagine. Sometimes we would have to get her out of trouble, like the night Lester and I chucked out a Dutch fuckwit who was threatening to punch her.

I was the Frightwig drummer for Cecilia's song at the gig in Zurich. The number was going over well, and my buddy Bernard Stippa, who was along as a roadie, was at the side of the stage, grooving along. At some point, though, Cecilia started getting seriously hassled by this Swiss Sid Vicious wannabe and his Nancy Spungen wannabe girlfriend. The geek kept trying to grab the mike, and Cecilia kept telling him to fuck off. She and the geek got into a tug of war with the mike. Then Cecilia let go of it. Wham! It smoked the pinhead right in the schnozz, and his nose started bleeding like fuck. Oh-oh, I thought to myself, here comes trouble. When Sid Junior regained what little sense he had, his girlfriend urged him to get up on stage and even the score. He started to climb up, but Bernard got a running start from the drum riser, and he plowed the geek right in the face. The peabrain went flying ass

over tea kettle about fifteen feet back into the crowd. After that we called Bernard "Bernie, the one-punch German boxing champ."

After four more German shows, we worked our way north to Denmark, playing on a cold day at an outdoor show in Copenhagen for 5,000 Danes. We

Wimpy and Shithead. *photo: Bev Davies*

played at the Ungdomshuset again too. After soundcheck, the people at the venue served us dinner – oatmeal. I was always game for any kind of food, having spent most of my twenties living on potatoes, but Dimwit looked at his bowl of mush with cold contempt. He lit a smoke, then extinguished it in the porridge, leaving the butt sticking out. Lester, rightly so, got pissed off at him. He and Dimwit exchanged some unpleasantries, and the conflict seemed to end there, or so I thought.

After our set was over that night, we went backstage with the crowd yelling for more. But the mood among us was foul. Dave and I were willing to go back out, but Wimpy and Dimwit were not. Lester finally pushed Wimpy, yelling at him, "Get up there and play!" We did play a few songs, but our heart wasn't in it.

The arguing and bitching continued backstage. Finally Lester snapped, "Okay, you guys don't want my opinion? I won't give it to you! From now on, I will only collect the cash and count the beers!" And he meant it. For most of the tour that followed, he would march up to us after a show and say things like "You have 400 Deutschmarks and twenty-seven beers" in a sullen, expressionless manner. In the van, Lester wouldn't say a word or crack a smile; Dave and I tried hard to coax anything out of him, but nothing worked. Lester had come up with an incredible number of good ideas for the band, but now his stubborn streak was getting in the way of that.

The next part of our tour took us to Sweden. One day, we were heading north in the rain on the main highway when the back tire of the truck in front of us threw up a rock. I don't know what kind of cheap glass the Ford Motor Corporation was using over there, but thousands of cracks instantly spread over our windshield. At the time, I was driving, going sixty miles an hour, and I had a one-inch hole to see out of. I managed to get the van off the road without killing us. When we stopped, we knocked the broken glass out. There were no service stations about, so the only thing to do was drive without a windshield until we could find one.

It was late October, and bloody well freezing. Everybody bundled up as much as they could. I put on a toque and a scarf, and wore sunglasses to keep the wind and rain out of my eyes, but I had to take them off about once a minute to wipe them dry on my pants. The highway ran through a lot of little Swedish towns, and every time we came to a stoplight, Laura, Cindy, and I would stand straight up through where the glass used to be and wave at the local yokels. A couple of them were so surprised by this they tripped and fell over on the sidewalk. After 100 kilometers of this fun, we happened upon a Ford dealer that luckily had a replacement windshield in stock.

An English fan named Little Dave had come out to see our show in

Stockholm, and he hitched a ride from there with Frightwig to our next show back in Berlin. It was an arduous journey – 1,200 kilometers of driving plus a bunch of border crossings and a ferry ride. During the trip, Little Dave had an allergy attack, becoming sicker by the minute. It looked very grim for him through the East German corridor, where you weren't allowed to stop. He was in a state of shock by the time Bernard Stippa got him to a hospital in Berlin. Little Dave barely made it, but luckily he pulled through. Little Dave has since become a friend.

Frightwig was ending their part of the tour, so we said goodbye to them in Berlin, and the next day we left for Poland. The Polish promoters had sent a letter giving us permission to play there to the Polish embassy in Bonn, where we picked it up. We were very excited. No punk bands other than our pals Youth Brigade had ever played in the still-communist country. Polish Prime Minister General Jaruzelski had only recently lifted martial law, which had been invoked after the general strike at the end of 1981.

It only took an hour to get to the Polish border. We showed the border guards the carnet (the list of all our equipment and its country of origin) and our letter of permission. They waved us through to a booth, where we were told we needed to show our "papers." I strolled confidently up to the counter, but a frustrating "conversation" ensued, in which neither party understood a single word that was being said. The woman behind the counter was trying to communicate something about a document for the van I was missing, and I kept trying to tell her those were the only documents I had. Both of us got louder and louder.

After about half an hour of this absurd business, somebody came along and told me we needed to buy Polish auto insurance; our U.K. insurance wasn't good enough. It was a scam to get western currency into Poland, just like all the traffic tickets we had been getting in the east. We also had to buy gas coupons at an inflated exchange rate. We did both of these things, then made one more purchase: a bunch of booze to celebrate our entry into a Warsaw Pact country.

We made our way along the highway to Poznan, having a merry old time. We didn't have a show that day, but we did have an appointment to meet our Polish tour manager. Then, without warning, our party was wrecked. The two-lane highway made a sudden jog around some road construction, and Dave missed the turn. We smashed through a wooden barricade, ending up high-centered on a big pile of dirt. The bass guitars and the cymbals slid forward with the impact and nailed Lester and Luxury Bob on the backs of their heads.

Once we'd determined that nobody was seriously injured, we piled out of the van to survey the damage. Gertie's new windshield was cracked, and the hood was badly bent. The wheels were buried in the dirt. We used a cymbal stand and the tire jack to dig the wheels out so we could back up out of the dirt pile. When we were free, we got the fuck out of there.

I took over the driving. Our accident made us wary of the Polish road system, and by now it was dark and foggy. Also, the hood was still damaged, so from time to time it would, without warning, fly open while we were driving at sixty miles per hour. The highway went right through a bunch of little towns, and you had to slow down in a big hurry, which I found out only too quickly. I'd be flying along, then have to slam on the brakes to avoid a horse-drawn coal cart or a drunk staggering along the road.

We finally got into Poznan, but had no clue where we were going; we didn't have the address, just the name of a club. The others were too freaked out to leave the van, so I got out and asked a nearby soldier, but he turned out to be drunk, and he didn't speak a word of English. I could hear some music, though, so I headed off down the street, following my ear. I soon came to the door of an odd nightclub with no sign out front. It was strange. From the foyer, I could see a jazz band; they sounded just like Jan Gabarek on acid. There were two or three shitty little stage lights which gave the band an eerie glow. When I spoke in English to the people at the door, they hailed me like a long-lost comrade. But their behaviour was odd. Someone would go to hand me a drink, then, with some trepidation, pull it back and ask me, "You have ads?"

"What?" I replied.

"You have ads?' they'd repeat.

After three drinks had been pulled back from me, I finally figured out they were asking if I had AIDS. I guess the new media in the east had created the impression that everybody in the west had AIDS, and that you could catch it easily, such as from drinking glasses. Their reactions made the club seem even more surreal.

I finally communicated to them that I was in D.O.A. and I was looking for our tour manager, Wojeck. Ah ha! They said I was in the right place. Somebody led me to the club's office, where they pointed him out. The poor guy was slumped behind the office door, passed out. When they finally roused him, he leapt to his feet and hugged me. Then he grabbed the bottle of vodka he had half-drained while waiting for us and offered me a drink. I told him straight-away that I didn't have AIDS. He looked relieved. Wojeck spoke limited English, so I asked him what the plan was. He insisted we have three or four drinks before discussing it. What could I do but comply?

Quite a period of time had elapsed since I'd left the van, and the others were very glad to see Wojeck and me. We all went back to the club and downed a few turbo colas: Coke or Pepsi and vodka. We stayed in a couple of tiny little apartments that night.

Our four gigs in Poland were all bizarre. We were guided everywhere by our comrade Wojeck, and we were always the only band playing. Shows  with crowds of around 300 people would start at six PM. Audiences didn't know any of our songs, but there were two they related to instantly: one was "Dance o' Death," a song which spoofs televangelism, for which I dressed up like a Catholic priest and gave a "sermon" on stage. In a country of forty million Catholics, that was bound to be fascinating. The other song they really got into was "General Strike," which had been partly inspired by the general strike in Poland in 1981. After a show, everybody knew those two English words.

Shithead delivers his "sermon."

Poland was an interesting country, and we found the people very resilient. Their unfortunate lot in history was to be geographically situated between Germany and Russia. That had meant a lot of fucking armies going back and forth. Under the communist regime, a huge portion of the economy was underground or "black market." The store shelves were bare, but if you asked the right person they could get you whatever you wanted. The petrol lineups were a mile long, so Wojeck made an "arrangement" for us in Warsaw: a guy drove up with a huge gerrycan of gasoline and filled up most of our tank for cash.

Lineups were a central feature of Polish life. In a grocery store, there were different lineups for each category of food: bread, meat, cheese. To us spoiled North Americans, the quality was generally poor and the selection terrible. One thing we never saw readily for sale was beer, and a person can only drink so much vodka. But one day Laura and I saw some little brown bottles behind the counter in a store. I kept gesturing until the shopkeeper sold them to us.

I cracked one of those babies open as soon as we got outside. Blaah! It didn't taste like beer. Laura took a sip, and she wasn't sure if it was beer either. Wojeck was more enthusiastic. "Oh good! Thank you very much. Polish beer." He happily glugged down the rest of the six-pack as we drove to the next town.

Because of the fucked-up Eastern monetary system, the money we got paid for each show was really hard to spend. We were impressed when Lester told us we were making 25,000 zlotys a gig. It didn't matter when it turned out to be only US$25. We would usually end up at a nice restaurant and spend our Polish money there. We all bought a few souvenirs and Dimwit bought, for twelve dollars, a trumpet that would have cost three or four hundred dollars in Canada.

On our last day in the country, I met up with the musicians from Dezerter, one of the best bands ever to come out of Poland. They played punk, but always put some inventive twists into their songs. A couple of years earlier, Dezerter had put out a 7-inch single that sold close to 50,000 copies in Poland. But after martial law was imposed, it became increasingly difficult for them, or any other bands with political lyrics, to release anything. I agreed to take some cassette tapes of theirs back to Canada and produce a new album for them. Later, Tim Yohannon, of *Maximum Rock 'n' Roll* fanzine, agreed to bring out a Dezerter album on their label, as long as I got all the lyrics translated into English. Finally, I found somebody who could do it, and Cecil English and I went into Profile Studios to put together an album. I am proud of the project, and it was well worth the effort. Incidentally, Dezerter is still going strong. In 1998, we played with them in Poznan; it was D.O.A.'s twentieth anniversary and Dezerter's fifteenth.

We had a couple more shows in Germany following our trip to Poland. On the way there, we took a tour of the death camp, Auschwitz. It was a sobering experince. The level of cruelty and the complicity of those involved should never be tolerated on this earth. I have never heard anything so quiet as our group when we left Auschwitz. There was total silence in the van. I am glad I saw it for myself.

During this time, Gertie had been running very poorly, and we deduced that the van was running on two cylinders, not four. As we left Germany and were climbing up through the Alps on our way to Italy, I got Dave to stop at a gas station for some beer. When we piled back into the van, only 100 meters from the border, Gertie didn't have enough power to get up the hill. Dave stayed behind the wheel while the other seven of us got out and pushed the van all the way to the Austrian border.

We got Gertie out of the Alps and onto the northern plain of Italy, around Milan. The van wasn't running well, but at least it was moving. We stopped for lunch at an Italian truck stop. These are some of the best in the world, very quick food and great coffee. Laura and I bought some olives, a bottle of Chianti, and a Tom Jones cassette! As Gertie got rolling again, we put in the cassette and everybody started drinking vino and singing along. I know Tom

Jones is Welsh, but somehow he helped to make the trip all the more Italian.

In Pisa, we met up with Antonio from the Cheetah Chrome Motherfuckers, who got Gertie into a garage for repair. The news was bad; we had blown the top of the engine, and it was a miracle we hadn't ended up stranded on the highway somewhere. To make matters worse, the parts had to be ordered from England, and they would take a fucking week to get there! The Italian and French parts of our tour would be over by then, but if we didn't get the van fixed, our entire investment would be down the drain.

We had some time to kill, so we took a tour of the Leaning Tower of Pisa. What an incredible sight. We looked around the tower at the surrounding scenery for a while and Dave launched a mini-parachute man off the top. We were headed down when we came across Dimwit on the outer deck, on his hands and knees. There were no hand rails there, and he had a look of sheer terror in his eyes. We got him to his feet and helped him get down.

With the van in the garage, the tour had to be conducted by train. We took guitars and a change of clothing. We soon discovered a problem, though – we usually had three or four connections to make each day, and the Italian trains were never quite on time. So we almost never made it to a venue before ten PM. We would be absolutely starving by then, but there was no time to eat before we rushed on stage. After each show there would be a prolonged discussion among the organizers of the shows about where they shoud take us to eat and how the D.O.A. group would be housed for the night. These discussions could take up to an hour and a half. We would just sit there on our guitar cases drinking wine on empty stomachs.

Our show in Allassio, on the Italian Riviera, was a sad time for Laura and me. She was leaving again; this time she and Cindy were heading down to Greece to stay with a friend for a few months. The show itself was bizarre. It was held in a huge carnival-type tent that could hold about 1,000 people, but at soundcheck we discovered the amps they had for Dave and me were tiny. Our guitars that night must have sounded like mosquitoes buzzing around under the big top. Then about 200 policemen arrived and stood shoulder to shoulder around the perimeter of the tent. It sure made for an intimidating atmosphere, but we had a hard time not laughing at their uniforms, which made them look as if they were really in the circus.

We missed our first show in France, in Clermont-Ferrand. The train connections just didn't get us there in time. The promoters were angry. Then our next show, in Grenoble, was wrecked by some brainless French skinheads. From there we took a fast train to Paris. All we saw of the city was the Metro. The Paris promoters, Mickey and Valerie, got us to jump the turnstiles with our guitars to save the fare.

175 I The Endless Tour, Part Two

The funniest part of our French adventure was when Wimpy left an expensive borrowed sleeping bag on the fast train from Paris to Dijon. He couldn't decide if he should get back on the train to retrieve the sleeping bag and risk getting whisked away to the next town, or just forget about it. He was hopping back and forth between the train and the platform like a chicken. I think it's called the "I'm a little drunk and I don't know what the fuck to do at the French train station" dance. The train roared away with the bag.

The show in Dijon was marred by skinheads as well. Just as we were starting to play, Luxury Bob told off a couple of them he saw pissing in the corner of the club. The same geeks came up to the stage and started kicking Luxury as hard as they could. I cuffed one of them in the head, and they backed off when we threatened to shit-kick them. We put Luxury back near Dimwit for protection.

The French part of the tour was over when we got word that Gertie had been repaired. Lester had left by then, and the rest of us split up. Hutch, Luxury Bob, and Wimpy took a train to Aachen to stay with our German tour managers for a few days. Dave, Dimwit, and I took the train to Pisa.

We picked up the van and started driving north to Aachen. Everything was cool until we reached the Italian/Swiss border. Then we got in some real shit. Whenever we crossed a border, we had to show our carnet, the small book listing the band's gear. With this, the border guards could make sure you entered and exited the country with the same stuff, and had not sold anything. We had given the guitars, the snare drum, and the cymbals to the other guys to take to Aachen, so I had gotten our friend Antonio to write us a note in Italian that would explain the situation to the fascists at the border.

It took six different border guards before one of them finally understood. Even then, he had to take me and the carnet to the "big bossio" of the frontier. The big jerk blew his top. He got up from his desk and screamed first at me and then individually at each of his six subordinates who were standing there. He pounded his fist on the table and repeatedly slapped down the carnet. He acted like we had been pissing all over the Sistine Chapel. After about an hour of this, they fined us some lire and let us go.

We were braced for more trouble when we got to the Swiss border, but the guard there stamped the carnet after half a minute and then told us to enjoy our journey. *Arrivederci*, baby!

Our show at the AJZ in Bielefeld was the last gig scheduled in Europe. The show went very well, but the next morning when Bob went to bring the van into the inner courtyard of the squat, he couldn't get it started. A mechanic told us the motor was kaput. This time we had thrown a rod. Fuck!

That mechanic in Pisa isn't on my Christmas card list anymore. Fortunately, we were saved by a Scotsman named Eric, who drove us back to London in a rental van. Bill Gilliam later arranged for a flatbed truck to bring Gertie back to London. I guess he wanted to give her a decent English burial.

Our friend Todd picked us up at JFK Airport in New York City. Our vehicles were jinxed that year. We discovered the Blue Bullet was also running very poorly, and we had to call AAA just to get out of the city. The officials at the Canadian border went nuts on us. They didn't believe the prices we told them we'd paid for the Marshall amps or for Dimwit's trumpet. Next, they landed on the Alternative Tentacles mail order catalogues that came inside our LPs. "Are you sure this isn't obscene material?" accused one of the fuckwit guards, having looked at song and album titles like "Cruxifucks," "Too Drunk to Fuck," and "Let's Fuck." I told him he was missing the artistic point of it all. Then the head cheese called Hutch and me into his office. He had a sly look on his puffy face as he fingered a small leather elephant that Hutch had purchased. "What have we here?" he asked with great excitement. He squeezed the elephant, and as he did some of the dark-brown contents squeezed out between the stitches. "Aha! What's this?"

"It looks like a seed," I said.

The head cheese took out his knife and cut it in half, then smelled it. Yep! It was just a harmless seed. He looked disappointed, and they finally let us go. Welcome back to Canada.

We played a show in Ottawa, then set out for Quebec City. About ten miles out of Ottawa, we heard a big bang from the Blue Bullet's engine. Things then got very quiet, with the van rolling along on momentum. Dave pulled it over to the side. The Blue Bullet was dead! We got a tow truck and took it back into Ottawa, where we left it at a garage. We did some quick calculations and decided to play just enough shows to get us back to Vancouver. We rented a van and played the shows we'd booked in Quebec and Montreal. We also had a good show at Bullwinkle's in London, Ontario. The support there was great, October Crisis and Idiot Savant.

The Endless Tour was over. We had played 132 shows in 105 different cities in thirteen countries on different continents. We'd covered 63,000 miles, about two-and-a-half times the circumference of the earth. We'd gotten our asses kicked a few times, but we'd done most of the ass-kicking. And we'd had a gas.

CHAPTER THIRTEEN

TO HELL 'N' BACK

We put our gear into a container at the airport in Toronto. It went home and so did we. We'd been travelling for most of the year, but thanks to ticket costs, vehicle rentals, and blowing up two different vans, we were broke! A quick jaunt to California gave us a little bit of dough. Laura and Cindy arrived home from Greece on Christmas Day after a fog-delayed landing. We had a great reunion. Shortly after that, I moved out of the Plaza, and Laura and I rented a place in East Vancouver. It was a good change.

D.O.A had a couple of things going on. "General Strike" was released on a U.K. compilation called *We Won't Be Your Fucking Poor*. A video called *The Warrior* had resulted from a show we'd played at the Stone in San Francisco in 1985. Lester was quite busy, so we started working with Cattle Prod Productions, run by Mark Smith and Jay Scott. But we had no new record coming out, and we wanted to get something happening. We popped into Profile Studios to do a demo. We were seeking a new label. Alternative Tentacles had been good to us over the preceding four years, but there were forces in and around the band that felt we should be looking to hit a grand slam with a bigger record company. Looking back now, I think that was a foolish philosophy. But the demo at Profile would mark a major change in our recording life. It was the first D.O.A. session with Cecil English, a great guy and a fine producer. Over the next fifteen years, Profile would become a home away from home for the band. D.O.A. would record seven albums there, five of them produced by Cecil.

Mark and Jay booked us a hellaciously cold tour of the Prairies at the end of February of 1986. It looked like a trip that would make us some dough, but at our final rehearsal the night before, Dimwit announced he was leaving D.O.A. Thanks for the advance warning, we grumbled. Dimwit made us an offer: if we paid him $700, he would do the trip. Dave was incensed at this kind of blackmail, and Wimpy and I weren't too happy either. But we agreed to Dimwit's demand. We rented a truck for the ten-day trip, and we made enough to pay our bills and Dimwit. It was a rotten ending to a long partnership, but we should have seen it coming. The tension and endless travel of the previous year had taken its toll.

We had gone through two of Canada's best drummers, Biscuits and Dimwit, and now we needed a new person in that spot. We tried out a kid named Kerr Belliveau, but that only lasted about three weeks.

In the meantime, a big thing was looming on the British Columbia political scene. Bill Bennett's Social Credit government and the city of Vancouver were hosting a world's fair called Expo 86. They were full of bullshit about how it "would put Vancouver on the map and make us a world-class city." One fact they downplayed was how many people would be evicted to make room for the tourists flooding into town. Expo 86 was adjacent to Vancouver's Downtown Eastside; the hotels there had become like rooming houses for poor, elderly, and disabled people. Some of them had been there since the end of the Second World War.

The hotel owners saw a chance to do surface renovations and make a quick buck, and they kicked out many of these long-term residents. Hundreds of people were evicted. Finally the breaking point came: eighty-seven-year-old Olaf Solhiem, a forty-year resident of the old Patricia Hotel on Hastings Street, died after being evicted. The news hit the people of the city hard. Olaf had been disabled in his youth in a mine blast; he had given all he could to Canada, and his eviction notice was the thanks he got.

Lester came up with another of his good plans in response to all of this dirty dealing, a crisis EP called "Expo Hurts Everyone." The D.O.A. track was "Billy and the Socreds," a reworked version of Credence Clearwater Revival's "Willy and the Poorboys." Also on the 7-inch EP was "Tyrannosaurus Rex" by Rythm Activism, "Sha La La La La" by Mecca Normal, and "The Old Mangled Man" by Stu Leal, all excellent Vancouver musicians. Dave Lester whipped up a cover for the project in no time flat. The benefit single was distributed throughout B.C. by Sudden Death Records and friends, and helped keep the heat on the Social Credit government.

We were still looking for a drummer when we heard that Jon Card,

formerly of Personality Crisis and SNFU, had moved to Vancouver from Edmonton. He'd often eaten and drunk us out of house and home at the Plaza in the early eighties. We asked Jon if he wanted to play drums for us, and it was a go. As the years went by, he joined the Montgomery brothers as one of the great drummers of D.O.A.

Around that time we were approached about doing a benefit in Lillooet, in B.C.'s southern interior. Near there lay the last unlogged watershed in the region, the Stein Valley. The show was scheduled for May 17 at the old Lillooet high school gym. We arranged for Greg "Two Shirts" Hathaway, from Roots Round Up, Rhythm Activism, and Mecca Normal to play as well. Rhythm Activism was a highly political, experimental duo featuring Norman Nawrocki and Sylvain Cote. Mecca Normal was another great experimental duo made up of Jean Smith and Dave Lester (who had designed a bunch of D.O.A. record covers). Hathaway had a solid, rootsy guitar sound.

We didn't have instructions about where the gym was, but we figured it would be pretty easy to find in such a small town. The first thing saw as we pulled into Lillooet was a line of logging trucks that stretched as far as the eye could see. Some were loaded with dead trees, and many of them were decorated with big signs like "Save Our Jobs," "Log the Stein," and "Loggers Unite." I spotted one sign that looked progressive, until I read the fine print. The big letters said "Earth First," but the smaller ones read, "Log the other planets later!"

I'm no Sherlock Holmes, but I could tell we were in for trouble that night. We could see the high school from where we were, but the road to get there was fucked up with construction. We stopped to get directions. Jeff Dixon, our roadie, and I hopped out of the truck, and immediately four loggers made a beeline for us. Before I could say, "Excuse me," one of them jeered, "This must be the fucking band nobody in town wants to play tonight." Another one of the rednecks spoke up. "Let's send these turkeys back to Expoland." Jeff and I looked at each other, wordlessly endorsing the axiom, "He who knows when to get away, lives to fight another day." We thanked our kind hosts, hopped back in the truck, and drove off.

We got down to the gym all right, and there we met the ecology-minded

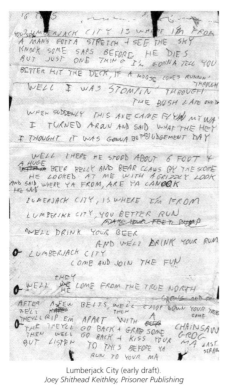

'6 '5
YOU3+ LUMBERJACK CITY IS WHAT I'M FROM
A MAN'S GOTTA STRETCH + SEE THE SKY
KNOCK SOME SAPS BEFORE HE DIES
BUT JUST ONE THING I'M GONNA TELL YOU
BETTER HIT THE DECK, IF A MOOSE COMES RUNNIN
                                    THROUGH
WELL I WAS STOMPIN THROUGH
                THE BUSH I ATE OWL
WHEN SUDDENLY THIS AXE CAME FLYIN MY WAY
I TURNED AROW AND SAID WHAT THE HEY
I THOUGHT IT WAS GONNA BE THE JUDGEMENT DAY

WELL THERE HE STOOD ABOUT 6 FOOT 4
A HUGE
BEER BELLY AND BEAR CLAWS BY THE SCORE
HE LOOKED AT ME WITH A GRIZZLY LOOK
AND SAID WHERE YA FROM, ARE YA CANOOK
HE SAID
LUMBERJACK CITY, IS WHERE I'M FROM
LUMBERJACK CITY, YOU BETTER RUN
          DANGE YOUR FEET TO PUMP
WELL DRINK YOUR BEER
          AND WELL DRINK YOUR RUM
LUMBERJACK CITY
          COME AND JOIN THE FUN
          THEY
WELL WE COME FROM THE TRUE NORTH
          STRONG AND COL
AFTER A FEW BELTS, WE'LL CHOP DOWN YOUR TREE
WELL HACKED   THEM   SOME
THEY'LL RIP EM APART WITH A
THE THEY'LL GO BACK + GRAB SOME CHAINSAW
THEN WELL GO BACK + KISS YOUR GROG MA LAST
BUT LISTEN TO THIS BEFORE YA   STRAW
          RUN TO YOUR MA

Lumberjack City (early draft).
Joey Shithead Keithley, Prisoner Publishing

side of the local population. As we were doing our soundcheck, I got a call from a Vancouver TV reporter who'd heard there was going to be trouble at the concert that night.

In the end, the loggers never showed. But what they did do was stop a lot of kids from coming to the concert. The loggers' argument was, "These punks and hippies are taking food off our tables by jeopardizing our jobs." Having grown up in a resource-based economy like British Columbia's, I didn't have anything against the loggers, and I would never want them not to have jobs. But we can only gouge the earth for so long before it starts gouging us back. After the concert, all the bands went to one of the organizer's backwoods property and had a hootenanny. Laura and I pitched a tent in the woods, confident the bears would be frightened off by all the bloody noise the motley crew of punks and hippies were making.

As a footnote, I've said this before and I'll say it again: many things in life have to do with timing. In 1986, a bunch of redneck loggers wanted to kill us. The next year, the Stein Valley became a *cause celebre*. Some high-powered show-biz and eco types got John Denver to come up and play a big "Save the Stein" concert. They did this two years in a row, and eventually most of the logging was stopped, with the help of the local First Nations people. In any war, somebody's got to go out and make the initial charge. D.O.A. was cannon fodder more than once over the years.

Folk singers Pete Seeger and Arlo Guthrie had been hired by Expo 86 to do a concert, and some people from the Vancouver Downtown Eastside Residents Association (DERA) contacted the musicians and asked them to do a benefit concert for the people being evicted from the area. They agreed. Jim Green, the head of DERA, asked if D.O.A. wanted to open the show. Open a show for one of my idols, Pete Seeger? We jumped at the chance. Arlo Guthrie was cool in his own right, but he was also the son of one of America's two greatest lyricists, the immortal Woody Guthrie. (The other being Bob Dylan, of course.)

It wasn't quite that simple, however. The Vancouver Parks Board objected to D.O.A. playing the benefit concert, which would be held at Malkin Bowl in Stanley Park. Their peabrained rationale was that our music would scare the animals in the nearby zoo, and that D.O.A.'s fans would run amuck and trample the park's flowerbeds to death. Jim Green stuck up for us, and a compromise was reached. Jon could bring his drum kit and Wimpy his electric bass, but Dave and I would play acoustic guitars. This was definitely a first for D.O.A.

Pete Seeger and Shithead, 1986.

Ten thousand people showed up for the concert. The highlight of our short set was "Billy and the Socreds." The crowd just howled and cheered and sang along. I never did hear if the animals got upset, and the flowerbeds still looked okay when we left the stage. Seeger and Guthrie turned in a whale of a performance that was charged with emotion. Pete said afterwards that he'd liked our set. I met him again eleven years later and was amazed to find he

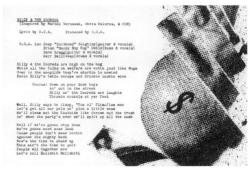

remembered D.O.A. and the show that day. The concert in Stanley Park was free, but the organizers raised over $10,000 by passing the hat. The money went directly to the Expo evictees.

We were still looking for a record deal, and Lester had managed to get us booked into the New Music Seminar, an influential music convention in New York City. It was a big deal to play there at the time, especially for unsigned artists. As a lead-up to the convention, Lester, Mark Smith, and Jay Scott booked us the "To Hell 'n' Back" tour, named from the title of a song I had recently written. As support, we brought along No Means No from Victoria. We didn't know it yet, but they would become one of the best bands ever to come out of Canada.

We played a bunch of shows through the midwest, working our way eastward. On July 13, we played a big show at City Gardens, in Trenton, New Jersey, with MDC, Corrosion of Conformity, and No Means No. The old City Gardens was in a trashy area of a trashy town, but the shows there were usually solid.

Twenty-five hundred people turned out for a show the following night at the Ritz in New York as part of the New Music Seminar. D.O.A. and No Means No played with Celtic Frost, Red Cross, and Danzig. Chuck Biscuits was now drumming for Danzig, so it was cool to see him. He had altered his style since he'd left D.O.A.; gone were the Keith Moon rolls. But he was still incredibly powerful.

After that show, we signed a five-record deal with Profile Records in New York (no connection to Profile Studios in Vancouver). Chris Williamson, who had promoted some of our shows in New York, had a sub label with Profile called Rock Hotel Records. Our label-mates included the Cromags, the Nils, and Peter and the Test Tube Babies, among others. Unfortunately, signing that deal would turn out to be a bad move.

The next day, however, I did the smartest thing I've ever done in my life. I phoned home and asked Laura to marry me. She wanted to think it over, so I called her twenty-four hours later from a laundromat in Washington, D.C. Laura said yes, making me a very happy man. Dave and Hutch went to the liquor store next door and came back with some room-temperature almond champagne, an awful concoction that was a far cry from the fancy French stuff. Dave popped the cork and we all had some out of plastic cups he had procured.

We hit Philadelphia, Richmond, and Raleigh on our way south, then arrived in Atlanta. We were booked into a joint called the Metroplex. The club had a big hole in the ceiling, so rain would pour straight down onto the dance floor. A smashed-up building across the street was inhabited by Nazi skinheads. Not a very pleasant venue, all in all. Following that, it was Newport, Kentucky; Columbus, Missouri; and Kansas City.

Just outside of Lawrence, Kansas, we appeared at the Outhouse, in what became the most famous rock 'n'roll cornfield in North America. We had joined up with CCM, the great Italian hardcore band, for a bunch of shows. A map took us to this cinderblock building sitting all by its lonesome in the middle of a hot, dry cornfield. We were bewildered. "Man, the show can't be here," someone said.

But that was the place, all right. We had to quickly put on some insect repellant, since the skeeters and the chiggers were ready to eat us alive. This further added to the smell of the combined entourage of D.O.A. and No Means No; we called ourselves the "Dirty Dozen" (Canadian version).

A ton of people showed up, and we would play the Outhouse a few more times over the years. There were two great things about the venue: there were no neighbours to be bothered by noise, and you couldn't wreck the place since it was made of concrete blocks. Hutch said there should be a series of these kinds of places opened up across the land, so that the youth of North America could have a good time wherever they lived.

That night we made the long drive to Denver. Denver is like the western crossroads of the U.S., the end of the great plains and the start of the magnificent Rocky Mountains. It's always been a jumping-off point for those people fleeing the east, everyone from wagon-train riders to Jack Kerouac's Beat generation.

Denver does attract all types of people, though, as we would discover that night. We were playing at a rundown theatre in Five Points, one of the city's roughest neighbourhoods. About 400 kids showed up, and the gig was rocking. There was an orchestra pit right in front of the stage left over from the days of silent films.

However, before long, a bunch of racist skinheads showed up. Not all skinheads are racist – some of them are totally cool – but these skinheads were far from it. Their *modus operandi* was to get down into the orchestra pit and gang up on people, really roughing them up. It was sickening. I asked these guys a few times to cool it, but they were oblivious. Our music was never meant to be a backdrop for senseless violence, so I finally stopped the show.

I asked the Denver audience if they wanted to be pushed around by these bullies all year round. The crowd started yelling at the skinheads. I also pointed out that the racist gang consisted of fifteen people, and there were about 385 other people there who weren't part of it.

"You punks have pretty good odds on getting the better of these racists!" I said.

Dave burns his guitar in San Francisco, 1986. *photo: Bev Davies*

The crowd got louder and angrier, and the skinheads realized they were surrounded. Their biggest guy and obvious leader started making his way through the orchestra pit towards me. I leaned down to try to talk some sense to him, putting my hand on his shoulder in a peacemaking gesture. Fearful, he pulled back. I caught his muscle-shirt in my hand, and it ripped right off his back. Without thinking, I held the shirt up for all he crowd to see! The crowd cheered. The skinheads were furious. After giving us the Nazi salute, they made a beeline for the exit. A couple of locals told me after the show that the head skinhead had been planning to come back and stab me, but he and his gang had been arrested for giving the guff to some African-American cops out front of the theatre.

We wound up the tour shortly after that and headed home. Our press release announcing the deal with Profile Records got a fair bit of ink. We went back into the studio to record the first album. We'd decided to title it *True (North) Strong and Free*. The word "north" was really small on the cover, so the label pitched it as *True Strong and Free*. It was produced by D.O.A. and Cecil English at Vancouver's Profile Studios. We recorded ten songs that Wimpy and I had recently written. We used Dimwit's drum track for "None But the Brave" and Kerr Belliveau's tracks for "To Hell 'n' Back" and "Power Play." Jon Card drummed on the rest of the songs. Content-wise, it was the most Canadian album we had ever done, but the funny thing was the record was never released in Canada, as Profile Records in the U.S. either couldn't, or wouldn't, make a deal with a Canadian label.

The buzz was growing about our session and the record deal. I got a call at home one day, and the guy on the other end of the line said he was Randy Bachman and that he wanted to come out and jam with D.O.A. "Who is this really?" I said.

"It's Randy Bachman!" the guy replied.

"Fuck off!" I shot back. "Who is this really?" After a few minutes of

this, I was convinced: it was Randy Bachman of the legendary Bachman Turner Overdrive (BTO and the Guess Who). I was stunned to hear what he had to say. He'd been told we were recording his song "Takin' Care of Business" for the album, and he wanted to jam it with us. Naturally, I said

D.O.A. and Randy Bachman take care of business in Vancouver, 1986.

sure! It's not every day that a rock legend calls you up and asks to jam! We agreed he'd join us for an all-ages gig at a Vancouver club called the Edge.

The big day arrived. A new band started by Paul McKenzie, the Guttersnypes, played, and Greg Hathaway opened the show. Bachman was there with his guitar. When our encore came, we got him up to join us and it was smokin'. No wonder. Bachman has been a great guitar player ever since his early days in the Guess Who.

Soon afterwards, we embarked on a cross-Canada tour as early promotion for *True Strong and Free*. Our show in Hamilton was at a dumpy joint named Chuggie's. Problem Child, the opening band, used some colourful language during their set; a "fuck" here, a "shit" there. Reasonable in my books, but the woman who owned the bar came up to me and said, "Isn't that language disgusting?"

"What's disgusting?" I said. "These guys are good!"

"The language they're using!" she said. "That's what's disgusting! D.O.A. isn't like that, is it?"

"Oh no!" I replied. "Of course not!" She knew fuck-all about punk rock, that's for sure.

My usual stage patter employed colourful language as well, in addition to our usual complement of songs like "Fuck You" and "Fucked Up Ronnie." When I went to get paid after the show, the bar owner was seething. She lectured me for about ten minutes, holding the filthy lucre just out of reach, until she finally relented and paid us.

While we were in Ontario, I got some shocking news – Laura was pregnant. I wasn't too supportive initially – too scared, I guess – but I called her back after a bit and told her that I thought it was good. It's not for everybody, I know, but I think kids are great.

At that time, there was a massive worldwide effort underway to force

Drug review • Lesser's love • The Nails • Fashion

NOW

free

DOA drives
hardcore home

the racist South African government to free Nelson Mandela and end apartheid. The movement was gathering momentum, but there was still much suffering in the black townships. When we were approached to play a benefit for OXFAM in Vancouver, with the money going directly to the purchase of an ambulance in South Africa, we were honoured to play. It was an eclectic bill, with Death Sentence, Randy Bachman and Denise McCann, 54-40, and D.O.A. The benefit raised $10,000.

The big day in Laura's and my life was fast approaching. We were set to be married on November 29. The night before, our friends arranged a "roast" for us at the Smilin' Buddha. The list of speakers included Buck Cherry from the Modernettes, Les Wiseman from *Vancouver Magazine*, Scary Failure, and Ken Lester. The gang from Reno had brought a case of the same brand of almond champagne we'd drunk in Washington when I told the band Laura had accepted my proposal. At the end of the evening, Dave Gregg brought out a special gift everybody had chipped in for: a guitar with the body made from a toilet seat! I gratefully accepted it, with a few tears in my eyes. (I

used this guitar onstage while playing "Great Balls of Shit." It worked fairly well.)

Laura and I got married at the hall in Confederation Park in North Burnaby, the park where I had learned to play lacrosse as a kid. It was a civil ceremony,

Shithead holds up his toilet seat guitar at his and Laura's pre-wedding roast at the Smiling Buddha, 1986. *photo: Bev Davies* since neither of us believe in God, and afterwards the two of us danced to John Lennon's version of "Stand By Me." Dave Gregg's band, the Grooveaholics, featuring Dave, Jon Card, and Ron Allan, with Ian Tiles as master of ceremonies, were on for the rest of the evening. I got up with the band and sang Johnny Cash's "Ring of Fire" for Laura.

Time was moving on, and we were all changing as individuals, including those in and close to D.O.A. Hey, that's cool. It's inevitable. To me, we were living up to the phrase "to hell 'n' back." D.O.A. could take on any kind of adversity, conquer it, and adapt it to suit our own purposes. Anybody can, if they use their spirit and mind in a strong and positive way.

We're Drivin' to Hell n' Back

we drive at night, drive at night,
go right past you and clean out of sight
take the dark passage through the empty night,
hit the highway with all of our might
like a freight train rollin' down the track,
we'll knock you right over
and give you a whack
yeah, we're drivin' to hell n' back

like a war, like a war,
gotta push ahead like we done it before
you know the count and we know the score,
yeah, gettin' ready for the fun in store
I got no time to get unpacked,
gimme some room, gimme some slack
yeah we're drivin' to hell n' back

yeah we're drivin', yeah we're drivin',
keep on drivin' to hell n' back

push it to the limit, push it to the limit,
it's a new frontier, can't wait a minute
I got some room, I gotta admit,
so climb on board and get on it
if your holdin' back and things are black,
it must be time to lose the pack
yeah we're drivin' to hell n' back

drive at night, drive at night,
blast right past ya an' clear outta sight
take the dark passage through the empty night,
hit the highway with all of your might
ain't stickin' around to catch no flak,
from a losin' proposition
that's beginnin' to crack
[famous shithead jowl shake]
yeah we're drivin' to hell n' back

Joey Shithead Keithley, Falling Apart Songs

Dave parodies Dylan. *photos: Iain Ross*

CHAPTER FOURTEEN

TRUE STRONG AND FREE

At the beginning of 1987, we got rid of the old Iron Lung van that we had bought off Shanghai Dog the previous year. Good riddance to bad rubbish. We bought a school bus for $3,000. Dave and a couple of buddies painted the thing red. It looked sharp. There was a sign above the hood, the kind long-haul truckers put on their rigs, that read "Miss Piggy." I can't remember how it got there, but we were soon to find out it was a prophetic warning. It was another rock 'n' roll lesson we learned the hard way: DON'T TOUR AROUND IN OLD SCHOOL BUSES. THE SCHOOL DISTRICT HAS SOLD THEM OFF BECAUSE THEY ARE UNRELIABLE HUNKS OF SHIT.

Rock Hotel/Profile Records were set to release *True Strong and Free*, and a good tour had been organized to promote it. This was also the first D.O.A. release to come out as a compact disc. But still another rock 'n' roll lesson awaited us. Record companies are eager to do promotional work when a record first comes out, but MOST FUCKING RECORD COMPANIES ARE FUCKING LAZY; THEY WILL NOT FOLLOW UP AND WILL DO SWEET FUCK ALL, SIX MONTHS AFTER THE RECORD HAS BEEN RELEASED. It was D.O.A.'s fate to learn that lesson over and over again.

We set out in early March for a fifty-five-day tour of the U.S. that we called the "True North Strong and Free Crusade." Our pal Iain Ross, who played in Curious George, made us some T-shirts before we left. Featured on the front was a big red school bus; the back showed the bus in flames. (Another warning we ignored.) The crew this time was big. Mike Lambert from Winnipeg was road managing, Chris Crud was our roadie, Hutch was still mixing, and Tony, a buddy of ours from Vancouver, made his first and only trip with D.O.A. as the merch guy.

We had our first problem with Miss Piggy only 400 miles from home. The bus broke down in front of a convenience store in a little hick town in Idaho. Mike Lambert raised the hood to start working on it, and before long three cop cars pulled up. Five cops jumped out, a couple of them with their guns drawn. They rounded us up and told us to put our hands in the air. They'd received a call that we were trying to rob the convenience store. What a well-planned robbery that would be; we had the world's slowest getaway vehicle, and it was broken down, to boot. We explained all this to the cops. They calmed down and put their guns away. There was only one problem, though. Card had gotten really drunk that day, and now he started pulling a routine, saying stuff like, "What right do you have to hold us up like this? We have work permits." Sheer stupidity. So the cops decided to search the bus, probably figuring they'd find some drugs. When the first guy inside saw the big cloth rendition of Elvis we had hanging behind the driver's seat, though, he called off the search. I've got to thank the King. The King lives! Dave got really pissed off at Card and castigated him sharply. Card, never one to back down, told Dave to "eat shit!" The two of them didn't speak to each other again for the rest of the tour.

It was a long drive cross-country to Rhode Island, where the tour was scheduled to start at the Living Room in Providence.

At soundcheck in Providence, I pulled out my new favourite guitar. It was one of the first Les Paul Juniors ever made, a rare TV model. I tuned it up and put it back in its case. But when we started the set that night, my first chord sounded like the strangest jazz chord ever. I grabbed my other guitar and the rest of the set went fine. After the show, I checked the Les Paul to see what had happened. Apparently the cold and moisture in the equipment bay of the bus had caused the glue that held the fret board onto the neck to come almost completely unstuck. I had never seen anything like it.

The next day we went to the Profile Records office in New York. They had a pile of telephone interviews lined up across the country. We did so many of them, I was hoarse the next day. As Dave and I were leaving the office, Dee Dee Ramone came in. Dave and I re-introduced ourselves – we had played four shows with the Ramones earlier in the decade, but we did not expect him to remember us. We asked him what he was up to and he said, "I got this new record, man! This new rap record called *Funky Man*. It's going good. Yeah, I'm here to promote it, man." I said that's cool, then I asked him what was happening with the Ramones. He replied, "I got this new record, man. It's a rap record. I'm here to promote this new rap record, man." Dave said that's cool. We tried some more small talk and we got the same reply about three more times. Dave and I looked at each other and shook our heads, then headed down the stairs to the street. Little did we know that later that year, MTV would name Dee Dee's single and D.O.A.'s "Dance o' Death" as the two worst rap videos of the year. Cool!

In New York we headlined a show at the Ritz with the Descendants and Firehose, the band that was born out of the great Minutemen. The tour took us around the midwest, then down south. We ended up at the Metroplex in Atlanta again. This time, the support was the Melvins and Frightwig. That show was highlighted when Frightwig got locked in their van, and five or six skinheads tried to flip it over by rocking it from side to side. They were trapped inside, screaming. Card noticed what was going on, came and grabbed a bunch of us, and we put the assholes to flight. Years later we were back in Atlanta and it was the old 688 Club, run by a shirtless, fucked-up cocaine dealer with a handgun in the waistband of his pants. He spent the evening running around the club and not making a lot of sense. Weird town, Atlanta.

We played two shows at the Cameo Theatre in Miami. The afternoon before our first show, a kid got stabbed at a rap show matinee at the Cameo. The cops wanted to cancel the D.O.A. show because of that, but said they would let the show go on if the promoter paid $120 for two Miami cops to do security. The promoter said it was extortion and he would rather cancel. That would have been fine for him, but we had driven a really long way to get there, so D.O.A. paid the $120 and the show went on.

Back on the road, Dave, who drove half the time, insisted on playing two Madonna tapes he had over and over again. This drove everybody else completely nuts as we gigged our way across the south to Texas. In Dallas, we parked the bus in front of the Theatre Gallery to catch some zzzs before the show. All of a sudden a bunch of racist assholes showed up and started preaching from their version of Hitler's handbook to the waiting crowd, talking about how immigrants were taking the jobs and were out to destroy the American way of life. During the show later, the same racist rednecks were on the dance floor sucker punching people and generally being jerks. I decided to dedicate "Fuck You" to them. The whole crowd stopped dancing. While singing, I made sure that they knew every "fuck you" was for them. The biggest guy, their leader, came towards the stage, followed by his minions. He grabbed my mike and tried to shove it through my teeth as I swung my old 1972 SG guitar and nailed the asshole in the side of the head,

snapping the neck of the guitar. The guy obviously had a hard head. He backed off and challenged us to the floor for a fight. In turn, I challenged his gang to come up on stage. By this point, I was holding my mike stand with the heavy base up, ready to decapitate the

Shithead, 1988. *photo: Villiam*

geek. Jon, Wimpy, Dave, and Luxury Bob were also armed with cymbal stands, guitars, and mike stands. It was a standoff. Finally, the doorman, who was a weightlifter well over six-and-a-half feet tall, came onto the dance floor, grabbed the leader of the racists, and dragged him out out of the club. The minions followed and smashed our bus window on the way out.

We then played shows in California with some great bands: T.S.O.L., MDC, Naked Lady Wrestlers, Verbal Abuse. Before we headed north, we gigged in Reno, and hit the casinos afterwards. Wimpy and I were lucky at the tables, but Card wasn't. Just before we headed out, he started mouthing off about how Wimpy and I had won with band money and that he wanted a share of our winnings. Wimpy told him to shut up, so Card took a swing at him. But he was so drunk that not only did he miss Wimpy's chin, he lost his balance, staggered pitifully, and fell backwards and smacked his besotted head on the cement curb. When he staggered to his feet he said, "Fuck this town! I'm gonna roll this town!" He then walked into the middle of Virginia Street, the main drag, and rolled down the middle of it, five-dollar chips and change falling out of his pockets. We just about pissed ourselves laughing before coming to our senses and dragging him into the bus before he got run over or arrested.

May 27, 1987 was one of the best days of my life. Laura gave birth to our first child, a healthy little guy we named Jake Aaron Keithley. Now there were three of us. Like I said, parenting is not for everybody, but if you are cut out for it, there is no greater joy than helping your kids and watching them grow. This was the start of my experience, and I am grateful for it.

Meanwhile, things were becoming somewhat frayed with our manager. Ken Lester had put eight solid years of work into D.O.A. and come up with some very good ideas and directions for the band. But he was starting to lose interest, so we hired a new guy to do our booking, Laurie Mercer. Laurie worked at Sam Feldman's agency, and he also managed No Means No.

We had still not gotten a release for *True Strong and Free* in Canada

or in Europe. Profile Records in New York were very uncooperative about licensing, and Chris Williamson seemed more interested in promoting another band, the Cro Mags. That really sucked, but we kept moving forward as a band. In

The D.O.A. Murder Squad practicing just before annihilating the Bruce Allen-coached CFOX Radio hockey team. *photo: Bev Davies* our stage show we sharpened our ridicule of the religious right, which had gotten very powerful in the U.S., after having the puppet Reagan as President for the last six-and-a-half years.

We had lined up some funding to make a video, and I cooked up an idea involving hockey and what we touted as Canada's *real* national anthem, "Takin' Care of Business." I had started playing hockey again after a ten-year hiatus. Dave, Wimpy, and I would meet every Friday night at Burnaby's Four Rinks, the largest ice complex in the world. We'd play hockey from midnight till three AM, and sometimes even later if the iceman hadn't woken up from his nightly nap. After that, we'd drink beer till four or five in the morning.

In the video, D.O.A. faced off against a gang of evil businessmen. We wore our red mac jackets as D.O.A. hockey jerseys. The evil moneyhawks, the four horsemen of the apocalypse, wore suits with their names on the back. They were coached by Lester, and the D.O.A. team, the "Murder Squad," was coached by Randy Bachman. We shot the video at Bob Montgomery's Boys' Club and a local arena. It came out great and got lots of airtime. We were still waiting for *True Strong and Free* to be released in Canada.

That August, we organized a benefit show at Vancouver's Graceland club called "No More Censorship." On the bill were D.O.A., No Means No, Death Sentence, RRU, and the Hellcats. The show was terrific, and it raised about $5,000 for Jello Biafra's defense fund. He had been charged with distribution of harmful matters to minors after a San Fernando, California girl purchased

a copy of the Dead Kennedys album *Frankenchrist*, which included a poster of a painting by avant-garde artist H.R. Giger that featured depictions of male and female sexual organs. The DKs and Alternative Tentacles had huge legal bills mounting up and the possibility of a large judgment against them in the American "legal" system. Luckily, the case ended in a hung jury; Biafra had won, even though he wasn't completely vindicated.

On October 23, we started the D.O.A. and No Means No North American "Tour de Force" tour. It was booked by Laurie Mercer without any support from Profile Records at all. It started in Tacoma, Washington, which went fine, but on the next night in Portland, a bunch of racist skinheads decided to show up. The bouncers at the club refused to do anything about them, and it was one of the few times where D.O.A. walked off and refused to play. In California, we started having more problems with Miss Piggy; the timing gear was now gone. So we left Hutch and Bob Montgomery behind with the bus and hopped in with No Means No to make a show in Hollywood. It wasn't the last time they would save our bacon. A couple of days later, Miss Piggy was fixed and Hutch and Bob met us further along.

In Salt Lake City, we were booked into Alice's Restaurant, the place immortalized in the Arlo Guthrie song. As the words go, "You can get anything you want at Alice's Restaurant," and apparently one of the things the locals had been getting there was an ample supply of any drug they wanted. When we showed up to play, the place was ringed by cops and TV cameras. The media were in a feeding frenzy, asking the kids about their drug habits, and whether D.O.A. was what they liked to listen to when they were high. (Music from the sixties works better for that kind of thing, in my opinion.)

As we crossed the midwest, Miss Piggy was having to visit a mechanic once a week. In mid-November, when we got to New York City, the big red bus broke down again. We got it fixed, only to have it break down yet again in Pittsburgh.

Card and Hutch.

Our last show on the American leg of the tour was in Boston, and then we headed up to Halifax, Nova Scotia. Card drank a pile of booze along the way. It didn't seem like a big deal; the trip would take twenty hours, and it was our day off. Card was always good about not drinking before a show. But once we'd crossed the border, Card got a horrendous nose bleed. We tried and tried to get the blood to coagulate, but nothing worked. We finally got him into the main hospital in Halifax, where Hutch's mom was a nurse. They packed his nose so full of cotton it looked like he had a fucking grapefruit attached to his face. Card had to stay in the hospital for a few days, so we asked John Wright of No Means No to fill in for the next couple of shows. He did an admirable job. We burned down the Old Flamingo Club in Halifax, then played in Fredricton, New Brunswick and Quebec City. Laura and baby Jake met us in Quebec City. Card rejoined us in Montreal.

It was really cold out east, and all I had was this horribly beat-up old jacket I had bought in some second-hand store for two bucks. In Toronto, half a dozen cabs blew right by when I tried to flag down a ride for Laura, Jake, and me; I looked like a homeless guy. Laura had to hail the taxi instead. We were staying with Melanie Kaye, a longtime Toronto scenester and D.O.A. supporter, and the super in her building had a whole bag of blue leather jackets that had been ripped off from nearby George Brown College. The price was right, so everybody in the band bought one.

The next night, D.O.A. drove down to London, Ontario, for a show at a joint called Mingles. We walked into the club looking like a football team in our new leather jackets. My jacket was #89, and it said on the sleeve that the my specialty was "Signwriting." Fucking Signwriting? What kind of college do you attend to learn that? I'd have preferred something like "nuclear fission" or "robotics." Anyway, we weren't in that joint more than two minutes before some other guy came in wearing a George Brown jacket. He waved and yelled, "George Brown, fuckin' rocks!" We looked at him like he was from outer space. There was a moment of stunned silence, then he slunk off with his beer. I guess he realized we were from the EXTREMELY UNFRIENDLY class of '87.

We played about another ten shows on the way back across Ontario and western Canada. I guess they were good. Hard to tell sometimes, when you do so many. We finished off the year with a New Year Eve's show at the Luv-a-fair in Vancouver. The support was Crash Bang Crunch Pop (yeah, just like the cereal); it was the new band featuring Ron Reyes of Black Flag. Ron had moved up to Canada; the band was good, but it didn't last. At the crack of midnight, it was 1988. The year was over; we had done some different things, but nothing ever really remains the same. The status quo for D.O.A. was about to get shaken up in the new year.

D.O.A. had come a long way since we started. We had put out five albums and played a helluva lot of shows around the world. It had always been a real test keeping D.O.A. rolling, but somehow the ideas and the philosophy of the band were enough to keep it all sticking together. Things had changed for Wimpy and me in particular. We were both fathers now. Dave seemed to be going off in another direction and Ken Lester was fading out of the picture.

In a way, you could see it coming. The landscape for D.O.A. was going to change tremendously.

If You Don't Like D.O.A. Dial 1-800-EAT SHIT

CHAPTER FIFTEEN

WHAT THE FUCK!
THINGS CHANGE!

We were exhausted after touring so much, so we laid low for the next couple of months, playing the odd show here and there. One highlight was a late February show at 86 Street in Vancouver, with Bolero Lava, an all-woman pop band. Card's girlfriend, Laurel Thackery, played guitar with them. On February 24, we played at Graceland in Vancouver with Soundgarden as support. They were a good band, just about to take off.

Then something unexpected came along. The previous year, our old pal Bruce Paisley, who was working for a big music promotion company in Vancouver, had played a trick on Ken Lester by telling him he'd lined up D.O.A. to open for David Lee Roth in front of 10,000 people at Vancouver's Pacific Coliseum. Roth was still big-time stuff in those days, and Lester ran around telling anybody who would listen. He was really pissed off to learn it was a hoax. So when Bruce called us at a gig in Victoria to say David Lee Roth

would be in Vancouver the next night and wanted D.O.A. as the support band, Lester replied sarcastically. Bruce had a hell of a time convincing Lester it was a legit offer. Some guy from Skid Row, Roth's current support band, had fallen off the stage and broken his bloody leg, so Roth needed somebody to fill in on short notice. We quickly agreed. It would be a big show – they had sold 10,000 tickets – and with our music being so different from Roth's, there were bound to be some fireworks.

We met Roth's road manager at the soundcheck. There are some showbiz types who make your skin crawl, and this guy was one of them. He obviously felt he had to lecture us on the dos

and don'ts of a big-time rock show. I didn't bother telling him that our old roadie, Bob Montgomery, had had the manager's number one boy in a headlock some years back.

We hung our usual D.O.A. backdrop on the huge scrim behind the stage. It looked like a postage stamp up there. The concert promoters hadn't announced in advance that we were taking Skid Row's place, and they didn't tell the audience until five minutes before we were scheduled to go on. A murmur went through the crowd, who had clearly come expecting a big dose of schlock rock.

D.O.A. blasted away in our usual obnoxious fashion. Some poodle-do geeks started yelling at us and giving us the finger, and some of them threw coins onto the stage. In between songs, Dave would bend down to pick up the money, then offer comments like, "Thank you, now I have enough for dinner." A couple of guys at the front kept trying to gob on us. Finally, the monitor guy grabbed one of them by the collar and smoked him in the face four or five times. As the geek's knees buckled, the rest of the D.O.A. haters stepped back. They and their poodle-dos wilted faster than posies in the midday Australian sun. The most fun song to play that night was "Fuck You," which we naturally aimed at the audience members who were clearly hating us.

Once we got off stage, I put away my guitar and wandered around in the bowels of the Coliseum. I ran into Roth's road manager, who said I was in a restricted area. I waved my backstage pass at him and laughed. Still, he told me to leave. I told him to fuck off. He tried to push me out, and I resisted (what did he expect?). Before I knew it, there were six heavies surrounding me. They escorted me back to our dressing room and then kicked me out of the Coliseum. A few minutes later, I was joined at the back door by the rest of my comrades. That was it, our big-time "rock" experience. Fuckin' great! At least we knew which side we were on.

During this time there was a raging debate about whether Canada should enter into a free trade agreement with the U.S. All of us on the anti-free trade side knew that the deal was a great giant scam by banks and big business to take raw resources out of Canada and ship them to the States. Anti-free trade activists were organizing three concerts, to be held simultaneously in Montreal, Toronto, and Vancouver. D.O.A. gladly agreed to do the Vancouver show. This gig also led to my first speaking engagement. I went to Langara College in Vancouver to speak at an open forum on the adverse effects free trade would have on Canadian culture and the arts. A radical element of the student association thought it was a good idea. Sadly, the fight was lost as Canada's prime minister, Bullshittin' Brian Mulroney, signed the free trade agreement with his pal Ronald Raygun.

Later on, this deal was expanded into NAFTA, the North American Free Trade Agreement, which allowed the U.S. to exploit both Canada's natural resources *and* Mexico's cheap labour pool. These days the issue has become even bigger with the advancement of the WTO (World Trade Organization), and associated schemes like APEC (Asia Pacific Economic Cooperation). These organizations are not set up to help the average person, but rather the fat cats and their cronies who enrich themselves even further at the people's expense. The modern "free traders" would rather have the West deteriorate to Third World standards if it means improving their bottom line.

What the anti-globalization forces want is "fair trade," not free trade. We need to support our brothers and sisters around the world in forming strong trade unions and getting enforceable environmental standards.

Some battles have been lost, but not the war.

The David Lee Roth experience had been bizarre, but July of 1988 would bring something equally odd. D.O.A. was asked to play the Vancouver Folk Festival. I know I am in the minority, but I do see folk music and punk music as being closely related. They are two of the few forms of protest music still alive and well in western culture; musically they are worlds apart, but philosophically they are close kin. So being invited to this prestigious celebration by festival director Gary Cristall was cool. We played the main stage to a generally positive reaction, although some packed up and left in disgust (and I can't remember ever having turned down my amp quite that low). On one of the side stages, we played with Rick Scott, formerly of the Pied Pumkin String Ensemble. I had really liked Pied Pumkin as a teenager, so that was a thrill. Pied Pumkin and D.O.A. were the first Vancouver bands to put out their own independent records in the seventies. DIY all the way.

We started doing a bunch of recording at Fort Gore. Wimpy and I had written a pile of new songs: a couple about South Africa, a few that were a little more rock 'n' roll, and a whole lotta punk rock. Dave had gotten hold of an 8-track machine, and he would usually run that while Card, Wimpy, and I put down the beds. Dave got pretty good at running the tape machine, but he was spending less and less time with us learning and practicing the new songs. This led to a bit of a disconnect between Dave and the rest of us, exacerbated by the fact that Card and Dave still weren't getting along.

This tension wasn't helped by our legal troubles. We were in the middle of another battle with David Ferguson and CD Presents, this time over the ownership of the songwriting and performance rights on *Bloodied but Unbowed*. We had a very able lawyer, Pat Nichols, but the battle raged on and on. At the same time, we were trying to secure our release from Profile Records in New York. They had put out *True (North) Strong and Free* (except in Canada) and refused to do another, yet we couldn't release any new albums until we had secured an outright release. It was a fucking horrible situation. To top things off, Jon and Laurel were due to have a baby in a few months, and this legal bullshit was stopping us from being able to make a living.

So we did what we normally did when we needed money: we booked a North American tour. This time around, we were behind the wheel of a brand-new van. Miss Piggy had been costing us a fortune in repairs, and the time had come to buy a decent vehicle. We decided on a new step van. We paid a pile of dough for it, but it had an aluminum body that we figured wouldn't rust away. We are still driving the same van today, fifteen years later, and it runs like a top. It got its name when Art Bergmann borrowed it for a tour. The van looks like a big white milk truck, so Bergmann named it after the World's Toughest Milkman, Reid Fleming, the main character in a great fucked-up comic book by the very talented David Boswell.

Our tour started in Missoula, Montana at a show put on by the Rockin' Rudy record store. The next night we played in Rapid City, South Dakota, at a benefit for groups trying to stop strip mining in the Black Hills. From there, we played the midwest all the way to the east coast, with bands like Agent Orange and Scream. Back in Canada, a number of gigs happened during an insane heat wave. During a show at the Siboney Club in Toronto,

the club was so stiflingly hot that Death Sentence drummer Doug Donut, suffering from heat exhaustion, fell off the back of his drum stool. We ran around opening doors to get him some air.

Back in Vancouver, we got a call from MuchMusic, Canada's version of MTV, asking us to be

Shithead preaches to the fans. *photo: Laurence Acland*

part of a special they were taping in Prince Albert, Saskatchewan. Prince Albert, a little town north of Saskatoon, is also the home of a maximum security prison. The prison was having its third annual Jailhouse Rock concert, and they had invited some local rock bands to play during the day. The bill was D.O.A. and the original lineup of Bachman Turner Overdrive, with a bunch of local bands to start. We had made several attempts to play prisons in B.C., but the authorities had always said we were too political. This Prince Albert jail crew was not a collection of guys who hadn't paid their traffic tickets. Dinner was prepared by the Lifers Club, and the guy who cooked our steaks had murdered a couple of people. So we knew we shouldn't argue if we thought the steaks were too well done.

The show was being held in the exercise yard, smack dab in the middle of the prison. The local bands were halfway through when some big black clouds rolled in and it started to pour. The sound rental company hadn't brought any covers for the equipment, and the sound gear was getting soaked. The organizers dragged parts of it inside, then used some hair dryers to dry out the speakers. This delayed the proceedings severely. Lockdown in that joint was nine PM, and it was close to eight PM before they got the sound up and running. BTO hadn't played yet, so it looked bad for D.O.A. The lockdown time was a strict rule that *never* varied. Somehow, though, I managed to talk the warden into extending it that night by one hour. I suggested to him that there might be a riot if we didn't play. In the meantime, a bunch of prisoners were banging objects against their cell bars, chanting, "BTO – D.O.A. – BTO – D.O.A." over and over.

When it was our turn, we rushed up onto the stage and went for it. We had forty-five minutes. For our fourth song, we announced that we were going to do a country and western tune, and this got a huge cheer from the inmates. We played "San Quentin" by Johnny Cash, but I changed the words to "Saskatchewan Pen, I hate every inch of you. You've tortured me since 1972." After that, I fired up the chainsaw – it had become a staple of our set, something for me to joust the crowd with – and we launched into "Lumberjack City." We found out later the guards had been freaking out about the chainsaw, wondering how the fuck it got in there. I guess they didn't check Reid Fleming carefully enough. During our set, the warden told MuchMusic host Terry David Mulligan that next year they'd be sticking to country and western.

Our set went over well, but what followed was easily one of the best rock shows I've ever seen. BTO rocked so fucking hard I couldn't believe it. The way the sound echoed off the high brick walls of the inner courtyard was fucking great. The prisoners loved it. It was an escape from their bitter reality.

We dropped Dave off in his hometown of La Ronge, just north of Prince Albert, and Wimpy, Jon, and I drove off into the night. Not too long after getting home, the three of us came to a decision. We agreed that Ken Lester would no longer be D.O.A.'s manager. Lester had been with us for eight-plus years and had helped us immensely. He had been really creative, and he'd focused the band on many good ideas and causes, some of which we might have missed otherwise. But things had changed, and Lester had become the wrong person for the job. His priorities and lifestyle had done a complete 180 since I first met him. Dave disagreed with our decision when he returned. He was Lester's biggest supporter, and this was the breaking point for him. He quit.

Our final show with Dave was a benefit at the Maritime Labour Centre on Vancouver's waterfront. The workers at the White Spot, a historic local restaurant chain, were trying to get their first union contract. My brother Jef lined us up to play. It was a good show, and it raised lots of money for the cause. The most emotional moment of the night was formally saying goodbye to Dave. Wimpy gave him a hug, and so did I. I've missed the guy ever since. We travelled many miles together. Dave was a smokin' guitar player, really energetic on stage, and he was and still is a solid human being. The pride of La Ronge, Saskatchewan. Here's to you, Dave!

It wasn't easy to find a replacement for Dave. We tried out twenty-seven different guitar players, finally settling on Chris "Humper" Prohom, who'd played with the Day Glo Abortions. Chris was talented and easy-going, so he fit in quickly.

Shortly afterwards, we played in Seattle at a place called the Underground. The promoter, Lori Lefavor, had put together an interesting bill. The middle support band was Coffin Break, a really good Seattle band, and the opening group was a band called Nirvana. The gig started early and I missed Nirvana. Too bad. I think that was only their second show ever. Nardwaur the Human Serviette, a noted Vancouver musicologist and music writer, claims that Kurt Cobain and Courtney Love actually met at a D.O.A. show in Portland.

Nirvana were really important in changing music, and I'm not even thinking about the vast number of records they sold. They changed the *sound* of what was acceptable on American radio. Previous to their making it big, the music that was acceptable was oldie stuff like the Rolling Stones and hard rock and metal from the eighties like Mötley Crüe and Van Halen. But those sounds were much tamer than the sheer aggression of Nirvana. A new generation had grown up with bands like Hüsker Dü, the Dead Kennedys, the Clash, and the Ramones, bands that were never

played on mainstream stations. But the early punk bands had paved the way, so once Nirvana became so hugely popular, it kicked the door wide open for well-promoted punk bands like Green Day and the Offspring, then Rancid and a revitalized Bad Religion. That in turn set punk up to become almost mainstream, with the likes of Blink-182.

In late October, our deal with Profile Records was officially terminated, ending two years of wrangling. We had most of an album done at Profile Studios with Cecil English, so we took six of the songs from those sessions and made up a demo. We'd been invited by the Refuse and Resist organization to play at a big political rally called Resist in Concert! in New York, so we thought we'd head over to L.A. afterwards to see about getting a record deal. Resist in Concert! was a cool event, definitely a left-wing affair, promoting an anti-war, anti-violence, and resistence agenda. There were about twenty

bands, and the list of entertainers and speakers included Sinead O'Connor and Susan Sarandon. The following night we played at CBGBS, the only time we've played that historic club in our twenty-five-year career.

We flew back to Seattle and did a few gigs on our way down to L.A. Two of our shows there were acoustic. This was the start

D.O.A. (l-r Shithead, Prohom, Card, Wimpy) at the
Resist in Concert! show in New York, 1988. *photo: Eileen Polk*

of "Drunks on Acoustic." The idea was to get as fucked-up as possible, then play bad country and western. We did this for fun and as a change-up for D.O.A. fans. Once in L.A., Restless Records offered us a record deal. Overall, it was a good trip.

Nineteen eighty-eight was close to being over. Dave was gone, Ken was gone, and Profile Records was gone. Gone, gone, gone, like a wild goose in winter. What the fuck! Things change.

CHAPTER SIXTEEN

NOT SO QUIET ON THE WESTERN FRONT

We kept up with our Drunks on Acoustic shows. It was a good sideline without the pressure of making a gig a blockbuster event like a D.O.A. show usually was. The act actually got slightly more professional. Before too long, the Drunks got a break. Our old buddy Gary Cristall invited us to play at a festival called Mayworks, an annual celebration of working people. Cristall had seen us play as the Drunks and liked it, but our songs were all in the "ridiculous country and western" category. He threw some "Wobblie" songs at us instead. The Wobblies were members of the IWW, the International Workers of the World. In the early part of the twentieth century, they were instrumental in helping to achieve decent working conditions for women and men in North America. A lot of Wobblies paid a heavy price for being activists in a very conservative time, and many received long jail sentences. Some of them paid with their lives. One of these people was Joe Hill, who was the songsmith for the IWW. He took old Baptist hymns and rewrote the words so they made sense and turned them into popular anthems. In 1914, Joe Hill was arrested for murder in Utah. Many believed that his arrest was retribution by the state of Utah for his organining efforts in the mining regions there. In 1916, he was executed by firing squad.

We took it seriously when Cristall asked us to learn some of the songs from that era. For our Mayworks show, the set list looked like this: "Banks of Marble," "Dump the Bosses off Your Back," "The Preacher and the Slave," "Union Maid," and "Billy and the Socreds." It took me back to the music I had listened to as a teenager: Woody Guthrie, Bob Dylan, Leadbelly. The set went over great, and the Drunks started to sober up.

Following the Mayworks show, D.O.A. played a Peace Benefit in a hockey arena in Parksville, B.C., a little town outside Nanaimo on Vancouver Island. Parksville is close to Nanoose Bay, a base for Canadian Armed Forces submarines. American nuclear-powered and nuclear-armed subs came to dock there and test their firepower, so there was an active no-nukes movement afoot.

D.O.A. has played about 200 benefit shows over the years, and half of them have been really well-organized. The other half were put on by well-intentioned people who had absolutely no idea how to stage a concert. The Parksville show was one of the latter. The doors were supposed to open at seven PM, but when we arrived at four PM, there was no sound system and the stage hadn't even been built. We humped our gear in, then set to building the stage.

The sound system finally arrived, but the guy installing it was a bit of a know-it-all, and he wired the sound in a very dangerous fashion: the entire power supply of the arena was hooked up to run through the system. Our pal Cecil English, who was helping, rewired the system so it was safe for the bands, but the other guy took offense at this and restored his original wiring when English's back was turned.

Everything was finally ready for soundcheck. I'd asked the organizers to hold the doors till eight PM, and it was now 7:40. I was sitting in the stands waiting for Humper to finish his guitar check. Humper could be real a joker at times, the proverbial life of the party. So when I saw him doing a funny dance at the mike, I yelled down at him to get on with it. "We're really late already!" I said. "Quit fucking the dog!"

But he wasn't jacking around. He was getting electrocuted!

He'd had his hands on his guitar strings when he touched the mike with his lips, and he was getting a powerful shock. He finally fell face forward on his guitar, breaking the connection. We rushed onstage. He was alive, but he was white as a ghost. We carried Humper into one of the hockey

dressing rooms underneath the stands and propped him up on a bench. He looked like the hockey player Donald Brashear after he got McSorleyed. The entire power of the arena had just run through his lily-white body.

By this point, the assembled throng was pouring through the door for the concert. D.O.A. was supposed to go on at ten PM and it took Wimpy, Jon, and I, the next two hours to convince Humper to go back on that stage. He finally agreed, but he didn't go near the fucking microphone.

That summer, a movie being shot in Vancouver took on significance for the musical community. The film

Shithead rocks. *photo: Sylvie E. Thorne*

was *Terminal City Ricochet*, and fledgling film producer John Conti approached D.O.A. about doing part of the soundtrack. He also offered me a part in the film.

The movie was set in a futuristic city run by a corrupt mayor, his corrupt police force, and his super-corrupt secret police force. Sounds like a lot of cities we know today. Jello Biafra was starring as the head of the dreaded Secret Police. I played one of his brutal enforcer cops, Officer Friendly. My partner was the great Gene Kiniski, former professional wrestling champion of the world.

Shithead and Gene Kiniski on the set of *Terminal City Ricochet*.

Ken Lester was one of the writers of the film, and he and Conti suggested that D.O.A. and Biafra collaborate on a song. We performed together on "That's Progress," a song Biafra had written. D.O.A. also recorded the Subhumans song "Behind the Smile" and the Who classic "Won't Get Fooled Again" for the film, but the licensing rights for the Who song turned out to be too expensive (although the D.O.A. version of the Who classic later appeared on *Greatest Shits*). The film was not exactly a cinematic triumph, but the soundtrack album, released by Alternative Tentacles, was powerful.

Biafra and all the guys in D.O.A. had really liked the way "That's Progress" turned out. Biafra was coming back to Vancouver to do more stuff with the movie. Lester and I suggested to Biafra that we try to record some more songs together, so we worked out a recording schedule with Cecil English. Alternative Tentacles put up the dough. It was good bloody timing. Biafra had some excellent songs already written.

We had one week to learn the songs and another week to record them. Biafra didn't play an instrument, so he would hum the melodies and the guitar lines into a cassette deck. He'd play that for us, then Humper, Wimpy, and I would sort out everything for the guitar and the bass. Biafra was quite exacting about the process. After having worked with him so closely, I find his former bandmates' claims that he never wrote any of the music a bunch of malarkey. Biafra had absolutely no problem writing music to go along with his scathing lyrics.

My favourite of the songs we did with Biafra was "Wish I Was in El Salvador." The most challenging one was "Full Metal Jackoff." Biafra hummed some of the parts, but he didn't really have a feel for what he was trying to get across. The song really needed some drive and I came up with a syncopated rhythm for the song, which was almost fifteen minutes long. When we got into the studio with the song, Biafra had it pretty well worked out. He sang in the isolation booth, and the four of us were in the main recording room. Biafra acted like the conductor: if he held his hands in the air, we would do a verse; if he held them out sideways, we would do the chorus; and if he pointed down, we did the bridge. We got it on the first take. Card's right arm (the one that hit the cymbals) was ready to fall off, but he persevered.

The recording was easy, but the mixing was a different story. English and I would arrive at the studio at noon. Biafra lived by an insomniac's clock. He'd get there between eight and ten PM and keep us mixing till six in the morning. After a few nights of this, I started leaving at midnight. The album was completed in about ten days. Biafra took the tapes back to San Francisco, where he got the incredible Winston Smith to do two great pieces of art for the front and back covers. *The Last Scream of the Missing Neighbors* took off like a rocket in Europe and did well in North America as well. It is the best-selling album I've ever been involved with.

In September that year, Laurie Mercer, our booking agent, officially became D.O.A.'s new manager. Laurie was consistent and hardworking, and would go on to manage the band till 1998.

The Drunks on Acoustic were asked to play an "End the Arms Race" benefit in September at the Arlington Caberet in Vancouver. The opening acts were the Raging Grannies and a good local band, the Hard Rock Miners, a kind of hyped-up acoustic jam band. The show was well-attended, and it raised some money for the cause. But the most notable part of the evening was the book that came out of it. It was at this show that Michael Turner, a poet who was also a member of the Hard Rock Miners, got the inspiration for his book *Hard Core Logo*. The book features a long-time punk band that had been together for twelve years and was doing acoustic shows. The name of their band was Hard Core Logo, and the lead singer's name was Joe Dick. It all sounded strangely familiar.

The book was made into a movie of the same name by Toronto director Bruce McDonald in 1995. It is an enjoyable punk rock movie, but something got lost in the translation. McDonald captured the crazy band antics of west coast hardcore in the eighties, but he missed the social and political angle of bands like D.O.A., Black Flag, and the Dead Kennedys, the confrontation and purposeful defiance of authority that made "hardcore punk" one of the most radical movements of the time.

Environmental causes were picking up steam, and one serious issue in B.C. was the damage caused by the pulp and paper industry as it pumped crap into the air and dumped toxic effluent into waterways. A number of studies pointed to higher-than-normal cancer rates among people who lived close to pulp and paper mills, and there was serious evidence that fish and shellfish were being adversely affected.

One of the groups fighting the companies was an outfit called Environmental Watch, which was spearheaded by Terry Jacks. As a member of the Poppy Family and as a solo artist, Jacks had had monster hits in the sixties and seventies (including "Seasons in the Sun," a number one hit in the U.S.), and was now using his fame for a good cause. My pal Dale Wiese suggested we get in touch with Jacks about organizing a local benefit concert.

Jacks liked the idea but thought we should make it bigger. He called up Bruce Allen, and Laurie Mercer, Jacks, and I went to a meeting at Allen's office. Bruce was on the phone when we got there, doing what he does best – yelling at and threatening the person on the other end of the line. When he finished, he hung up, swung his chair around, and said in a loud voice, "All right! Who the fuck are we going to save today?" After a bit of jawing, it was decided that we would try for two nights at 86 Street, with Bryan Adams as the headliner.

The shows were set for mid-October. Bryan Adams and D.O.A. would play both nights, and the other guest bands were BTO, Barney Bentall, and a rock 'n' roll outfit Laurie was managing called the Scramblers. The event became a media circus. Both shows sold out immediately. For his part, Allen tried to con us into only playing one night, but I put my foot down: D.O.A. would play both nights. On the second night, during Bryan

Adams' encore, I got up and traded verses with him on "Stand by Me." The event helped to focus media attention on the pulp and paper industry. Eventually, thanks to a lot of good old-fashioned hard work by a lot of organizations, the industry changed their procedures to a cleaner process. The good side won for a change.

After the show, Terry Jacks suggested we record a version of his song "Where Evil Grows," which we had played at the benefit. We recorded it with Terry producing and Cecil English mixing at Profile Studios. It was fun working with Jacks, and he was meticulous. The single was added to our new album, which we were calling *Murder*, as a bonus track. We shot a video for it too.

On November 6, 1989, a great thing happened. Laura gave birth to our second child, a beautiful baby girl. We named her Georgia, for American artist Georgia O'Keefe.

The "Where Evil Grows" video debuted on MuchMusic at the end of that month, and a few weeks later we embarked on a cross-Canada tour to promote the new album. It was a shitty and dangerous time of the year to be travelling. Reid Fleming broke down in Ottawa, stranding us there for a couple of days. I particularly remember one night as we were driving through Manitoba towards home. The temperature was −30°C, it was three in the morning, and everybody else was asleep under whatever blankets or scraps of clothing they could find. The rear heater was cranked on full, as was the front one. I was wearing two pair of socks, three shirts, my heaviest coat, a scarf, a toque, and longjohns under my pants. I had the radio tuned to some mouldy-oldie station, and I was kinda dancing in the driver's seat just to keep from freezing. To make matters worse, we were almost out of gas. Finally, a truck stop appeared on the horizon. I pulled in fast, burst out of Reid Fleming, and ran inside, where I kept hopping around to get the circulation back in my limbs. The gas station attendant didn't say a word. He had obviously seen this before.

This just reinforced another rock 'n' roll rule: DON'T TOUR CANADA IN THE WINTER, DUMBASS!

D.O.A. (l-r Wimpy, Shithead, Card, Prohom), 1989.

Another memorable evening on that tour involved something called the Winnipeg Handshake. We were playing the upstairs cabaret at a greasy joint called the Circuit Club. Down below was a dumpy little drinking hole. We pieced the following story together after the show. Two guys downstairs got into a disagreement about a cocaine debt. The guy who owed the coin ran upstairs to the Circuit, paid his ten bucks to get in, and grabbed a table near the bar. The second guy ran after him, paid his ten bucks, and advanced towards the first guy's table. As Greaseball 2 approached, Greaseball 1 stood up and pulled his weapon from under the table. He was holding a beer bottle by the neck, and the end was smashed off. Greaseball 1 then gave Greaseball 2 the Winnipeg Handshake: he jabbed the broken end of the bottle into Greaseball 2's eye. Greaseball 2 ran straight towards the D.O.A. T-shirt booth, and promptly bled all over the merch. Jay Scott, who was manning the booth, grabbed some T-shirts and held them up to the guy's eye to try and save it. The guy grabbed the T-shirts and ran out into the –35°C night, as did his assailant.

The one thing about being on the road for days at a stretch is it gives you lots of time to come up with ideas, and we decided to follow up on one when got back to Vancouver. We had never recorded a live album before. Cecil English set up a bunch of recording gear in his van and parked it in the alley behind Club Soda, where we performed at a show in December. He was able to get a pretty good recording, and *Talk – Action = 0* was ready for release. Restless Records released the album the next year.

The band, inevitably, went through a lot of changes that year. Personally, I had some real joy added to my life with the birth of my daughter Georgia. The band and I still had our ideals intact, a real "us against them" mentality, and we knew that we would, with the help of our families and friends, make it through any shit thrown our way.

CHAPTER SEVENTEEN

MURDER

We were finally back on track with some new releases. In February 1990, *Murder* was released by Restless Records in the U.S., Roadrunner in Europe, and Enigma in Canada. It was later released in Japan and Australia. And Alternative Tentacles had *The Last Scream of the Missing Neighbors*, our record with Jello Biafra, out there in the U.S. and Europe. We were out to get our fucking momentum going again.

We arranged a big release party at Vancouver's Commodore Ballroom for *Murder*, and then set off on a tour down the west coast of the States. One of our first shows was at the Country Club just northwest of L.A. We played with the re-formed Weirdos from L.A., and Blast. About 1,000 people showed up and made the scene, among them Keith Morris, who'd played with Circle Jerks and Black Flag, and Flea from the Red Hot Chili Peppers. It was a great show. The next day it was D.O.A. versus the Chili Peppers on the golf course.

In early April, we flew to London to start a European tour promoting *Murder*. The crew this time was an interesting combo. Hutch was mixing, Chris Crud was the roadie, and Jay Scott was the merchandiser. They were effective together. Bill Gilliam of Alternative Tentacles met us at the airport. It had been five years and it was nice to be back.

We bought some used gear and rented the rest. Charlie, from the UK Subs, had a Marshall cab and a fifty-watt Marshall head for sale, and as we

were driving across south London to pick it up, he pointed out a little pub where a guy had hung himself in the loo while Charlie and his blues band were playing. That was the inspiration for the UK Subs album *Another Kind of Blues*.

The Dutch agency, Paperclip, sent over a guy named Eric Mans to be our driver/tour manager. On the way out of London, we stopped at the Marshall factory again, and bought JCM 900s for Humper and me. The legendary Jim Marshall came out while we were making our purchase. "Wow," I thought. "He's a D.O.A. fan." But then Marshall whispered into the clerk's ear and I overheard him tell the guy to make sure we had paid for our gear. When we unloaded Mans's Mercedes van, Wimpy's bass head fell off the top of the pile of gear, just about broke Jay Scott's foot, and hit the ground with a resounding thud. It was fucked up.

We went over swell at our first gig in Ipswich. Next up was Birmingham at Edward the 8th's. Then we went to Sheffield at just about the same time British customs agents found the parts to the super gun Canadian Gerald Bull had designed for Saddam Hussein. The parts had been made in Sheffield. When we we got to the venue, Take 2, another Canadian decided to do some designing. The sound system at the club was pathetic to start with, but after Chris Crud had rewired it, it only had a quarter of the power. Some think the Mossad took care of Gerald Bull. I know we took care of Chris Crud.

The next night's gig was in Hebden Bridge, a little English town in the heart of the West Yorkshire moors. The venue was on Keighley Road, only ten miles from where my grandfather had grown up. I was very excited. At the same time we questioned the wisdom of putting on a D.O.A. show in the middle of nowhere. Our fears were allayed when we pulled up to the venue and saw a guy with a large mohawk passed out in front. His head was in the gutter, his body was on the sidewalk, and he was surrounded by a pool of puke. We knew then it would be a good show that night!

D.O.A. (l-r Wimpy, Shithead, Card, Prohom), 1990. *photo: Karen Lee Plessner*

The next night it was up to Scotland, our first time there, where we played in Edinburgh. The place was absolutely jammed. Following that we played Newcastle, Leeds, Newport, and Brighton, before driving back to London for a show at the London School of Economics. A strange place for a gig, but it was a great show. The support band was Fudge Tunnel. Punks climbed the yellow metal walls inside of the hall and jumped off of anything they could find.

Then we headed to the continent. After a show in Aalst, Belgium, we made our way to Amsterdam to play the famous Melk Weg (Milky Way). Rotterdam, the site of another gig, had an unbelievable number of tall people. Those Dutchies must have been eating a lot of their own dairy products.

After a show at the Kling Klang in Wilhelmshaven, Germany – their speciality was air hockey and weizen (wheat) beer – our next stop was Copenhagen, where we played at Loppen, a part of Christiana, the world's largest squat. It was a good show, but what was even more fun was running into the Beat Farmers, a cool L.A. band, in the lobby of our hotel. Country Dick Montana was a funny guy. He had had a tumour removed, and he took his shirt off right there in the lobby to show everybody the long zipper-like scar on his massive barrel chest.

"Wow!" I said to him. "The operation was a success! But are you aware that they stitched a real ugly head on top of your shoulders?"

Everybody laughed. Montana smirked at me for a second or two, then shot back, "Yeah, they only had Canadian heads available at the time." This time the laughter was even louder. I could only smile and say, "Touché."

We went to Sweden next for three shows in Malmo, Gavle, and Fagersta. (If you're ever in Fagersta, don't drink the Fagersta chicken drink. It tastes like shit!) Sweden produces some good hockey players, but the place is really fucking expensive. We could hardly afford to buy beer or a meal. One thing we did buy was homemade hooch you can get on the street in old Coke and Pepsi bottles. Luckily, nobody went blind.

Back in Germany, we played shows all over the country, and our old friend Michel, who managed our 1985 tour, arranged for us to play with D.R.I. and C.O.C. in Munich. It ended up being a fun night of "initial" bands.

We played two great shows in Berlin, one at TU Mensa (a venue on the campus of Technical University of Berlin) and the other at the Ex. Both of these shows were so well-promoted by Marc (from the band MAD) and Franko that the rooms were so packed as to nearly cause another riot. Partway through our German dates, Eric Mans went back to Holland and the Paperclip agency sent us a new tour manager/driver. This guy was cool, so we called him Daddio. Daddio could drive like a madman and chain-smoke like nobody else. After our shows, he would sit in his hotel room doing the books, smoking and downing vodka with wild abandon till four or five in the morning. Somehow he would get himself out of bed by eight AM and wake

the rest of us. On that tour we played knock poker (thirty-one) almost every night. Daddio never lost a game, and he must have doubled his pay with his winnings.

We were booked next for some shows in the former Yugoslavia. We played Zagreb, then a little village in Slovenia near the Italian frontier. We got there via a tiny road that wound up and up and up through vineyards. The stage was in an open courtyard where there was a basketball court. Three kids were playing while their grandmothers were minding them. We wondered who the fuck had booked us there as we went off to dinner with the promoters. But when we came back, there were about 1,000 leather-jacketed punks crammed into the courtyard.

The wee village had no beer, so the promoters gave us a case of wine instead. No problem, we thought. But two-fisting with wine was somewhat different than drinking beer the same way, as Wimpy was to discover. We took the same winding road back, and as soon as we got to the hotel parking lot, Wimpy kicked open the door and puked everywhere. We concluded he was very considerate – he could have puked on all of us. Once we got inside we opened some more wine and Jay Scott pulled out the merch money, and it covered the entire table.

From there, we drove to Italy for shows in Milan, Bologna, Pisa, and Torino. The Italian shows were fuckin' chaos, as usual. The sound systems weren't working, the crowds were huge and out of control; just the way I like it. Switzerland was next, with shows in Basel and Geneva, one of which was produced by a wiccan cult. Laura and I spoke on the phone regularly, and she had told me she had taken baby Georgia to audition for a movie. They liked Georgia, and she got the part. The movie was *Look Who's Talking Too* starring John Travolta and Kirstie Alley. It was an exciting time for the Keithley clan.

The Murder tour moved into France, where we played Pontalier, Lyon, Paris, and a club called Le Balthazar, near Cremont Ferrand, which was billed as the smallest club in Europe. It *was* fucking tiny; good thing

Dave wasn't still in the band, or he would have had to sit down to play. The show at Le Balthazar was on June 3, the day I turned thirty-four. When the promoter showed us the rider, it looked almost as if he'd known it was my birthday beforehand. There was a nice selection of cheese and some beautiful choclate éclairs stored in a little cupboard in the band room. There was just one problem: every bit of food was covered with these fucking French ants! We pointed this out to the promoter. With a haughty French laugh, he picked up an éclair, brushed off the ants, and sank his teeth into it. We took the leftovers with us, to save dough at the horribly expensive French gas stops. The van was filled with requests like "Monsieur, pass le French ant cheese, *s'il vous plaît.*" It was funny, but every time I took a bite I seemed to feel those little buggers running around in my intestinal tract.

Our last show of that tour was in London at the Venue in New Cross on June 7. The show was packed and we played a raunchy set. I was hoarse as hell. There was a shitty aspect to the show. The club had hired rugby hooligans to do security. We couldn't see much from the stage, but Jay Scott had a bird's-eye view of what was going on from the closed-circuit camera in the club's office. The bouncers were roughing up the punks at the door and bashing anybody who had been thrown out of the pit. One kid got really hurt, and somebody called the cops. Scott could see the bouncers running to throw their brass knuckles and the small truncheons they had been carrying into a bucket. The bucket was hidden in a back room before the cops arrived, and the bar manager purposely helped hide the bloody evidence.

Daddio drove us to Heathrow the next day. We had a lot of stuff to carry through the airport, especially Chris Crud, since he had been buying trinkets for everybody back home. Every time we went through security, Chris had to remove all of his punk-rock garb for the metal detector, which really slowed us down. One wise-cracking immigration official grabbed Crud's passport. Crud's last name was Englemann. The official looked at the passport, then at Crud's tam and kilt, and sneered, "Herr Englemann? That don't sound too Scottish to me!"

By now we were in serious danger of missing our plane. We snatched up our packages after the final x-ray check and raced through the huge terminal, reaching the right gate just before the final boarding call. All of a sudden Crud realized he had left his box of trinkets at the last x-ray machine! He turned and started running back. I was carrying all the tickets, but there was no time to sort out whose ticket was whose. Crud was my buddy, so I bolted after him, trying to bring him back. Finally, he got too far ahead. When I got back to the gate I was completely winded. I asked the attendants to look out for a little guy in a tam and a kilt. The four of us had just entered the gate when one of those golf carts came flying up, with its stupid yellow light flashing. It was Crud with his box of trinkets. He had made it with thirty seconds to spare.

It was good to be home. It had been a long trip, and a tense one at times. We had reasserted ourselves in Europe again. But I couldn't ignore the fissures that were again cracking our fortress. And the kids had really grown while I was away; I'd really missed them and Laura.

We had a new agent, Allison Hamamura (who eventually became a very successful A&R person in L.A.), who booked us an American tour. We deadheaded out to Winnipeg, played one night at the Spectrum that turned out to be Bif Naked's first gig singing with Gorilla Gorilla, and then crossed the border into North Dakota. That night we played in Minneapolis, then drove down to Madison, Wisconsin, where we were scheduled to meet up with Negazione, one of the original great hardcore bands from Italy.

The promoters were late, so we waited in the club's parking lot. After a bit, Negazione showed up. There was nothing to do, so Negazione pulled out a soccer ball. What else? So it was D.O.A. against Negazione, and within three minutes, Negazione had a 3–0 lead. I could see things were just going to get worse, so I said what any red-blooded Canadian would say in that situation: "Let's play hockey!"

We got some sticks out of Reid Fleming (they came everywhere with us) and gave Negazione a crash course in ball hockey. We tried to even things up by giving them our merchandiser. It was a lot of fun.

The gig itself that night was very disorganized. When we went to get paid, the promoter had only thirty percent of what D.O.A. was owed, and no money at all for Negazione. I got mad and yelled, but to no avail. I gave Negazione what they were supposed to get from what I got. Before we left town I suggested we stop at the house where the promoter was having a party. When we saw that they had a keg of beer, we said we would take that as compensation. We ended up giving the keg away to some friends, but getting it made me feel better.

The next night, our show in Green Bay, Wisconsin, was cancelled, and the show in Milwaukee was very so-so. We were hitting a string of duds. Either we were out there at the wrong time, or the midwest was no longer a great place for D.O.A. At our gig at St Andrew's Hall in Detroit, the sound kept crapping out. We did have a fun show in Chicago, though. We had been hired by the Exit Club to play a boat cruise up Chicago's Gold Coast. The bands were Negazione, D.O.A., and Pegboy, featuring half of the old Nayked Raygun and one ex-Bloodsport member, both long-time Chicago stalwarts. About 200 people crammed onto the boat. Wimpy taught Humper, Card, and I the theme song from _Gilligan's Island_, but we butchered it because the boat was swaying so damn much.

Our shows in Cleveland and Cincinnati were not well-attended, and the hot and humid weather contributed to everybody's crankiness. On July 28, we played at the old Brookwood Hall, just outside of Dayton, Ohio. Thankfully, the Dayton faithful did not disappoint us, and we were ready to burn down the stage after Negazione turned in an inspiring set. Dayton was always a key place for D.O.A. For that show, it felt like old times.

We were about halfway through our set when some fuckwit started grabbing the mike stands. I told him to stop, but he kept doing it until he hit Humper in the teeth. I lost it, and with my guitar still on, I went to get the guy. But I made a mistake then that I had never made before or since: I went after the prick with my upper body instead of my feet. I was slugging him in the head, and he was lying on a sea of people swinging back at me. He was wearing some protruding rings that really gouged my face up, and I was bleeding pretty badly. I paid for defying a basic rule of fighting: DON'T LEAD WITH YOUR FACE!

I slept in the van that night. The next morning I woke up early and drove around thinking. D.O.A. had had a really good run, and we had always tried to do the right fucking thing whether the situation was fucked up or not. We acted on gut instinct, but this seemed to be it. I called Laura to talk it over. I'd been playing in the band for thirteen years, and I shed some tears while we were on the phone. Laura encouraged me to do what felt right.

I called a meeting with Wimpy, Card, and Humper that afternoon, and told them I didn't want to carry on with the band. We still had two weeks of shows booked. We played half of the remaining shows and told our booking agent, Allison Hamamura, to forget the rest. My heart just wasn't in it.

On the day of our final show, August 17, in Allentown, Pennslyvania, Tax from Negazione got word that his mother had died. He wasn't surprised, because she had been ailing, but still he was grief-stricken. That night, he did one of the bravest things I have ever seen. He got up there and played his heart out. Our pal Christeen Aebi, who had driven down from New York to see the show, got up and sang "Midnight Special" with us.

Humper stayed out east to visit some relatives, as did Brian Thalken, and we dropped our sound man, Chris Heck, in Dayton. Once he was gone, the van was very quiet. We drove the last 2,000 miles in a strange and unfamiliar silence.

We didn't announce anything officially when we got back to Vancouver, but word got around about the band's demise. Out of the blue, we got a phone call from our old pal Dirk Dirksen. He wanted D.O.A. to play a show in San Francisco that he would produce into a video. So Laurie Mercer booked us a farewell tour down the west coast, the place where we had really gotten our start. We took some old friends along to enjoy the last hurrah. Ken Chin, lead singer of SNFU, was merchandiser, John Wright, of No Means No, was our roadie, and Craig Bougie, the soundman for No Means No, did the mixing. The *Vancouver Sun* even paid for our buddy John Mackie to report on four days of the trip.

We started the tour in Las Vegas, then played Tijuana, Mexico, at a place called Iguana's, with L7 as the support. We did gigs at Bogart's in Long Beach, always a great club, and Club Lingerie in Hollywood. Then it was time for the show in San Francisco at the DV8 Lounge. Dirksen and his partner Dameon had a mobile truck set up outside the club to capture shots from all the cameras that night.

It turned out to be a spectacular event. We played for well over an hour, then Jello Biafra came on the stage for the encore. It was 1990; the build-up to the first Gulf War had begun, and Biafra launched into his poignant piece "Die for Oil, Suckers!" It went on for a good twelve minutes before Bougie at the soundboard started turning Biafra down. I did the riff from "Full Metal Jackoff," and the encore went on and on.

We played the next night at the Cactus Club in San Jose, where I sold the infamous D.O.A. backdrop. Then it was on to the old WOW Hall in Eugene, Oregon, with our pals the Detonators. Portland was next, then the Waterfront in Seattle. Before the show, John Wright had showed me a hole in the fly-wheel cover of the chainsaw, and when we did "Lumberjack City" on stage, I accidentally stuck my ring finger on my left hand – the hand I fret the guitar with – down the hole, taking part of it off. Holy fuck, did that hurt. I ran backstage and cursed my head off. The guys from Subvert were back there guzzling our beer. In a rage, I picked up a bunch of beers and smashed them against the wall. The Subvert guys freaked out and ran out of the room. It wasn't fair. D.O.A. might be over, but I didn't want to be so disabled that I couldn't play guitar any more. The show had lurched to a stop. Finally, I wrapped some bandages around my finger and we finished the show as best we could. I didn't bother going to an American hospital as we were heading back to Canada. Luckily, my injury wasn't as bad as I'd originally thought.

The following weekend D.O.A. played The Last Hurrah at the Commodore. The support was great – GBH and Aversion. I arranged for Humper to play most of the leads, since my finger was still fucked up. The Commodore was totally fucking packed. People drove and flew in from everywhere. Almost right at the start, some geek chucked a beer can at me.

He must have been thinking that kind of thing was punk rock. We had just finished our third song, but I stopped the band and warned the audience about that shit. As soon as I said something, another pencil neck hucked another beer can and nailed me in the chest. There was dead silence in the room. I just stared out at the crowd. An ugly fucking scenario went through my mind: for a brief moment I wanted to find the puke who had thrown the can. For an instant I wanted to unload thirteen years of trying my guts out. I wanted to show them the blood, the sweat, the lost teeth. I wanted to rip that geek apart.

But, luckily for him, the idea left me. For a while, though, I burned. I ripped apart, I had that insanely fucked-up, take-no-prisoners attitude one more fucking time. I let the geek smirk, as if he had gotten away with something. I refused to dignify his stupidity with a response.

We played our set, and then encore after encore. We drew out every last bit of energy the crowd, and we, had. We were dead.

I felt like a soldier finally coming home: badly wounded but still standing, bloodied but unbowed.

Then it was really over. All the gigs, all the travel, all the albums, all the songs, all the mayhem, all the camaraderie, all the fallen comrades, all the upheaval, all the spent emotion. And not one drop of any of that could have or should have been taken back.

In the end I'd learned, if nothing else, that if you work hard enough at something, you can change the way things are. You can take one idea and spread it around the world. Together, we can move mountains, truly.

D.O.A. (l-r Shithead, Ken Jensen, Wimpy) in Vienna, 1994. *photo: Manfred Rahs*

CHAPTER EIGHTEEN

LIFE AFTER DEATH

This chapter is here to let you know there is life after death, or at least there was for me after D.O.A. broke up in 1990. Who knows, if enough people buy this book, maybe I'll take some of the fucked up stories from the last thirteen years and work them into another book!

After we decided to dissolve D.O.A., I tried my hand at acting. That went okay for a while, but I soon got tired of auditioning for bit parts on bad American productions (the TV show *Wiseguy*, for example). Two years after the breakup, in the summer of 1992, I called up Wimpy to see if he wanted to get D.O.A. going again. He said sure.

Now some may ask, why start up D.O.A. again? Well, in the nineteen months that we weren't together, nobody had come along to take our place. There weren't any new, loud, rippin', obnoxious rock bands that would gleefully send a punk boot right into the establishment's groin! That was the main reason why.

I wanted to get back to the fundamentals of being a three-piece, so the only thing Wimpy and I needed was a drummer. I didn't think Jon Card would be interested, so I looked around for a bit. I called up John Wright from No Means No, who recommended Ken Jensen, a kid from Victoria who played in Red Tide. Ken turned out not only to be a great drummer but also one those rare, easygoing guys. He was a great fit.

So D.O.A. was once again ready to go. Laurie Mercer was willing to manage us, so the next thing we needed was a record label. We called up Restless Records and asked if they wanted to put out another album. They were cool about it, so we started recording at Profile Studios, with John Wright producing and Brian Who Else engineering. The recording sessions went smooth and fast. The only hitch was that while we were recording, Restless got bought out by another record company. We were left high and

Ken Jensen, 1993.

dry yet again! Luckily, Mercer worked out a deal with Jello Biafra and Bill Gilliam from Alternative Tentacles; they saved our bacon. We titled the album *13 Flavours Of Doom* and were quite happy with the results.

The new album launched us into a bunch of really successful tours over the next couple of years in Canada, the U.S., Europe, and Australia. For a change, we were actually getting paid decently for our efforts. In the summer of 1993, we recorded another album with the same production team and the same lineup. Jensen's drumming had gotten stronger, and he even wrote a couple of good songs for the album. The final recording sounded quite different from a lot of our earlier releases, but it still worked. We also continued with tradition and took a couple of songs from the session to release as a benefit single to raise funds to help the fight to save old-growth forests in Clayoquot Sound, an area on the west coast of British Columbia.

In August 1994, tragedy struck: we got the news that Dimwit had overdosed on heroin and died. I couldn't believe it. One of my lifelong friends was gone. Dimwit was not an addict, only an occasional user. But he had gotten a hot shot of junk – it was a little too pure – and that was it. Let that be a warning to anyone who might think junk is "cool." It ain't. I've lost too many friends to that shit, and you don't have to be a junkie to die from heroin; it can happen with just one hit. My song *Junk City Nowhere (Vancouver)* is about Dimwit. I have a hard time playing it for myself, let alone on stage.

That fall we decided to add a fourth band member. We asked the very talented Ford Pier, who had played with Roots Roundup and Junior Gone Wild, if he wanted to play guitar with us. He said sure and, like Jensen, turned out to be a great addition, adding a lot of energy to D.O.A.'s live shows.

On January 30, 1995, I was sitting down to watch the Superbowl on television when the phone rang. It was Tom Holliston from No Means No who told me that Ken Jensen had died earlier that day in a house fire. I was in shock. I called Wimpy and met up with him and Tom at Ken's house in East Vancouver. It was terrible to look at; it was charred and still smoking. Apparently, the night before somebody had dropped a cigarette on the couch and it had smoldered for hours before coming ablaze. Ken got overcome by the smoke and fell down the stairs. Again, I was in shock at the sudden loss of a friend. Never again would Ken be the wonderful human being that he was. Luckily, four others living in the house, including No Means No's Craig Bougie, awoke in time and escaped by jumping off the roof. A simple smoke detector would have prevented it all.

Eventually, Wimpy and I got into the basement of the burnt-out house to survey the damage. We had been practicing in Ken's basement, and we discovered that all of our equipment had been destroyed by the water the fire department had used to fight the inferno. Later, a bunch of good people in cities like Toronto and Vancouver, to name only two, organized several benefit concerts to help D.O.A. replace or repair our equipment. They raised a lot of cash and I am eternally grateful to all those who helped. We ended up with more money than we needed, so we bought a huge box of smoke detectors and took them down to the Carnegie Centre – the

JUNK CITY NOWHERE (VANCOUVER)

© Joe Keithley, Falling Apart Songs (SOCAN)

Hadn't seen you for a while
But things still felt close
But when your brother Bob called me
I felt a big chunk slip away
A big chunk of me died that day

When Bob felt your hand
It was ice cold
The junk had done its business
You got a hit that was too bold
An' they say the coast ain't that cold

chorus:
Somehow – every score will even out
'Cause anytime – it can all screw up
Too much junky business in Vancouver town
Some call it cool
But I just call it, I just call it Nowhere

In Dimwit's shed we started
Cheap guitar and a drumset
An' we made a lot of big plans
Now our plans are a dead end
And I feel that I'm kicked & dead

'Cause you had to go score
Some call it dangerous fun
But I just call it crap
It's another way to lose
An' what we lost was you

chorus

D.O.A. (clockwise from top left Ford Pier, Shithead, Brien O'Brien, Wimpy), 1996. *photo: Jan Berman*

community center in the Downtown Eastside – and gave them out to folks who needed them.

John Wright agreed to fill in on drums for the next record, both as a tribute to Ken and because he's a super guy. We called the new album *The Black Spot*. Brian Who Else engineered again and it was released on Laurie Mercer's short-lived Essential Noise label.

Soon after the release of *The Black Spot* in the spring of 1996, we got a new drummer: Brien O'Brien, from Curious George, a solid guy and a cool drummer. And on July 27, Laura gave birth to a really cute baby boy. We named him Clayton Tyler. I'm a lucky guy. What an amazing thing, to have three great, healthy kids.

That summer I got involved trying to save a second-growth forest in our neighbourhood. A bunch of fuckheads from a few high-tech companies wanted to cut down the trees so their employees could have a "park-like" setting to work in. Then, the Green Party asked me to be a candidate for them in the upcoming provincial election in British Columbia. At first I declined, but later changed my mind, figuring that I could really stir up some shit. That proved to be the case. I liked the Green Party because it was so new that they had not yet become corrupted, like all the bigger political parties. I could operate like a maverick. In the end, out of a field of six candidates, I came in fourth – not bad! I had been bitten by the political bug. A couple of years later, I ran (unsuccessfully) for Burnaby city council.

Back to D.O.A. We toured quite a bit, but by the end of 1996, Wimpy had again had enough. He decided to pack it in. Ford left at the same time. It was really too bad, but these things happen.

Brien and I forged ahead, though, working on new songs in his basement. Laurie Mercer encouraged me to start playing solo acoustic shows, so I gave it a try. They went well. I was nervous as shit at first, but I soon got the hang of it. I played the Vancouver Folk Festival and did a lot of

cool benefit gigs for anti-globalization events.

Late that year, on the advice of Fat Mike from NOFX and Fat Wreckords, I brought Sudden Death Records out of dormancy and got serious about it. (It's worked out well; by the end of 2003, we have released fifty-three albums from such artists as D.O.A., d.b.s., the Real McKenzies, the Damned, Ripcordz, Ford Pier, and Dog Eat Dogma. Thanks for the idea, Mike.)

The first two new Sudden Death releases were D.O.A. albums: *The Lost Tapes*, a collection of old and rare tracks, and a new studio album, *Festival of Atheists*. Brien and I had recorded the new album with Cecil English at Profile Studios. He played the drums while I did vocals, guitar, bass, and helped Cecil to produce. We had a lot of fun with the whole concept of *Festival of Atheists*, as we spammed right-wing Christian evangelical organizations with emails, urging them to join our nightly onstage rituals of atheism. One group in the Yukon held a prayer meeting outside our show there and tried to stop the kids from going into the arena. They even splashed holy water on the arena doors! But the show went on, much to their dismay.

Before D.O.A. could properly tour again, we needed a new bass player. Kuba stepped in and would be a member of D.O.A. for four of the next five years. The new line-up toured Canada, the U.S., and Europe. But it was this last trip that finished Brien O'Brien; two days before we were supposed to leave on a California tour, his back gave out for the last time. (Too much riding around in crammed little vans, said the doctor.) I asked Jan Rodgerson, from Dog Eat Dogma, if he would fill in on drums. He did and he's been our drummer ever since. Darn good thing, too! He's a solid person and has easily followed in the tradition of great D.O.A. drummers. Hey, he can also fix a van in an emergency, which is an essential skill for D.O.A. members! All he needed was a new handle, so we named him The Great Baldini, after his smooth pate.

You know, I have a million stories (maybe only about five percent of

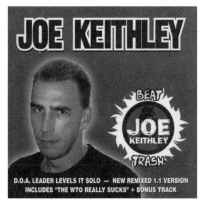

D.O.A. (l-r the Great Baldini, Kuba, Shithead) with an NYPD fan, 1999.

them are in this here book). Our old soundman, Bob Cutler, suggested that I start doing spoken word performances. "Yeah," I said, "look at Rollins and Biafra. They're doing pretty well with that shit!" So I did a few performances that combined spoken word with some of my acoustic songs. They worked pretty well, so Cecil English and I recorded an album of spoken word and acoustic songs in 1999. I called the whole happening deal *Beat Trash*. Hey, a solo record. Cool!

The fall of 2000 was a busy time. I got a job as a talk show host on a new Internet station based in Vancouver called *MyCityRadio.com*. It was a riot. I would interview politicians, actors, comedians, and we would have bands play live on the street. I had old friends like David Spaner, Jack Rabid, and Greg Potter as regular guests. But it was short-lived. Ten months later, the station went belly-up, leaving us employees high and dry.

I felt Kuba had hit a plateau as a bass player, and sacked him, then asked Randy Rampage if he wanted to play bass for us again. He said yes right away. We had a lot of fun playing shows with Rampage. The passage of time and the wear-and-tear of life had taken its toll, but he was still the same I-don't-give-a-shit wildman he had been in the early days.

To top the fall off, there was also another provincial election. I again ran for MLA (Member of the Legislative Assembly) in my riding of Burnaby-Willingdon under the Green Party banner. As part of my campaigning, I played my guitar at Skytrain stops, handed out leaflets, put up campaign

signs, answered constituents' questions about policy, and made speeches at the all-candidate meetings. I worked my ass off. This time I came in third, with fifteen percent of the vote. Not bad. What it really proves is that people will vote for shitheads, but not necessarily Joey Shithead!

In 2001, D.O.A. recorded a new album. It was weird: it took the longest goddamn time of any album I had ever been involved with. We were all working at other jobs, so we had no time to record. But in the end, it was worth it. We called it *Win the Battle*. It turned out to be the best album we'd released since 1982's *War on 45*. The Canadian version of *Win the Battle* even included a duet with our pal Bif Naked on "All Across the U.S.A.," and the resulting tour took us to Japan for the first time. That was a riot.

At the end of 2001, Rampage went back to being a longshoreman and Kuba returned to the band. We did a shitload of shows around the world supporting *Win the Battle*. That tour took its toll; it was Kuba's last stand. When it was over, he was out for good. But not D.O.A., which lives on.

And so the story continues. I can't believe more than twenty-five years have passed since that first day D.O.A. jammed at 343 Railway. There have been a lot of ups and downs over the years, but through it all, I'm proud of what we've accomplished. We had a blast. We still are.

Already Dead

too many geeks, too many miles.
too many stagedives into the pile.
too many beers, too many cops,
too many rednecks at the truckstop
they hate our guts, don't like our kind,
but we turned the tables on some real swine

can't kill us, already dead.
too much shit, that's in our heads
don't give a fuck, what they said,
cause we're all, already dead

got no style, no grand finale,
just hearing loss and an old Rand McNally
too many scams, too many creeps,
lotsa fastfood, nowhere to sleep
they say we're wrong, gonna burn in hell,
here's a noseload, choke on it pal.

Joey Shithead Keithley, Prisoner Publishing

APPENDICES

APPENDIX I

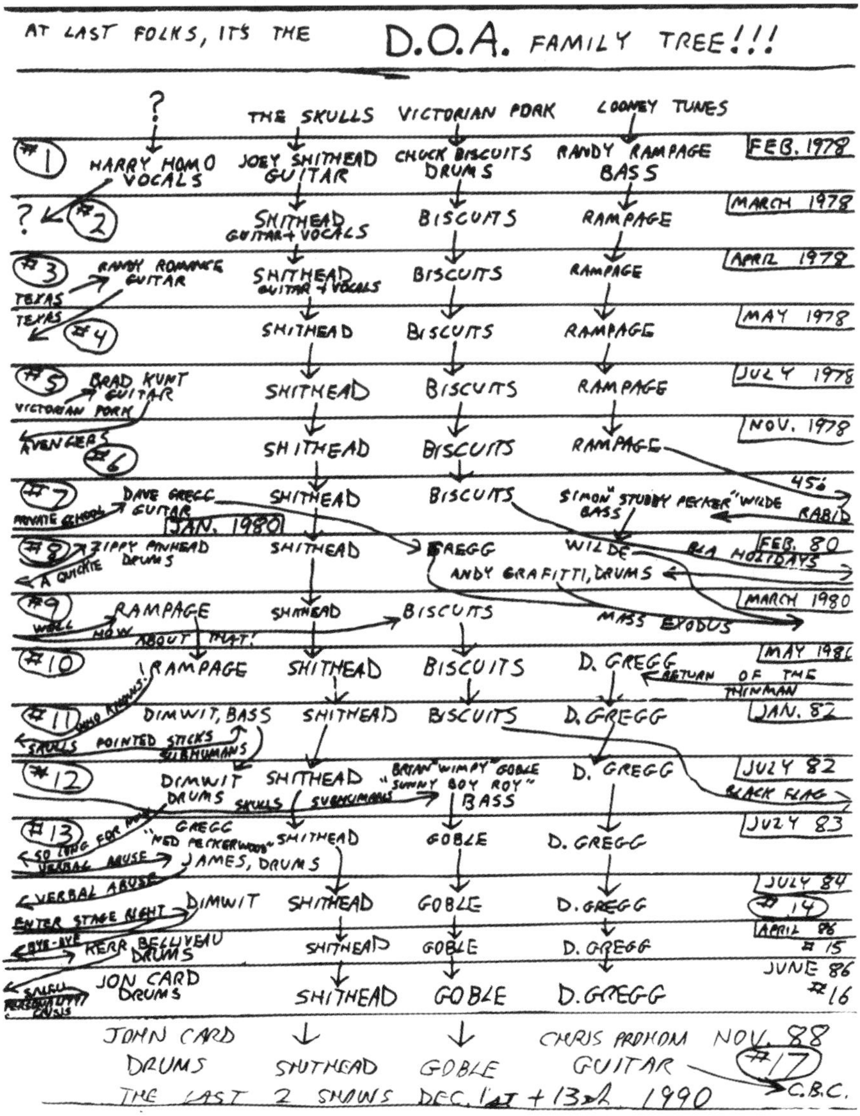

AT LAST FOLKS, IT'S THE D.O.A. FAMILY TREE!!!
?
THE SKULLS
VICTORIAN PORK
LOONEY TUNES
#1
HARRY HOMO VOCALS
JOEY SHITHEAD GUITAR
CHUCK BISCUITS DRUMS
RANDY RAMPAGE BASS
FEB. 1978
#2
SHITHEAD GUITAR + VOCALS
BISCUITS
RAMPAGE
MARCH 1978
#3
RANDY ROMANCE GUITAR
TEXAS
SHITHEAD GUITAR + VOCALS
BISCUITS
RAMPAGE
APRIL 1978
#4
SHITHEAD
BISCUITS
RAMPAGE
MAY 1978
#5
BRAD KUNT GUITAR
VICTORIAN PORK
SHITHEAD
BISCUITS
RAMPAGE
JULY 1978
#6
AVENGERS
SHITHEAD
BISCUITS
RAMPAGE
NOV. 1978
45's
RABID
#7
DAVE GREGG GUITAR
PRIVATE SCHOOL
JAN. 1980
SHITHEAD
BISCUITS
SIMON "STUBBY PECKER" WILDE BASS
#8
ZIPPY PINHEAD DRUMS
A QUICKIE
SHITHEAD
GREGG
WILDE
FEB. 80
ANDY GRAFITTI, DRUMS
MASS EXODUS
#9
RAMPAGE
WELL HOW ABOUT THAT!
SHITHEAD
BISCUITS
MARCH 1980
#10
RAMPAGE
SHITHEAD
BISCUITS
D. GREGG
RETURN OF THE THINMAN
MAY 1980
#11
DIMWIT, BASS
SHITHEAD
BISCUITS
D. GREGG
JAN. 82
SKULLS POINTED STICKS SUBHUMANS
#12
DIMWIT DRUMS
SHITHEAD
"BRIAN "WIMPY" GOBLE "SUNNY BOY ROY" BASS
D. GREGG
JULY 82
BLACK FLAG
SKULLS / SUBHUMANS
#13
GREGG "NED PECKERWOOD" JAMES, DRUMS
SHITHEAD
GOBLE
D. GREGG
JULY 83
VERBAL ABUSE
VERBAL ABUSE
ENTER STAGE RIGHT
DIMWIT
SHITHEAD
GOBLE
D. GREGG
JULY 84
#14
BYE-BYE
HERR BELLIVEAU DRUMS
SHITHEAD
GOBLE
D. GREGG
APRIL 86
#15
JON CARD DRUMS
SHITHEAD
GOBLE
D. GREGG
JUNE 86
#16
JOHN CARD DRUMS
SHITHEAD
GOBLE
CHRIS PROHOM GUITAR
NOV. 88
#17
C.B.C.
THE LAST 2 SHOWS DEC. 1st + 13th 1990

D.O.A.   REFORMED   SEPT. 92
KEN JENSEN   JOEY SHITHEAD   BRIAN GOBLE   (#18)
  DRUMS   GUITAR + VOCALS   BASS + VOCALS

1994   SIMON WILDE DIES FROM A BRAIN TUMOR R.I.P.
   1994 DIMWIT OVERDOSES R.I.P.   JUNIOR GONE WILD
KEN JENSEN   SHITHEAD   GOBLE   FORD PIER   ROOTS ROUNDUP
                                   GUITAR   SEPT. 1994
                                               (#19)

JAN. 1995 KEN JENSEN DIES IN A HOUSE FIRE   R.I.P.
SUMMER/FALL 1995 D.O.A. RECORDS "THE BLACK SPOT"
   WITH   JOHN WRIGHT OF   NO MEANS NO

CURIOUS GEORGE   NOV. 1995
   → BRIAN O'BRIEN   SHITHEAD   GOBLE   PIER   (#20)
      DRUMS

   ADIOS BRIAN WIMPY ROY GOBLE / SO LONG   NOV. 1996
EVIL TWANG ←   FORD PIER SHOW BUSINESS GIANTS
                                           → SOLO CD

SUMMER + FALL 1997 BRIAN + JOE RECORD FESTIVM OF ATHEISTS
   BRIAN O'BRIEN   SHITHEAD   WYCLIFFE   OCT. 1997
                                 BASS   (#21)

   BRIAN O'BRIEN   SHITHEAD   KUBA   JAN. 1998
   ← RETIRES   BASS   (#22)

DOGRAT DOGMA THE GREAT BALDINI   SHITHEAD   KUBA   JAN. 1999
   →   DRUMS   (#23)

   THE GREAT BALDINI   SHITHEAD   RANDY RAMPAGE   SEPT. 2000
                                    BASS   (#24)
                                               → OUT AGAIN

   THE GREAT BALDINI   SHITHEAD   KUBA   JAN. 2002
                                   RE-ENTERS ON BASS   (#25)

BIF NAKED   → AND OUT AGAIN
ECONOLINE CRUSH
   → DAN YAREMKO   SHITHEAD   GREAT   JULY 2003
      BASS   BALDINI   (#26)

DISCOGRAPHY

Year	Album	Format	Label
1978	Disco Sucks	4 song 7-inch EP	Sudden Death Records
1978	Prisoner/13	7-inch single	Quintessence Records
1979	World War 3/Whatcha Gonna Do?	7-inch single	Sudden Death Records
1980	Something Better Change	album	Friends Records
1980	Triumph Of The Ignoroids [live]	4 song 12-inch EP	Friends Records
1981	Hardcore 81	album	Friends Records
1981	Positively D.O.A.	5 song 7-inch EP	Alternative Tentacles Records
1982	War On 45	8 song 12-inch	Faulty Products (US) Alternative Tentacles Records (UK)
	[tracks and covers are different on US and UK versions]		
1982	Right To Be Wild (Burn it Down/Fuck You) [benefit]	7-inch single	Sudden Death Records
1983	General Strike [benefit]	7-inch single	Sudden Death Records
1983	Bloodied But Unbowed [tracks are different on US and UK versions]	album	Alternative Tentacles Records
1985	Let's Wreck The Party [US and UK covers are different]	album	Alternative Tentacles Records
1985	Don't Turn Yer Back On Desperate Times	4 song 12-inch EP	Alternative Tentacles Records
1986	Expo Hurts Everyone (benefit) [with three other artists]	4 song 7-inch EP	Sudden Death Records
1987	True Strong and Free	album	Rock Hotel/Profile Records
1989	Last Scream Of The Missing Neighbors with Jello Biafra	album	Alternative Tentacles Records
1989	Where Evil Grows	casette single	Enigma Canada
1990	Murder	album	Restless Records
1990	Talk - Action = 0 [live]	album	Restless Records

1991	Greatest Shits	album	QQYRQ Records
1992	Dawning Of A New Error [compilation]	album	Alternative Tentacles Records
1992	13 Flavours Of Doom	album	Alternative Tentacles Records
1993	Loggerheads	album	Alternative Tentacles Records
1993	The Only Thing Green [benefit]	7-inch EP	Alternative Tentacles Records

1994	It's Not Unusual, But It Sure Is Ugly	5 song 7-inch EP	Alternative Tentacles Records
1996	The Black Spot	album	Essential Noise
1996	D.O.A./Show Business Giants [split]	5 song 10-inch	Essential Noise

1996	Marijauna Motherfucker [benefit] split with Colorifics	7-inch	Canabis Canada Records
1997	D.O.A. split with Hanson Brothers	7-inch	Empty Records
1998	Festival Of Atheists	album	Sudden Death Records
1998	The Lost Tapes	album	Sudden Death Records

| 1998 | D.O.A. split with d.b.s. | 4 song 7-inch | Empty Records |

1999	Beat Trash [Joey Keithley solo]	album	Sudden Death Records
2000	Nervous Breakdown split with Dog Eat Dogma	7-inch	Sudden Death Records
2001	Just Play It Over And Over Again	5 song 7-inch	Sudden Death Records

2001	Win The Battle	album	Sudden Death Records
2001	The End, live 1990 with Jello Biafra	DVD	Rhino Records
2003	War and Peace	album	Sudden Death Records
2003	Greatest Shits [tracks different than CD version]	DVD/VHS	Sudden Death Records

2004	Positively D.O.A. (singles 78-83)	album	Sudden Death Records
2004	D.O.A.	new studio album	Sudden Death Records
2004	Joey Shithead Keithley [solo]	new studio album	Sudden Death Records

TRIBUTE ALBUMS

2001	We Still Keep On Running With D.O.A. 7 bands covering D.O.A. tunes		Base Records (Japan)
2003	Let's Start The Action international electronic tribute to D.O.A.		Sudden Death Records

ACKNOWLEDGMENTS

I would like to thank all of my family, my friends, D.O.A. members past and present, and all those who helped D.O.A. along the way. I would also like to thank the countless fans that have supported D.O.A. and myself over the years.

And thanks to Barbara Pulling for her editing expertise, and to everyone at Arsenal Pulp Press.